SILENT VIGNETTES

Stars, Studios and Stories from the Silent Movie Era

BY **Tim Lussier**

FOREWORD BY LON DAVIS

Published in the USA by:
BearManor Media
1317 Edgewater Dr #110
Orlando, FL 32804
www.bearmanormedia.com

Paperback ISBN 978-1-62933-773-9
Case ISBN 978-1-62933-774-6
BearManor Media, Orlando, Florida
Printed in the United States of America
Book design by Robbie Adkins, www.adkinsconsult.com

*This book is dedicated to the memory of
Diana Serra Cary (Baby Peggy)
whose friendship and kindness
I will always treasure.*

Acknowledgments

❧

It would be impossible to name everyone who has contributed in some way or another to the Silents Are Golden website and, thereby, to the research and writing of the chapters in this book - to all of whom I owe a great deal of thanks. However, I would like to acknowledge a few people who were instrumental in getting this book published:

Lon Davis, author, historian and friend who not only provided his editing skills, but also graciously gave his advice and guidance over a period of several months to see this book finally in print.

Scott H. Reboul, editor extraordinaire, who spent many hours scrutinizing every detail of the book to ensure correctness, clarity and accuracy.

Robbie Adkins, whose experience, professionalism, and design skills have made a much more attractive book than I had ever imagined.

Ben Ohmart, BearManor Media owner and publisher, who kindly and enthusiastically accepted my manuscript for publication.

TABLE OF CONTENTS

Acknowledgments. iv

Foreword by Lon Davis vi

Preface by Tim Lussier. viii

Chapter 1: The Incomparable Betty Compson 1

Chapter 2: The Boy and the Girl: Harold Lloyd and Bebe Daniels 8

Chapter 3: Buster Keaton is All Wet 18

Chapter 4: From Demure to Tempestuous: Chaplin's Silent Ladies 32

Chapter 5: The Divine Corinne Griffith 41

Chapter 6: The Tragic Flugrath Sisters: Edna, Viola and Shirley 49

Chapter 7: "Heaven Flower Beauty": Francelia Billington 55

Chapter 8: Harold Lockwood—A Tribute 63

Chapter 9: The Lubin Manufacturing Company: Its Rise, ... 71
    Its Reign, Its Requiem

Chapter 10: The Silk Hat Comedian: Raymond Griffith 77

Chapter 11: "Garbo: The Official Dream Princess of the Silent Drama 84
    Department"

Chapter 12: The Reluctant Star: Nils Asther 91

Chapter 13: The Mysterious Death of Olive Thomas. 98

Chapter 14: Pickford's Patriotism 104

Chapter 15: Pretty, Funny Ladies 111

Chapter 16: The Dapper Reginald Denny 124

Chapter 17: Stuntmen: Risking Their Lives to Thrill Moviegoers 132

Chapter 18: Vitagraph: Three Men and Their Baby 150

Chapter 19: Reginald Hitchcock and Alice Taaffe: The Most Ideal Union . . .161

Chapter 20: Three Crusty Characters 170

Chapter 21: The Fair Virginia Brown Faire 178

Chapter 22: The Novak Sisters, Part I: Jane. 200

Chapter 23: The Novak Sisters, Part II: Eva 253

Chapter 24: The Novak Sisters, Part III: Fade-Out .284

About the Author 290

Index 291

Foreword

౭ఌ

The last thing I am is tech savvy. So, when the Internet made its debut, I paid it no mind. But when my wife, Debra, and I finally broke down, tuned in, and logged on, we were both immediately hooked. It turns out that cyberspace is a veritable bonanza for aficionados of silent film. There are dozens of wonderfully informative websites, none more attractive or accessible than SilentsAreGolden.com. The webmaster of that worthy site is my good friend Tim Lussier.

On the first of each month for almost a quarter of a century, Tim has faithfully posted material pertaining to the silent era: insightful film analyses, interviews, news on the latest DVDs, book reviews, and just about anything else one could ever want to know about that most glorious period of filmmaking. When Kevin Brownlow, the dean of the silent film community, asked me to recommend a reputable website where his distinguished colleague, H.A.V. Bullied, M.A., might post his unpublished essays on some of the greatest American and European films of the 1920s, I did not hesitate to suggest Silents Are Golden. Thanks to Tim, the ninety-five-year-old Dr. Bullied was able to fulfill his lifelong ambition of bringing these long-suppressed articles (along with an introduction by no less than *Metropolis* director Fritz Lang) to a wide audience.

But Tim is much more than an online publisher. He is a collector, an educator, and a writer, one whose enthusiasm for silent films comes through in every line of his unpretentious prose. His insightful articles on actress Virginia Lee Corbin (written with the full cooperation of Virginia's surviving sons) led to the publication of the first-ever biography on that quintessential flapper. *Bare Knees Flapper: The Life and Films of Virginia Lee Corbin* was published by McFarland & Co. in 2018. The book was well reviewed and launched Tim Lussier as a respected silent film historian. So dedicated is he to his subject, in fact, that he personally paid to restore one of Corbin's feature films, *Headlines*

(d. Edward H. Griffith, 1925), held at the Library of Congress in Washington, D. C., and released it to the silent film video market.

Tim's latest literary contribution is this compendium of lively essays, collectively entitled *Silent Vignettes*. Herein you will find the legends—Pickford, Chaplin, Keaton, and Garbo—as well as fascinating profiles on such frequently overlooked players as Reginald Denny, Francelia Billington, Virginia Brown Faire, Harold Lockwood, George Fawcett, Viola Richard, and Anita Garvin. There is also an in-depth, three-part dissertation on the beautiful Novak sisters, Jane and Eva.

Whether you're going old-school—reading a genuine book with covers and actual pages made from trees—or you're using that newfangled thing called an iPad—another latter-day technology I swore I'd never use but have since heartily embraced—you are in for a treat.

Lon Davis

Lon Davis *is a former stand-up comic who has written extensively on film history. His first book was* Silent Lives: 100 Biographies of the Silent Film Era *(BearManor Media, 2008). He has also edited over three hundred academic books on the performing arts, American history, and English literature. He and his wife, Debra, co-wrote the 2020 documentary film* This is Francis X. Bushman, *based on their authorized biography* King of the Movies *(BearManor Media, 2009).*

Preface

எ

An 8mm film from Blackhawk Films entitled *That's My Wife* (1929) starring Laurel and Hardy started it all 46 years ago. Shown in total silence on a borrowed 8mm projector, I was enthralled. Since then, I have worked my way through film, then videotape and into DVD and Blu-Ray collecting every silent film, feature and short that I could find. It's my drug of choice—I'm addicted.

I love all silent films. There's something about the tenor of the time—the world these people lived in, whether real or fantasized on the screen. Movies are an amazing thing. They are a window into a time long ago—not only to see cars, fashions, buildings, houses, decorating styles, etc.—but to see how people thought, what was important to them, how they viewed work, relationships, history, and yes, even sex.

I'm amazed at the rapid progression in the quality of filmmaking and storytelling in just a 30-year period. To see a film from 1898 and one from 1928 is almost mind-blowing. Many silent films from the late 1920s can stand toe to toe with films of today in terms of storytelling and cinematography. And to think they are telling these stories in total silence—simply amazing!

There are so many great actors and actresses from this period, too, and—in my humble opinion—this period offers the best comedies ever made. It's a little hard to believe that names like Pickford, Fairbanks, Chaney, Chaplin, Keaton, Valentino and others still live today—100 years or more since their heyday. But then again, how could they not? They are alive on the screen—as if we were looking into the window of someone's home and watching them eat a meal, dance, kiss, argue, fight, make up.

I have to admit I get just as excited when I discover a hitherto unseen film with one of the "second echelon" stars, as well as one of the "big" names, such as those mentioned above. A poverty row-produced film, seen for the first time, is a joy to behold. Why? One reason is most of them have great stories. Yes, they are often predictable and simple, but, nevertheless fun to watch—and it's that simplicity in storytelling and in production that I find charming.

It's by viewing these films, too, that I often discover someone on the screen with whom I wasn't previously familiar. Let's take Virginia Brown Faire, for example. The chapter on her in this book resulted from my discovery of this beautiful star in a couple of poverty row films, *Queen of the Chorus* and *The House of Shame*, both

1928. I had to know more, and, of course, I began searching for more of her films to see.

Although they are most identified with cowboy stars William S. Hart and Tom Mix, with whom they made several pictures, my interest in the Novak sisters came about from such films *The Barbarian* (1921) and *Laughing at Danger* (1924), both produced by independents.

Then there are those films that, seen for the first time, struck me as undiscovered gems. My first exposure to Raymond Griffith was a screening of *Paths to Paradise* (1925) at a film convention, a production I feel can stand with those of "The Big Three" (Chaplin, Keaton, Lloyd). That film resulted in the chapter on Griffith — I needed to know more.

Also seen for the first time at a film convention was *Docks of New York* (1928). Yes, I had seen Betty Compson in *Paths to Paradise* earlier, but her performance in this Josef von Sternberg drama was a revelation — thus my interest in knowing more about her. When I became aware that Harold Lloyd and Bebe Daniels could have possibly married if circumstances had been different, I had to dig deeper — and then decided to write about their relationship.

After viewing *Mare Nostrum* (1926), one of my favorite films, and *The Magician* (1926), I began to wonder about this ongoing relationship between director Rex Ingram and Alice Terry. Yes, I knew they were married, but I became aware of a devotion existing between them that I wanted to know more about. This, too, evolved into a chapter in this book.

Being an avid Buster Keaton fan, the more of his films I watched, the more I began to notice that water somehow played a part in so many of his gags. It may be rain, a waterspout, a lake, a waterfall, or whatever. Keaton may have suffered being wet in his films more than any other comedian — therefore, going through his films to seek out those gags was a joy-filled quest.

Years ago, I saw a short documentary on the Lubin Film Company on TV, most likely on PBS. It wasn't a first-class production, but it was enough to pique my interest in why this once-stalwart studio faded so fast. There's another chapter.

Therefore, each chapter has a genesis in my curiosity—the appeal of a personality that came across the movie screen, a presence, a performance, a beauty, a talent, or a mesmerizing tale. There are a variety of topics, stories, and lives offered in this book. It's just possible the reader may feel some of the same spark that inspired me to write these chapters—and then go on fact-finding expeditions of their own—whether through further reading or by viewing the films, themselves. I hope so.

Tim Lussier,
May 2021

Betty Compson's beauty is evident in this fan photo, c. 1921.

CHAPTER 1
The Incomparable Betty Compson
❦

*P*aths to Paradise (1925) with Raymond Griffith, and *The Docks of New York* with George Bancroft offer two polar performances by the lovely Betty Compson. As Molly, a jewel thief in *Paths to Paradise*, the winsome Miss Compson was perfectly teamed with Griffith, who played a rival jewel thief. As the two competed with one another to steal a necklace in a home where Compson posed as a maid and Griffith posed as a wealthy bon vivant, the screen literally lit up with personality, wit, and charm. Although Griffith was a top-rank comedian, he wasn't able to overshadow Compson's performance. She switched from a demure, obedient maid to a tough, determined burglar convincingly and adeptly while retaining her charming beauty throughout.

Of course, the more critically acclaimed performance is in *The Docks of New York*. She is Mae, a destitute girl who tries to commit suicide but is saved by a rough coal stoker named Bill (Bancroft), whose ship had just docked. Compson tugs at the viewer's heartstrings and draws forth a wave of sympathy for the poor, hopeless Mae, who has been beaten down by the Fates. The viewer wants to rescue her from her misery, especially when it appears that Bill is going to leave her and go back to the ship the morning after they are married.

Kevin Brownlow called *The Docks of New York* "one of the enduring masterpieces of the American cinema," adding that it was "the greatest film [director Josef] von Sternberg ever made." He said Compson's portrayal of Mae was "electric," and certainly it was and still is.

Early Performances

While attending high school in Salt Lake City, Utah, Compson played violin in the Mission Theatre orchestra, which accompanied the movies and the vaudeville acts appearing there. She was such a success that she teamed up with three young men and, accompanied by her mother, went to San Francisco to get bookings. No bookings were secured, however, and the three young men left the act. Compson did, however, manage to get a 15-week tour as a solo violinist act.

Back in Salt Lake City, she began touring with a couple of Pantages shows, doing her violin specialty. When the show played in Los Angeles, she made a screen test for the Christie Brothers. She finished the tour and received a call from Al Christie in Salt Lake City, offering her a contract.

Compson's given name was Eleanor Lucime Compson. It was Christie who christened her "Betty." She was a success in the comedies, and, in 1916, *Motion Picture News* stated, "Betty Compson grows more fascinating with each succeeding picture."

In John Kobal's book, *Hollywood, The Years of Innocence*, there are two nude photos of an actress taken by the Evans Studio in 1916. According to Kobal, the actress is identified on the slides as Betty Compson, who would then have been 19. Kobal feels "the attribution is open to question," but adds, "if it *is* Betty Compson, she wouldn't have been the first actress—or the last—to have begun her career by posing in the nude."

After making more than 70 comedies for Christie, she was fired in 1918 because she refused to make a personal appearance. Compson was almost destitute when she landed a role in the Pathé serial *The Terror of the Range* (1919). It was during this time that she began to make a lot of contacts with the up-and-coming stars of the day, such as Rudolph Valentino, Bebe Daniels, Gloria Swanson, and John Gilbert. It was also at this time that she met director (and her future husband) James Cruze.

Her Big Break

On December 23, 1918, she received a call from director George Loane Tucker. After meeting with her, Tucker offered her the role of Rose in *The Miracle Man*, for $125 a week. When it hit movie screens in August 1919, it made stars of Betty, Lon Chaney, Thomas Meighan, and Elinor Fair.

Tucker also directed her in *Ladies Must Live* (1921), and, by this time, Compson had fallen in love with the director. However, he was married, and she soon found out he was dying of cancer. Shortly before he died, he negotiated a new contract for Compson with Paramount. Although grateful for the favor, Compson was devastated by Tucker's passing.

Amazingly, Tucker had negotiated an astounding weekly salary of $2,500. In 1922 and 1923, she made seven films for the company, however, due to poor direction, her pictures were not successful enough for Paramount to offer her a raise, and she refused to sign without one. This may account for the fact that she went to England in 1923 and made three films there—*Royal Oak*, released in October 1923; *Woman to Woman*, released in February 1924; and *White Shadows*, released in May 1924. Interestingly, Alfred Hitchcock shared co-writing credits on two of the films. She became homesick, however, and returned to Hollywood, signing with independent producer Tilford Cinema Corporation for $3,500 a week.

After two films for Tilford, Paramount Pictures founder Jesse Lasky asked her to come back to his company; director James Cruze wanted her for his newest film, *The Enemy Sex* (1924). It must be noted that this was not her first film for Cruze; she had a small role in his 1923 comedy *Hollywood*.

The Enemy Sex premiered August 25, 1924 and was the first of 10 features she made for Paramount between 1924 and 1925, one being the previously mentioned *Paths to Paradise*. Another was *The Pony Express*, starring Compson and Ricardo Cortez. It was Cruze's attempt to recreate the success of his blockbuster hit, *The Covered Wagon* from 1923, but *The Pony Express* did not even come close.

Compson's biggest event of 1925 occurred on October 25, the day of her wedding to James Cruze. The story circulating in fan magazines at the time was that Cruze was directing Compson in a film (*The Pony Express*?) and had to demonstrate the lovemaking he wanted since the leading man wasn't meeting the director's expectations. The repeated how-to demonstrations helped to seal an attraction that had been going on for some time.

In 1928, Compson told an interviewer about the events leading up to the marriage: "I've been in love with him for a long while . . . It was from a photograph in a fan magazine—when he was an actor and long before I went into pictures . . . Some years later, I was dancing one night at an out-of-town café. Jim was there. I had never seen him before. He kept looking at me . . . Soon he came directly over to me and asked me to dance. We danced, then, and he asked me how I would like to play in one of his pictures. I said, 'Oh, yes!'"

Compson continued by saying that she went to Europe shortly after that, and she and Cruze did not see each other for some time. Then she got a call to test for a part at Famous Players for a film Cruze was directing. She didn't get the part, and it was the director's job to tell her so. "I sat in his office and cried. I was heartbroken and beyond caring what impression I was making. I'd wanted that part so much. He was so kindly, so sympathetic. I remember he said to me, 'Never mind. The next time we meet, you will be the star.' I was! Later he told me he fell in love with me then."

Compson went on to say there was nothing they could do about their love at that time because Cruze was married. But the next time she was on the Famous Players lot, he proposed.

In The Belle of Broadway *(1926), Compson successfully impersonates a Broadway star from the distant past. However, this leads to questions regarding how she could continue to appear so young.*

Poverty Row and a "Has Been"

Compson quit Paramount again in 1925. Her first film after *The Pony Express* was an English feature entitled *The Prude's Fall*; it was released in the U.S. as *Dangerous Virtue*, starring Jane Novak. The movie was being filmed in various European locations during the first quarter of 1925, so it must be assumed that Compson returned overseas during this time, although her part in the film was small.

Compson claimed in at least one article that she "quit" the screen after marrying Cruze, but she made three pictures in 1926 and five in 1927. During that period, she had one picture for Fox and two for Universal—but it seemed her light was beginning to fade since she was appearing more often in pictures for minor studios like Chadwick, for whom she made three films in 1927. There was one film for Columbia (still considered a Poverty Row studio) called *The Belle of Broadway*. (It is of particular interest to silent fans today because it was released in 2014 as a part of the Sony Choice Collection with an original score—apparently the Collection's only silent release.)

It soon dawned on the actress that studio executives considered her to be a "has-been." An article in the October 1928 issue of *Picture Play* magazine, stated, "A few years ago when Betty began to accept these quickie offers, comment was made that she was slipping. She was one of the pioneers to park her car unashamedly before the less pretentious studios. Then it became less reprehensible to appear in a quickie, and now it is almost fashionable.

"'What care I?' she asked . . . 'They offered me good money and 'my girl' (a term she used to refer, compositely, to all of her roles) some fascinating situations.'"

By this time, though, her marriage to Cruze had turned rocky, resulting in separations and reunions. When they finally split for good, Cruze went bankrupt, and the creditors descended on Compson, forcing her to sell quite a bit of her property to pay her estranged husband's debts.

Compson rebounded with the *The Big City* (1928), a Lon Chaney crime-drama for MGM. Remembering their days together in *The Miracle Man*, it was Chaney who had requested Compson as his leading lady. She almost played opposite John Gilbert in *Flesh and the Devil* when MGM was having some disagreements with Greta Garbo, but, of course, the disagreements were straightened out, and Garbo and Gilbert starred together, gloriously so.

Released in March, *The Big City*, although considered an average, run-of-the-mill crime-drama, garnered Compson good notices, thereby helping to re-establish her place in pictures. "A most surprising performance is given by Betty Compson," *Variety* said that this was "a much better piece of playing than Miss Compson was thought susceptible of performing. She makes this role very effective."

This was followed by four more "quickies" for minor studios. But she hit the jackpot again later that year when she was cast as Mae in Josef von Sternberg's *The Docks of New York*. The picture received better reviews than *The Big City*, but Compson's praises were somewhat scattered. One reviewer thought she was too attractive for anyone to believe that no one would have her. Another simply said her performance was "good." However, her next picture, and final release for 1928, garnered her the most attention of her career.

An Academy Award Nomination and Talkies

For her performance in *The Barker*, a First National picture with Milton Sills, Compson was nominated for the Academy Award for Best Performance by an Actress. In addition to Sills, the film featured Dorothy Mackaill and Douglas Fairbanks, Jr. It's the story of a sideshow barker (Sills), who wants his son (Fairbanks) to be a lawyer, but the young man ends up joining the carnival, too.

A print of Scarlet Seas *(1929), with Richard Barthelmess, survives in the Milan archive; the original score also survives, on Vitaphone discs. This would be Compson's last silent film.*

Compson is one of Sills's conquests, and when she is rebuffed by him, she pays another girl to "vamp" his son. Compson lost out to Mary Pickford in *Coquette* (1929) for the Academy Award. (The second Academy Awards honored films released between August 1, 1928, and July 31, 1929.)

The Barker *had some talking sequences, and Compson's voice came through so well she was offered many parts in sound films. She appeared opposite Richard Barthelmess in *Scarlet Seas* (1929), which was released with a Vitaphone track of music and sound effects, but no talking sequences. However, her next film, *Weary River* (1929), again with Barthelmess, included dialogue. As a matter of fact, she was so busy during this time that she turned down a part in Lon Chaney's second (and final) sound film, *The Unholy Three* (1930), recommending her friend Lila Lee as Chaney's leading lady.

Reflection

Looking back over her career while she was filming *The Barker* in 1928, she said, "My wickedness has kept me going. I wouldn't have lasted more than five years, possibly not that long, as an ingénue. Yet you cannot call 'my girl' a stereotyped vamp. She has a business, a 'racket' of some sort, whereas the vamp's only occupation consists of breaking up homes. 'My girl,' unless moved by jealously, doesn't stoop to such petty tricks. She never does dirty work just to be mean. She has no yellow streaks. Often, she is a victim of circumstances. She is morally 'bad' through love, or she is placed among crooks and knows no better life." She added, "I have tried to be good a time or two, but I was only sappy, never convincing. 'My girl' is a spirited person. She *has* to think."

And into the Sound Era

Compson is credited with 45 films in the 1930s and another 15 in the 1940s before playing in her final film in 1948, having segued easily into sound films, albeit without the star power she had in the silent era. In addition to the film roles, she performed on the stage and joined a vaudeville circuit. She also began a cosmetic line that cashed in on her name.

Shortly after her divorce from Cruze, she married Irving Weinberg, divorcing him later. During the 1940s, she married Filvius Jack Gall, a professional boxer. Together, they started a business called Ashtrays Unlimited, which made personalized ashtrays for hotels, restaurants, etc. She continued the business on her own after her husband's death in 1962.

Compson passed away April 19, 1974, at 77 years of age and financially secure. She once commented, "There will never be a benefit performance for Betty Compson"—and there never was.

SOURCES
PERIODICALS
The Big City review. *Variety* (March 28, 1928).
Gebhart, Myrtle. "Her Ten Crooked Years." *Picture-Play* (October 1928).
Hall, Glady. "Betty Compson Tells Her Untold Tale." *Motion Picture Classic* (December 1928).
Some Chaperone review. *Motion Picture News* (January 1, 1916).

BOOKS
Bodeen, DeWitt. *From Hollywood: The Careers of 15 Great American Stars*. New York: A.S. Barnes and Company, 1976.
Brownlow, Kevin. *The Parade's Gone By*. New York: Bonanza Books, 1968.
Kobal, John. *Hollywood, The Years of Innocence*. New York: Abbeville Press, 1985.

INTERNET
The American Film Institute Catalog of Feature Films. AFI.com.
"Betty Compson." *The Internet Movie Database*. IMDb.com.

CHAPTER 2
The Boy and The Girl: Harold Lloyd and Bebe Daniels
☙

By early 1915, Harold Lloyd and Hal Roach had exhausted Lloyd's mildly successful character Willie Work. So, Lonesome Luke, a copy of Chaplin's tramp with clothes in reverse (too tight instead of too baggy), was born. The first of these films, entitled simply *Lonesome Luke*, was released on June 7, 1915.

Hired At 14

After about a half-dozen or so of the Lonesome Lukes, Virginia "Bebe" Daniels was hired to be Lloyd's female lead. The October 16, 1915, issue of *Moving Picture World* lists the troupe as Harold Lloyd, Harry "Snub" Pollard, Bud Jamison, Earl Mohan, Gene Marsh, Arthur Harrison, and Bebe Daniels.

Bebe was only 14 years old when she and her mother visited the Rolin Studios for an interview with Lloyd and Roach (Lloyd was 22 years old in 1915). She was no novice actress, having appeared on the stage for the first time at 10 weeks of age, and in films about seven years later. "When I was eight," she said, "my parents decided there was a good future in picture work, so for several years I played child parts at Vitagraph, Ince and Pathé. The work was fascinating to me and much easier than the stage."

Getting money occasionally from film work was okay with Bebe's mother, but when she realized she wanted to do it full-time after signing with Roach, Mother said she "never thought Bebe would sink that low."

Typically, the purpose of a "leading lady" in these early, knockabout comedies was simply to give the main character a pretty girl to "play off of," that is, she served about the same purpose as any other prop in the film. A 1916 Lonesome Luke entitled *Luke's Movie Muddle* (a.k.a. *Luke's Model Movie, Director of the Cinema* and *The Cinema Director*) is a good example of this.

In this one-reeler, Luke is a one-man ticket seller, ticket taker, and usher in a small movie theater. The eight minutes of mayhem show Luke rudely pushing customers into their seats, jerking hats off men's heads, quieting a talkative woman, fighting with projectionist Snub Pollard, and flirting with every pretty girl who comes into the theater. Bebe is one of these girls and occupies barely a minute of total screen time. Luke escorts her inside, jerking a man's handkerchief from his pocket to dust off her seat. Later, while flirting with the girl sitting in front of Bebe, he reaches around and absent-mindedly grabs her foot and starts swinging it back and forth. This incurs a slap from the incredulous Bebe. And that was her total contribution.

Commenting on Bebe's role in the Lonesome Luke series, Lloyd biographer Annette D'Agostino Lloyd said, "[S]he had little to do and no real responsibility, and the whole series can be seen as merely a training ground for her future talents."

Leonard Maltin observes, "The boy-girl relationship in these early comedies is . . . crude. Harold's pursuit of Bebe Daniels is merely a repetition by rote of the standard comedy formula and is never played for sincerity or believability. As star comedian, it was Harold's obligation to go after The Girl, no matter how outlandish the charade. Lloyd later commented, 'When I was Lonesome Luke or one of those other characters, love affairs were not real. They were travesties on the real thing.'"

In considering these films and the Lonesome Luke character, it obviously would have been quite impossible for any character development for Bebe. There was no character development for Luke beyond being offensive, abrasive, knockabout, and a study in perpetual motion—"a spinning top," to quote critic Walter Kerr.

The Boy with the Glasses

Although the Lonesome Lukes were profitable, Lloyd was seeking a deeper characterization than this Chaplin imitation could provide him. That was made possible through the development of "the glasses character," named for the horn-rimmed spectacles he always wore. In addition, Lloyd's more subdued persona allowed Bebe's role in the films to take on a broader personality. It was a gradual growth, since the early glasses character wasn't far removed from Lonesome Luke, but, as time went on, Lloyd began to create a character that was not grotesque, as were most of the comics of the day, but likeable, ambitious, and optimistic. He became known as "The Boy," and Bebe "The Girl," labels indicative of their universal appeal. (After Lloyd's near-fatal accident with a prop bomb in 1919, Bebe sent him a "get well" card addressed to "The Boy" from "The Girl.")

The glasses character was introduced in the fall of 1917, and, as noted, it was a gradual conversion as Lloyd and Roach wanted to test out the new characterization before putting Lonesome Luke to bed entirely. For obvious reasons,

Harold Lloyd as he appeared not long after adopting "the glasses character."

it proved to be the more successful of the two characters, and Lloyd was on his way to redefining silent screen comedy.

The Non-Stop Kid was released in May 1918 and shows how the story-line could now accommodate Bebe. The film opens with Bebe in a garden, surrounded by suitors on her 16th birthday. Her grouchy, domineering father runs Harold, as well as all the other suitors, off the property. Harold soon learns that her father has picked a Professor Noodle as her husband-to-be, and Harold poses as the professor to get into the home during a reception.

Notice there IS a story line here as opposed to the series of knock-about scenes strung together in *Lonesome Luke's Movie Muddle*. Also, the story is built around Bebe's character, and, although she doesn't have an active part in advancing the plot, she is necessary to it. This is similar to a scenario of an October 1918 release entitled *Why Pick on Me?* However, instead of being kept from Bebe by a stern father, he must outsmart a bigger, and more muscular, suitor for her affections. Once again, the plot is built around Bebe and her inaccessibility, but that's the kind of situation that Lloyd's glasses character dealt with best—overcoming overwhelming odds and exhibiting not only a quickness of body but a quickness of wit.

Overcoming adversity comprises almost the entire storyline of *Ask Father* (1919). Harold and Bebe want to get married, but Harold must go to her father's office to ask for her hand. However, the father has no interest in having Harold as his son-in-law. So, the film is basically a series of attempts by Harold to see the father and subsequently being thrown out each time by the office workers.

One of the most enjoyable aspects of these films is the regular close-ups of Bebe and her reactions to Lloyd's antics. Apparently, Lloyd learned early on that Bebe was one of the best at a variety of facial expressions—surprise, shock, laughter, pouting (especially pouting), etc.

A posed scene from Ask Father *(1919), with Sammy Brooks, Bud Jamison, Lloyd, and Daniels.*

Lloyd described her as "a dark, dewy, big-eyed child." Lloyd biographer Tom Dardis writes, "Bebe possessed an extraordinarily expressive face, her huge eyes well-suited to register the full impact of the wild antics of Harold and Snub Pollard. She was quite dark; the studios later liked to boast of her 'Castilian beauty.'" He added that she was "the perfect foil for Harold, especially her shocked or quizzical 'What can you be thinking of?' expression."

It's difficult to imagine that Bebe at the time was a 14-, 15- or 16-year-old girl. Lloyd's later leading lady and wife, Mildred Davis, was demure and somewhat childlike on the screen, but not Bebe. She was always self-assured in her roles, sometimes feisty, sometimes even mature, and much more worldly than her age would lead one to believe.

The Off-Screen Bebe

The real Bebe off the screen, however, obviously retained some of the immaturity one would expect in a young teenager. According to a 1918 *Photo-Play Journal* article entitled, "She Wouldn't Be Kissed," Bebe was among a group of movie stars who were selling kisses to raise money for the Red Cross. Kisses were going for as much as $30, a not-ungenerous sum in a time when $5 a day was good pay. Bebe was among the reserves waiting to have her kiss bid upon when she suddenly removed herself from the proceedings, placed $40 in the collection box and left. Asked by the writer why she was leaving, Bebe replied, "Why, all those men scare me to death, bidding and crowding for kisses. I—I—wanta go home. I will give the Red Cross 40 dollars for my kiss—I'd rather than sorta sell it."

Bebe liked moviemaking, and she liked working with Harold Lloyd, but from the very beginning, she had aspirations of being a serious dramatic actress. In 1917, she told an interviewer, "Of course I like my present work, but someday I want to do really big things. When I was a little girl, I played in a great many Shakespearean plays, and when I saw 'Viola' and 'Portia' and 'Juliet' presented in such a beautiful manner, I hoped with all my might that when I grew up, I, too, might play such parts. I've changed my mind a little since then. I wouldn't care particularly about playing in the Shakespearean roles, but I do want to play fine modern parts that require hard work. I'll never be satisfied until I do." This dream of hers would later play a critical role in her relationship with Lloyd.

The majority of the films she made with Harold Lloyd were based at the old Bradbury Mansion on Court Street in downtown Los Angeles, where Roach had large rooms in which to shoot, and a stage constructed in the yard. However, as with most comedies of that period, location filming was the preferred method. "Their work together was always kind of spontaneous, unpredictable fun," Dardis said. "Each week found the Rolin Company in some new and hitherto unexplored part of the greater Los Angeles area in quest of a locale for the stories they invented as they rode around the country that was a paradise in those pre-smog, pre-freeway days." According to Bebe, the locations were critical since they were often sought out before a story line had been developed. "[W]hen I worked with Harold, we never had a script. We always went on location and thought things up."

Bebe was ambitious, independent, and headstrong, so it was natural that she would become more of a contributing member of the team. As time passed, she became a regular participant in the discussions regarding her role, and it was not uncommon that she would argue with Roach and/or Lloyd. There exists a memo from Roach to his business partner, Dwight Whiting, from that period which states Bebe was the only member of the company not to get a paycheck on payday for refusing to perform once when there was a disagreement.

"For Lloyd, Daniels was the perfect leading lady at this time," observes D'Agostino Lloyd, "for her self-confident and cool style was the ideal foil for his emerging and growing character."

Bebe Daniels in a fan photo taken when she was a star of her own feature films.

Bebe may have still been a teenager, but she was proud of her work and had confidence in her talents as an actress. Without a doubt, she and Lloyd had their arguments, but there was a bond between the two—most certainly an affectionate one—that far exceeded any disagreements they may have had.

Boy Loves Girl, or Vice-Versa

Although he was eight years older than she, it is well known that a romance developed between Harold and Bebe. Their relationship, both professionally and personally, was mutually satisfying from the start.

"From the time we made the three pictures at San Diego in 1915, she and I had been pretty constant companions, one of our chief bonds of interest, a mutual love for dancing," Lloyd wrote in a 1928 memoir. "For a year or two before the war, dancing for cups was a craze in the picture colony. Bebe and I won 20 cups or more in competition against Wally and Dorothy Reid, Gloria Swanson and Wallace Beery and many other movie couples at the Sunset Inn, Santa Monica; the Ship Cafe, Ocean Park; Nat Goodwin's at Venice; Watt's Tavern and such popular resorts."

A chance meeting on one of these evenings in 1917 was to mark a major turning point in both Harold's and Bebe's lives.

As Lloyd told it, "Bebe long had had a natural desire to graduate from comedies into dramatic pictures. About a year before she left the company, we were dancing at the Sunset Inn in Santa Monica one night. We survived the elimination contests and defeated the Reids for the cup in the finals. [Cecil B.] DeMille, his scenario writer Jeanie MacPherson, and party were there, and the director broached the question of Bebe coming to him. She said she would like nothing better, but that her contract with Roach yet had a year to run. 'I will keep you in mind,' he told her, 'and when the year is up, we will see.'"

DeMille recalled in his 1959 autobiography, "Still another was a young girl I had noticed, without being overwhelmingly impressed, in some of Hal Roach's comedies. But when I saw her one evening at dinner at a restaurant, it occurred to me that there might be more behind those big, dark eyes and cupid's-bow mouth than a steady diet of comedy roles had brought out. Then and there I asked Bebe Daniels if she wanted to work for me. More honorable than some in those cutthroat days, she said that she could not because she was under contract to Mr. Roach. More than a year later, however, she came to see me, all dressed up in her mother's clothes to make her look mature enough for dramatic roles, and I gave her a small part in *Male and Female*."

There is evidence that Roach wasn't too happy with DeMille's overtures toward Bebe. Following the incident, Roach's business partner, Dwight Whiting, wrote a letter to Frank Garbutt, general manager for Famous Players, complaining about DeMille's conversation with Bebe since "raiding" was prohibited by the Hollywood Producers Association. Garbutt claimed in a response to Whiting that DeMille did not know who she was, and when they did learn she was under contract to Roach, quickly informed her they could not pursue the matter further.

A candid shot of Daniels, center, kidding around with Sammy Brooks and an unidentified extra during the filming of Captain Kidd's Kids *(1919). This was Daniels's last film with Lloyd.*

Recalling the incident 50 years later, Bebe said, "Hal and Harold both said, 'This is a great opportunity for you, and we think you ought to go.' Then I said, 'I'll wait until my contract expires,' which I did, and then I called up and asked if he was still interested, and he said, 'Very much so.'"

The entire episode seems very congenial and almost antiseptic. Biographer Richard Schickel expressed serious doubts that Bebe's decision to go with DeMille after her contract expired in 1919 was that simple. He noted there may be some truth to Bebe's claims of wanting to seek greater dramatic opportunities, "but it surely isn't the whole story. For one thing, Lloyd's career was obviously on the rise, and it was a strange moment for her to leave an actor with whom she was so closely associated." Bebe's last two films with Lloyd were his first two-reelers with the glasses character, *Bumping into Broadway* and *Captain Kidd's Kids*, both 1919. At this time, his popularity was greater than ever. In two years, he would achieve phenomenal success making feature films.

To Marry or Not to Marry

Schickel continued, "[T]he two had been great and good friends almost from the moment she had joined the company . . . Now suddenly, there was nothing between Harold and Bebe, and a larger explanation is required." Schickel stated flatly that Bebe wanted to marry Harold. Dardis agreed, "There is some indication that she was anxious to marry him, but he felt he was far too young to shoulder the responsibilities that went with marriage." It very well could be that Lloyd was reluctant to marry until he was on the financial footing he had been seeking for years. Yes, his popularity was greater than ever, but the tremendous wealth that he would know at the time of his marriage to Mildred Davis was a few years off. Lloyd's extremely practical and even tight-fisted nature probably wouldn't allow him to make such a major step at this critical point in his life.

D'Agostino Lloyd feels the love the two held for each other is evident on the screen. "Perhaps in no other film is the real-life relationship between Daniels and Lloyd more evident than in *The City Slicker* (1918) . . . Their love shows in simply the way they look at each other and the way they move together. In this, and the films that follow, the two seem genuinely affectionate toward each other. In *Count Your Change* (1919), Daniels is rescued from a thief by Lloyd, and the two share kisses and chocolates in the last few feet of film. If one had any doubt about their off-screen love, watch this film. The way Lloyd 'bites' Daniels' arm is downright titillating." She continues, "The off-screen love positively shone on screen, and their 'lovemaking' seems more natural and realistic than similar scenes between Lloyd and Davis or Lloyd and [Jobyna] Ralston."

Schickel said, "The trouble was that Lloyd, like his screen character, was quite insecure around women—at least at this time. He behaved toward Bebe as he behaved toward everyone else who was important then in his life—ingratiatingly."

Dardis observed, "It seems probable that, despite his tremendous fondness for her, Bebe posed a kind of threat to him—here was a young woman of only 18 and fully developed career plans of her own. This was scarcely what Harold wanted. There was also his timidity in making major decisions. His ambivalence toward Bebe Daniels can be seen as characteristic of his reluctance to make up his mind about things, a need to postpone a decision until he had examined the problem in all aspects, a process that Bebe must have found difficult."

Most likely, Bebe wasn't as concerned about honoring a contract in 1917 (especially if Lloyd and Roach encouraged her to go, as she claimed) as she was about her relationship with Lloyd. Maybe she was still holding out hope that they would marry. She certainly could have felt that it was too early to give up on their love.

However, by the time 1919 rolled around, Bebe was now a "mature" 18-year-old. The contract was up, and it can be safely assumed that she was ready to throw in the towel on getting a lifetime commitment from her leading man. It's obvious, especially from the earlier magazine interview, that Bebe's desire to be a dramatic actress was genuine, but one can't help but wonder how her acting career would have differed had she married Lloyd.

All Those Years Ago

Bebe always looked back on those early days with fond memories. She was hired at $10 a week and was earning $100 a week by the time she was 18, so it was a financially rewarding time, as well as personally and professionally. She credited Lloyd, Roach, and the whole experience with providing her the training she needed to move on in her career. "I was 14 when I went with the Rolin-Pathé comedies to play opposite Harold Lloyd, and I think this was the best possible training during my 'growing up' years, for comedy has taught me the values of lights and shade of emotional work that I probably would not have gained had I done only serious dramas. I loved it, too; it was a happy experience, for everyone in the company was so fine, and we were like a big family," she said in 1919.

More than 50 years later, Lloyd was in London when he paid Bebe and her husband Ben Lyon a visit. They had a pleasant time together, reminiscing about those early days in movies . . . and even though it had been 50 years since "The Boy" and "The Girl" had kissed or the young couple had gone out on the town for an evening of dancing, Lloyd was still wearing a ring she had given him during those carefree days together, and she still had all the trophies they had won in their dance contests.

SOURCES
PERIODICALS
Cheatham, Maude S. "Bebe, the Oriental." *Motion Picture Magazine* (November 1919).
Hilty, Bernadine. "She Wouldn't Be Kissed." *Photo-Play Journal* (December 1918).

Rolin Phunphilms advertisement. *Moving Picture World* (October 16, 1915).

Sheridan, Marguerite. "Mam'Selle Bebe BonBon." *Photo-Play Journal* (December 1917.)

Slide, Anthony. "Bebe Daniels: In Conversation with Ben Lyon and Anthony Slide." *The Silent Picture.* Spring 1971.

BOOKS

Bodeen, DeWitt. *From Hollywood: The Careers of 15 Great American Stars*. New York: A.S. Barnes and Co., Inc., 1976.

Dardis, Tom. *Harold Lloyd, the Man on the Clock*. New York: Penguin Books, 1983.

DeMille, Cecil B. *Autobiography*. Englewood Cliffs, NJ: Prentice-Hall, Inc., 1959.

Lloyd, Annette D'Agostino. *The Harold Lloyd Encyclopedia*. Jefferson, NC: McFarland & Company, Inc., 2004.

Lloyd, Annette D'Agostino. *Harold Lloyd: Magic in a Pair of Horn-Rimmed Glasses*. Albany, GA: Bear-Manor Media, 2009.

Lloyd, Harold. *An American Comedy*. New York: Dover Publications, 1971.

Maltin, Leonard. "Harold Lloyd: Comedy Through Characterization," in *Harold Lloyd: The King of Dare-devil Comedy* by Adam Reilly. New York: MacMillan Publishing Co., Inc., 1977.

Schickel, Richard. *Harold Lloyd: The Shape of Laughter*. Boston: New York Graphic Society, 1974.

Slide, Anthony. *Silent Players*. Lexington, KY: The University Press of Kentucky, 2002.

CHAPTER 3
Buster Keaton Is All Wet
ɛↄ

Here's a trivia question: How many gags did Buster Keaton perform that involve water?

You may be counting for a while, because out of 19 shorts and 12 features between 1920 and 1928, only three do not contain significant gags using water in one form or another.

Let It Rain

Let's start with rain. Name the shorts and/or features where rain was used in one or more sequences.

Ready? Okay, here goes.

- In *One Week* (1920), the first of his independent two-reel productions to be released, he and costar Sybil Seely are newlyweds who put together a prefabricated house themselves, with results that look like something out of *The Cabinet of Dr. Caligari*. While several guests are visiting during the housewarming, a terrible wind and rainstorm comes up, spinning the house round and round. Buster, Sybil, and the guests are thrown from the house, and all he can do is sit outside and wait for the storm to come to an end.
- In *The Boat* (1921), a storm sinks the *Damfino*, and Buster, his wife (Seely again) and two children are set adrift in a bathtub.
- In *The Navigator* (1924), he and Kathryn McGuire think they hear ghosts below and decide to sleep on the deck of the ship. As soon as they get themselves comfortably snuggled under their blankets, a big storm comes up, soaking them to the skin and sending them below again.
- In *The General* (1926), set during the Civil War, he has to abandon his train when the Union soldiers learn he is the only one on board. He escapes into the woods, and, as soon as he settles down into some sense of security, the rains begin to fall. Later, he rescues Marion Mack from a house where she is being held captive by the Yankees.

They sneak out of a window but must find their way through the woods during a heavy storm in the middle of the night. Finally, realizing they don't have a clue which way to go in the woods, they sit down on the ground, hold one another close, and simply wait out the rain.

- Although used to set a somber mood rather than for comedy, *Our Hospitality* (1923) begins during a terrible nighttime thunder-and-lightning storm. Buster is a baby (played by his infant son), and his father and Jim Canfield kill one another during the storm, assuring that the feud between the Canfields and the McKays will continue until Buster reaches adulthood.

The idea for The Navigator *(1924) came about after Keaton heard the ocean liner, the SS Buford, was going to be junked. He bought it, and his gagmen built a story around it. His co-star is the lovely and capable Kathryn McGuire.*

- In *College* (1927), he and his mother are walking to his high school graduation in a torrential downpour. Finally, he stops and purchases an umbrella along the way, but it seems too small to provide him or his mother with much protection. In at least three films, we see Buster walking in the rain, totally oblivious to the fact that he's getting soaking wet, and with no more concern than if he were strolling down the street on a clear, spring day.
- The next year, in *Steamboat Bill Jr.* (1928), we see an almost identical shot, this time without a mother on his arm. Buster is walking down the street to visit his father in jail. The rain is pouring, and Buster has that same all-too-small umbrella above his head.
- *The Cameraman* (1929) also includes a scene where he is walking down the street oblivious to the rain, but this time there's good reason. Co-star Marceline Day has just kissed him on the cheek, and he walks out into the rain, still in a daze from the show of affection.

Bag 'em With A Hook, a Gun, or Your Bare Hands

What about fishing? How many films can you name where Buster is fishing . . . and keep in mind he may not be doing it with a fishing pole each time!

- Although it may not qualify as fishing in its purest sense, the first time he catches a fish in a comedy is in *Convict 13* (1920). Buster has hit his golf ball in the water, and a fish swallows it. Determined to "play it as it lies," he dives, almost "fishlike," into the water again and again in search of the fish that has his ball—catching each one with his bare hands!

- The next year, in *Hard Luck* (1921), we find him fishing at a lake. Here the gag has him using a tiny fish as bait to catch a somewhat larger one. Not satisfied with the size of this one, he uses it for bait, throws it back in, and catches an even bigger one. Finally, he hooks one that is so big it snatches him through the air and into the water, but the line breaks, and we never see "the one that got away."

- In *The Frozen North* (1920), Buster is ice fishing. He is seated, back-to-back, with another fisherman, and their lines get tangled up together. With both men thinking they have caught a big fish, they begin tugging back and forth until Buster finally jerks the other man into one hole in the ice and up and out of the other hole.

- *The Balloonatic* (1923) has a lengthy sequence with both Buster and co-star Phyllis Haver fishing. Although Buster has no luck with a pole, he does catch several fish by grasping the oversized legs of the waders, flapping them and "shooing" the fish into a small rivulet, much as a lady would use her full dress to "shoo" chickens on a farm.

- In *Our Hospitality* (1923), Buster can be found on a rock ledge, fishing in a pool of water. He notices water falling from above and thinks it's beginning to rain. Suddenly, a huge rush of water falls in front of him, totally blocking him from view. Someone has blown up the nearby dam, creating a waterfall from the ledge above him. Of course, it serves a purpose. The Canfields are armed and searching for Buster so they can kill him. Just as the water hides Buster from view, we see the Canfields walk by. Close call!

- In *The Love Nest* (1923), Buster gets his fish in a different way. Armed with a rifle, he walks down the steps on the side of the ship and into the water. In a moment, we see a puff of smoke rise from the water, indicating he has fired the rifle. Seconds later, Buster walks up the steps from beneath the water with the rifle and the fish he has shot! In this same film, he gives another variation on fishing. The crew has spotted a whale and loads the harpoon gun. Buster is given the rope attached to the harpoon and told to tie it to the railing. Instead, he braces himself and holds the rope. Of course, when the harpoon is fired, he is jerked overboard. When next we see him, he is swimming back to the ship, pulling the rope behind him and leading the viewer to understand that he is bringing the whale back to the ship! A final gag in the film has Buster fishing with a traditional pole this time, but he unknowingly is atop a floating target the Navy is using for their maneuvers. Every time one of the shells being shot from a nearby ship splashes near the target, Buster thinks it's a big fish and turns to throw his hook in that spot.

- In *Daydreams* (1922), the tables are turned, and Buster is the "fish" rather than the fisherman. In this film, he is trying to hide from the police in the rotating paddlewheel of a steamboat. Trying to keep up with the motion of the wheel proves to be too much, and, tired and exhausted, he is thrown from the paddlewheel into the water. Next, we see an old fisherman on the dock take his "string" of fish, add one more to it, drop them back into the water, and continue fishing. Soon, he latches onto something that really tugs at his pole. He pulls back, and out of the water comes Buster, wet and bedraggled. He looks at Buster with interest for a moment, then takes his "string," runs it through one of Buster's lapel holes, and drops him back into the water with the rest of the fish he has caught.

Rowboat, Canoe, Whaling Ship, Ocean Liner, Steamboat . . .

How about boats? How many can you remember?

- In *The Boat*, Buster destroys his entire house while trying to extricate the boat he has just built from his basement. As soon as he, his wife, and their two children launch the boat for the first time, it immediately sinks. Although it is resurrected, it sinks for a final time during a terrible rainstorm (mentioned above). The bathtub they must use as a lifeboat may be considered a second boat in the film.
- The idea for *The Navigator* came about after Buster heard the ocean liner, the SS *Buford*, was about to be junked. He bought it, and he and his gagmen built a story around it.
- Much of the story centers around how he and co-star Kathryn McGuire use their ingenuity to survive on the abandoned ship

when they are set adrift, alone, with no power on the vessel. In the end, they are fighting off cannibals, who take over the ship when it runs aground. A ship figures in the final gag of the film, too. Buster and Kathryn are out in the middle of the water about to be overtaken by the cannibals when something begins to rise from the water and lift them into the air. It is a submarine, and they get inside just in time to evade their attackers.

• Although it may be argued that this does not constitute a boat, Buster himself is used as a seagoing vessel in *The Navigator*. He and Kathryn must get from the beach, where the cannibals are pursuing them, to the ship, which is a couple of hundred yards out in the water. Buster happens to be wearing a diving suit that is filled with air, so he simply lies on his back in the water. Kathryn, treating him as though he were an inflated life raft, climbs on top of him and she begins paddling back to the ship.

• There are two paddlewheel steamboats in *Steamboat Bill Jr.*, a brand new one owned by his father's rival, and the old "workhorse" that Buster's father, Steamboat Bill (played magnificently by Ernest Torrence), has been running on the river for years. This film may contain the most exciting use of a boat in one of Buster's films. A cyclone is blowing through the town and has caused the ground to give way beneath the local jail where Steamboat Bill has been incarcerated. The jail slips into the river and is slowly sinking. Realizing that his father will drown if something isn't done quickly, Buster swings into action. He rigs up the controls of the boat with a series of ropes so he can operate them from the wheelhouse while he steers, sets the boat in motion, and rams the floating jail. The structure is demolished, and, for a moment, we're not sure if Buster's father has survived the impact. However, we soon see a head bob up from the water amidst the rubble. He has survived, and, of course, Buster is the hero.

• Of the films that were built almost entirely around a boat, *The Love Nest* may be the least familiar. Buster's girl has jilted him, so he sets out in his small craft, *Cupid*, to sail around the world. He soon finds himself on a whaling ship run by a vicious captain (played menacingly by "Big" Joe Roberts). Buster wants to use a lifeboat to escape from the ship, but it is too heavy for him to move into the water. Therefore, he sinks the bigger vessel so the lifeboat can simply come to rest in the water as the big ship disappears into the ocean depths.

- *College* offers us a different kind of boat, a scull. The coach of the rowing team has been forced by the college dean to make Buster the team's coxswain. During the race, Buster pulls the rudder loose. So, he wraps the rope around his waist to tie the rudder to his backside, slips down the narrow stern of the boat and lowers the rudder and his buttocks into the water to steer the boat during the final moments of the race.

- One of the strangest scenes involving a boat appears in *The Balloonatic*. Buster is floating down a mountain stream in a canoe when he spies a rabbit on the shore. He paddles in the rabbit's direction, picks up his rifle, and suddenly we see him walking out of the water, the boat around his waist and his legs protruding through the bottom! Later, as he is going downstream, he fails to notice a small waterfall, and, when he goes over it, the boat capsizes. All we see is the

BUSTER KEATON in "The Balloonatic"

DISTRIBUTED BY ASSOCIATED
FIRST NATIONAL PICTURES, INC.

"Just a song at twilight."

In the final gag in The Balloonatic *(1923), Buster and co-star Phyllis Haver are unaware that they are about to drop over a waterfall. At the edge, the boat continues to float out into open sky. The camera pulls back, and we see Buster has attached his hot air balloon to the boat.*

upturned boat floating downstream and Buster's legs kicking in the air. The end of the film shows Buster and co-star Phyllis Haver in the boat with a canopy added to it. The couple floats lazily down the stream as Buster serenades Phyllis on the ukulele. The viewer is then made aware that they are heading straight for a huge waterfall. From a shot looking up, we see the edge of the boat appear as it eases out past the edge of the waterfall. Just as we think the boat should take a nosedive down the falls, it simply continues to float out into space. The next shot shows us that Buster has attached his hot air balloon to the boat, allowing them to float safely through the air!

- In *Seven Chances* (1925), he stands in a small, one-man boat with a rifle, trying to get a good shot at a duck that keeps "ducking" (no pun intended) under the water and popping up on alternate sides of the boat. Finally, Buster leans forward, peering into the water to see where the duck has gone. Unaware that he has leaned too far, the boat begins to take on water and eventually sinks.

In Sherlock, Jr. *(1924), Buster runs his car into the water, but, instead of sinking, it floats! To get things moving, he raises the convertible top in a perpendicular position so that it functions as a sail.*

- As mentioned previously, Buster evades the pursuing police in *Day-dreams* by hiding in the paddlewheel of a ferryboat. In *Our Hospitality*, he sets out in a small boat (actually it's a wood box, the kind in which you stack firewood) to escape the Canfields, but it capsizes, sending him adrift in the rapids. (More about this sequence later.)
- Buster used a boat, of sorts, for a gag in an earlier short, *The Play-house* (1921). After he has flooded the theatre, we see him floating through the water-filled orchestra pit in a bass drum, using a violin as a paddle.
- Here's a different kind of boat . . . Buster and Kathryn McGuire run their car into the water in *Sherlock Jr.*, but that's okay with Buster. The car floats (of course, it would in a Keaton film), so he makes the most of the situation and sets the convertible top in a perpendicu-lar position, so it functions as a sail!
- Probably the most unusual item Buster used as a "boat" was a horse! In *Hard Luck* (1921), he is crossing a river on a horse. First, we see Buster with a paddle, helping the horse along, and then we see him turned and facing the rear of the horse, stroking with two oars as if he were in a rowboat!

Is a Water Tower Funny?

Buster saw the comic possibilities in the old train water tower. He used one in two of his features and in one short. Can you name them?

- The first appearance of a train watering tower was in the 1922 short *The Blacksmith* (1922). Buster and his girlfriend, played by Virginia Fox, are being chased by an angry group out to avenge the wrongs Buster has done them. While he and Virginia stand beneath the water tower, debating their marriage plans, the angry group is sneaking up behind them. Buster, in his frustration with Virginia, is gesticulating wildly and accidentally pulls the rope to release the water from the tank. Their pursuers just happen to be directly below the spout and are drenched, allowing Buster and Virginia to escape.
- The second appearance of a water tower is in *Sherlock Jr.* Buster finds himself atop a railroad car. The train begins to move rapidly, but Buster doesn't want to go with it, so he runs toward the rear of the train. When he realizes the final car is approaching and the train is about to run out from under him, he grabs the rope on a train-watering tower. Just as the trains passes from underneath him, the

girl drains the pool to save Buster, but he is nowhere to be found. The next shot is of a large drainpipe emptying from the side of a hill, and here comes Buster in a rush of water, being deposited on the bank!

- For approximately six minutes in *The Cameraman*, Buster gives us one gag after another as he and his date, Marceline Day, try to enjoy themselves at a public pool. Buster's "dream date" runs into trouble after he and Marceline change into their bathing suits and walk out to the pool. A group of male admirers begin to follow the beautiful Marceline wherever she goes. When she tries to play catch with Buster in the water, the guys gather round him and snatch the ball away before he can get it. Marceline finally gets the ball through to him, but all at once, the guys pounce on Buster in an attempt to snag it. When they separate, Buster is nowhere to be seen. Suddenly, one of the guys does a back flip and Buster emerges from the water, gasping for breath.

- While taking a rest on a fountain in the middle of the pool, Buster and Marceline watch several well-built bathers diving from the high dive. Jealous at the attention they are getting from Marceline, Buster decides he will show her "some fancy diving." After climbing up and surveying the situation, Buster runs to the end of the board, changes his mind about diving, tries to make a sudden stop and gets all tangled up in his oversized bathing suit. He tumbles into the water and, when he emerges, his bathing suit is gone! He frantically looks around for it—no such luck. At one point during his search, a young lady rises from underneath the water directly in front of him. As she swims away, Buster furrows his brow and looks at her questioningly as if to ask, "What were *you* doing down there?"

- Later, he sees a rather large lady in a full, old-timey bathing suit that consists of pants and top with a voluminous skirt on it. Buster watches intently as she slips into the water. The next view of her is on the platform, legs bare and shouting, "I've been robbed!" Then we see Buster, wearing the lady's pants, which, by the way, extend up to his chest, running toward the dressing room.

And for Our Closing Number . . .

Here's the last bit of "Buster and Water" trivia. In what films does water play a part in a film's denouement?

- We've already mentioned the famous lost gag at the end of *Hard Luck*, the waterfall gag at the end of *The Balloonatic*, and the boat race at the end of *College*, as well as the films whose storylines are built around water—*The Boat, The Love Nest, The Navigator*, and *Steamboat Bill Jr.* All of these have endings that involve some activity in water. Of course, the one that qualifies as the most famous of all is in *The General*, when the train plunges through the burning trestle into the creek below. The final battle also takes place in and around this creek, and a reference was made earlier to the dam, which was destroyed by a cannon ball. The flooding that resulted sent the Union soldiers in retreat and saved the day for the Confederate army. Of course, it was Buster who accidentally sent the errant cannonball into the dam.

- Also mentioned was the scene in *The Playhouse* in which he used a bass drum for a boat, although it was not explained previously *how* he flooded the theatre. Virginia Fox was performing an underwater act in a huge, glassed-in water tank onstage. When she appears to be in trouble, he smashes the glass with a huge mallet, sending a torrent of water into the building.

- Although Buster used water gags and/or stunts at the end of several of his films, none was more spectacular than the one he used in the climax of *Our Hospitality*. The following is the sequence of events that led up to that final, spectacular stunt.

  1. Buster is on the side of a cliff. A rope comes down to him from above, and he ties it around his waist. What he doesn't know is that one of the Canfields, who are feuding with Buster's family, is on the ledge above with the other end of the rope tied around his waist.

  2. Canfield is trying to get Buster up and in position so he can shoot him. However, Buster jerks the rope, causing Canfield to fall.

  3. As he watches Canfield fly past him, Buster knows what is about to happen and braces himself. Since the rope is still tied to Buster's waist, Canfield's fall jerks him over the cliff as well and both plunge into the water below.

  4. Later, he has temporarily eluded his pursuer, but a length of rope is still tied around Buster's waist.

  5. He is continuing his escape on the train, but it derails, throwing him into the river.

6. Buster tries to find something to grab onto; he finally comes upon a log in the water and attaches his rope to it.

7. However, it dislodges, and both Buster and the log are being forced downstream by the rapids toward a huge waterfall.

8. Fortunately, one end of the log catches on something, while the other end, with Buster attached, swings out into space, extending itself beyond the falls.

9. Buster is dangling out in front of the falls but is able to work his way back up on the log and onto a small ledge.

Probably Buster's most spectacular water stunt was in Our Hospitality *(1923). He swings from a rope attached to an overhead log that is jammed at the waterfall's edge, catches the heroine (Natalie Talmadge) as she tumbles over the falls, and then deposits her on the rock ledge as he swings back.*

10. He struggles to remove the rope from himself and the log, without success. His girl (played by real-life wife Natalie Talmadge), who was coming to rescue Buster, has been thrown into the rapids, too, and she is heading for the waterfall.

11. Buster tries again, unsuccessfully, to remove the rope so he can get to her. Then he hits upon an idea. He moves back along the ledge, away from the falls, the rope still attached to the end of the log, which is extended out several feet in front of the falls.

12. He waits for just the right moment, and, when Natalie begins to go over the falls, he jumps from the ledge, swings by the rope in front of the falls, grabs Natalie the moment she goes over the edge and swings back toward the ledge where he deposits her in a beautifully rhythmic mid-air ballet.

Maybe It's Because "Buster" and "Water" Both End In "T-E-R"

In his autobiography, *My Wonderful World of Slapstick*, Buster reminisced, "The best summers of my life were spent in the cottage Pop had built on Lake Muskegon (MI) in 1908." Obviously, he looked forward to the recreation and enjoyment that was offered by such an environment and, as he noted, he spent much of his time boating and fishing.

Maybe it was these memories that led him to so frequently use water in his films, or maybe he simply saw the comic possibilities of that basic element. Whatever the reason, his comedies are filled with laughs, thrills, and, in some cases, gorgeous visual imagery because of water. If he hadn't felt as comfortable in that environment as he did, well, it just wouldn't be the same.

SOURCES
BOOKS

Keaton, Buster, and Charles Samuels. *My Wonderful World of Slapstick*. New York: De Capo Press, Inc., 1960.

Keaton, Eleanor, and Jeffrey Vance. *Buster Keaton Remembered*. New York: Harry N. Abrams, 2001.

CHAPTER 4
From Demure to Tempestuous: Chaplin's Silent Ladies
❦

Chaplin made five silent features in the 17-year period from 1920 to 1936, and although the Tramp character remained fairly consistent through each one, his leading ladies were a varied group, ranging from the demure to the tempestuous.

The Kid's Mother

It was only fitting that his first feature film included the beautiful Edna Purviance, who had been Chaplin's leading lady since his second Essanay short in 1915. Purviance will always have a special place in movie history because the years she served as Chaplin's leading lady are so important to the evolution of the Tramp. Although he created the character during his years at Keystone, the Essanay, Mutual, and First National years are when the character truly developed, and Purviance was right by his side, on and off the screen, through it all.

However, "co-star" may be too generous a word since the real co-star in his first feature, *The Kid* (1921), is Jackie Coogan. All things considered, Purviance's part as the kid's mother is almost incidental to the film, necessary only in setting up the story of the Tramp raising the child and his attempts to keep him.

Chaplin biographer's Theodore Huff, said, "Direction and acting, on the whole, are very fine. Edna Purviance's first emotional scenes, however, seemed rather stilted, even at the time of release." This may be somewhat true, but, as mentioned, her part was not a significant one, and she portrays the unwed mother very well. This type of role would be perfectly suited for the serene beauty of Purviance, who Huff also described as "demure and ladylike."

Purviance was not to serve as Chaplin's leading lady in any more of his films. It has been noted that she had begun to put on weight (her looks were sometimes described at this time as "matronly"), and her persona just didn't fit the 1920s flapper era. Chaplin's second wife, Lita Grey (she played a small part in the film's dream sequence), said, "During the shooting of the film, she had begun to drink, not heavily, but enough to displease Chaplin, who viewed drinking during working hours as unprofessional and therefore intolerable."

This is not a scene from a film; it is just Charlie Chaplin and Edna Purviance clowning around for the photographer. Purviance supported Chaplin in 34 of his comedies, the last time as the unwed mother in The Kid *(1921).*

Chaplin, of course, did try to promote Purviance's dramatic abilities by starring her in *A Woman of Paris* in 1923, but, when it came time to make his next film, *The Gold Rush* (1925), he moved to a younger leading lady with a completely different look.

The Dance Hall Girl

Georgia Hale proved to be a perfect choice as the dance hall girl in Chaplin's The Gold Rush *(1925). She admired Chaplin and proved to be a cooperative actress for the comedian, who sought perfection from his leading ladies.*

Georgia Hale had caught Chaplin's eye in Josef von Sternberg's *The Salvation Hunters* (1925). Following Chaplin's marriage to Lita Grey (she was to co-star in the film until she became pregnant with Chaplin's first child), Hale was selected for the role of the dance hall girl with whom the Tramp falls in love.

According to Huff, "In *The Gold Rush*, impersonating a hard, impulsive and fiery-tempered dancehall girl—a Chaplin heroine quite different from the pretty and agreeable Edna Purviance—Georgia Hale gives a performance of considerable verve although there are moments when she slips into some stilted conventions of the period."

Biographer Joyce Milton observed, "A former Miss Chicago, Georgia Hale was an interesting combination of glamour and midwestern straightness. She was well-cast as the fiery-tempered but good-hearted bar singer, and the shooting of the complicated dance hall scenes moved along briskly." Nevertheless, Hale's performance was praised by the critics, and reportedly she never gave her director and co-star a minute's trouble during the filming.

The pleasant working relationship between Hale and Chaplin was due in no small part to two factors—first, Hale was very candid about her admiration for Chaplin, which went back to her childhood days, watching him on the screen; secondly, the two developed a romantic interest in each other. In later years, Hale said, "You just knew you were working with a genius. He's the greatest genius of all times for the motion picture business. He was so wonderful to work with. You didn't mind that he told you what to do all the time, every little thing. He was infinitely patient with actors—kind. He knew exactly what to say and what to do to get what he wanted."

Hale looked the part of the tough dance hall girl (named Georgia in the film) and acted the part very well. It was no "push-over" role, either, calling for a varied range of emotions.

In dealing with ladies' man Jack Cameron (played capably by Malcolm Waite), the fiery temper comes through well, and her face portrays the anger superbly with narrowing eyes and tightly pursed lips. According to Hale, in one scene where she was required to slap the character of Jack, Chaplin had them do the scene so many times she really did become angry. The take that was finally used was when she has essentially lost her patience and gave fellow actor Waite a very hard, very real slap.

In another scene, Georgia goes to the Tramp's cabin and, finding a festively prepared table, realizes she had forgotten a promise to share New Year's Eve dinner with him. It is obvious she is disturbed by the hurt she must have caused him, and the fiery temper is displaced by compassion.

The final scene of the movie has her unexpectedly encountering the Tramp on a steamer heading back to the States (and not realizing he has become a millionaire since they last met). She gives a sensitive portrayal here at meeting the little fellow once again. Hale plays the part with a restraint that implies genuine surprise when she learns he is now a millionaire. Their final kiss to end the movie is touching.

Yes, Hale deserves praise for her part in the film, and, certainly, she brought much more to the role than the youthful-looking Lita Grey could have. Yet, as good as she was, Chaplin was to choose the weakest of his leading ladies for his next film.

The Circus Girl

The Circus was released in 1928, and the leading lady was another youthful teenage "find" of Chaplin's who had actually been recommended to him by his wife. Grey and Merna Kennedy were friends, and Grey felt she could trust Kennedy with her husband, but by the time the movie was finished, Chaplin and Grey's marriage was finished anyway.

Huff gave a somewhat less-than-glowing appraisal of Kennedy's work in *The Circus*. He noted, "Merna Kennedy, slightly reminiscent of Mabel Normand, though lacking her talent and personality, is merely competent." Obviously, Huff was referring to some of the physical similarities of Kennedy and Normand because Kennedy doesn't display any of the "life" or charisma that Normand had onscreen. However, his appraisal of a "competent" performance is accurate and about the best that can be said of it. For example, when she's called upon to cry, she accomplishes this by quickly throwing her head down

Merna Kennedy was not yet 20 years old when she supported Chaplin in The Circus *(1928), her first appearance on film. Her inexperience shows through in her performance, and, consequently, she receives the least praise of any of Chaplin's leading ladies.*

and hiding her face. When fear is called for (because of her abusive father), she throws an arm up as if to ward off a blow. With facial expressions so important in silent movies to convey emotion, Kennedy does merely a passable job.

This is disappointingly true in a scene where the Tramp shares his bread with her, admonishing her to eat slowly. She has been gobbling the bread ravenously because her father has denied her food since the day before. Throughout the scene, she stares blankly at the Tramp, showing no emotion whatsoever, whether he's chiding her or explaining how bad her eating habits are for her health.

This is not to say that Kennedy doesn't bring some girlish charm to the part (she was not quite 20 at the time); she also looks fragile and helpless enough when her abusive father is grabbing her by the arm and throwing her about. She's at her best, however, when called upon to be happy and giddy as she is in the closing scenes after marrying the tightrope walker.

All in all, Kennedy is attractive, and the fact that she doesn't give the most memorable performance of any of Chaplin's leading ladies could be due in no small part to the role she was given and the film in which she plays. Chaplin's next two films would give the leading ladies much more memorable roles.

The Blind Girl

Virginia Cherrill seems to have been a little unfairly maligned over the years because she was most likely Chaplin's least favorite leading lady, and she was not a professional actress. However, she turns in a commendable performance, *especially* when one considers she was not a professional.

Therefore, it stands to reason that Chaplin must be given a great deal of credit for the performance Cherrill gives as the blind girl of *City Lights*. Chaplin was doing this, too, under difficult circumstances since Cherrill was "addicted" to parties and good times—and was indifferent to her job as an actress.

Huff gave a little harsher appraisal: "All she brought to the part was good looks and near-sightedness, the latter a deficiency in general, though an asset for the particular role she was cast in." He then goes on to add, "Virginia Cherrill proved to be unusually effective as the blind girl, and certainly she is one of the most strikingly beautiful young women to ever appear in films."

Over the years, almost all Chaplin biographers have outlined the problems Chaplin experienced with his leading lady while making the film. One said, "She had given him trouble from the beginning . . . She was a party girl given to staying out most of the

Although Chaplin and leading lady Virginia Cherrill did not get along particularly well while filming City Lights *(1931), this looks as if it could be a candid shot of the two enjoying a lighter moment.*

night. Many mornings she would appear on the set somewhat worse for the wear, unfit for the camera which magnifies the slightest sign of dissipation."

Also, Cherrill did not revere Chaplin as did his other leading ladies. Because she was living on alimony, she wasn't impressed by her paltry 75 dollars a week salary. Early in the filming, she unwisely left the studio to have lunch with friends at a nearby restaurant, not realizing the entire cast was expected to remain on the premises all day. Then, another time, she elicited Chaplin's anger by requesting permission to leave early for a hairdresser's appointment. Chaplin complained often about her unprofessional attitude, but he had too much already invested in the film to change leading ladies.

According to biographer David Robinson, "From the start, he began to have doubts about Virginia. It has become legendary how Chaplin spent shot after shot, hour after hour, day after day, trying to get her to hand a flower with the line and rhythm he wanted, and to speak to his satisfaction a line—'Flower, sir?'—which was never to be heard."

Robinson contends the lack of affection between the two was a part of the problem, as well. In a telephone interview with Robinson in the early 1980s, Cherrill told him, "I never liked Charlie, and he never liked me." Even Chaplin did not lay the full blame on Cherrill, noting the fault was "partly my own, for I had worked myself into a neurotic state of wanting perfection."

At one point in the filming, Chaplin did fire Cherrill, but he was unable to find a suitable replacement (he even tried reshooting some scenes with Georgia Hale). He apparently realized he had shot too much footage with his original leading lady and simply wasn't satisfied with anyone else, in spite of the problems he was having with her. However, Cherrill did not come back easily. She had been coached by her friend Marion Davies on how to handle Chaplin and refused to return to the set until he had doubled her weekly salary.

Everyone agrees Cherrill portrays a blind girl very well, and one must admit that she demands the sympathy from the viewer that the part requires. As excellent as Georgia Hale was in *The Gold Rush*, she could not have played the part of the blind girl as well as Cherrill. Some rare footage shown in Kevin Brownlow and David Gill's wonderful documentary *Unknown Chaplin* (1983) shows Hale performing the final scene of the movie in which the blind girl has regained her sight and recognizes the Tramp as her benefactor by the touch of his hand. This is certainly one of the most moving and emotional scenes in the history of the movies, and Hale just doesn't seem to be able to "get" it. Cherrill, on the other hand, deserves much credit for her acting here, for the success of the scene rests totally on her reaction when she realizes who the Tramp really is.

The Gamin

Paulette Goddard was given a unique opportunity to portray a leading lady in *Modern Times* (1936) unlike any that had preceded her in a Chaplin film. Almost without exception, she receives high praise from authors, critics, and Chaplin fans for her spirited romp as the "gamin" in the last of Chaplin's silent features.

Silent film historian William K. Everson heaps high praise on the actress's portrayal. "Paulette Goddard's performance, a strange but wholly effective welding of Fairbanksian bravura and optimism with the wistful and defeatist pathos of Leni Riefenstahl's Junta from *The Blue Light* (1932), might well be listed along with Mae Marsh's performance in *Intolerance* and Eleanor Boardman's in *The Crowd* (though in a pantomimic rather than an acting sense) as one of the great performances of the silent cinema—and what matter that it was performed in 1936 and by an actress never a part of silent film?"

Huff said, "Paulette Goddard, different from both the old, passive Chaplin heroine, and the tempestuous Georgia, played the role of the gamin with vitality and spontaneity."

If Cherrill's lack of a personal relationship with Chaplin was a hindrance to her performance in *City Lights*, then just the opposite was true for Goddard in *Modern Times*, for the two were married right after the release of the movie, and she turned in a magnificent performance.

Goddard's is one of those performances that is so charming the viewer can't help but smile each time she comes on the screen. The viewer first sees her with raggedy dress and hair unkempt, stealing bananas at dockside. When she cuts them from the bunch, she places the knife between her teeth and throws the bananas to some street urchins on the dock level above. Her movements are quick, catlike. She glances around to make sure she's not caught. Her expression is one of determination and cunning.

Paulette Goddard as the spirited gamin in Chaplin's last silent film, Modern Times *(1936), was a hit with audiences. The comedian fell in love with his new leading during the filming, and they married shortly afterward. They would co-star in one more film together,* The Great Dictator *(1940).*

When her misdeed is discovered, her bare feet scurry over several small boats and away from the dock and capture. All the while, the viewer is thinking, "Gee, what a beautiful girl."

This first scene is a great introduction for her, and Goddard wins the viewer over immediately. It takes 20 minutes of film before she appears, but her presence is wanted back onscreen as soon as possible.

How old the gamin is supposed to be is unclear. She and her younger brother and sister are taken in by the authorities when their father is killed. So, it would be safe to assume she is under 18. Chaplin handles the relationship between the girl and the Tramp well, with no sexual connotations.

One of the most delightful sequences is when the Tramp takes a job as a night watchman at the department store. As soon as the store is closed and everyone leaves, he lets the gamin in, and they head for the lunch counter. Then, it's off to the toy department and a fantastic skating sequence (reminiscent of Chaplin's 1916 *The Rink*). After that, the gamin is seen wrapped in a white fur coat. She sits in the middle of a fabulous bed, fondling the coat around her neck and luxuriating in its expensive feel. Goddard is a joy to watch as she delights in the adventure of it all and enjoys a taste of a world completely foreign to her own.

Outside of just pure beauty, Goddard's most ingratiating trait is her smile. Each time she's around the Tramp, she bursts into a broad smile. Each time the Tramp is sent to jail, she's waiting for him when he is released (this, in itself, is endearing to the viewer). On one occasion, when he leaves the police station, she darts from an alley, sneaks up behind him and puts her hands over his eyes. When he turns to hug her, Chaplin wisely gives us a close-up of her face. That winning smile and her loyalty to the Tramp reaches out and draws in the audience.

So, who was the best of Chaplin's leading ladies? Just as beauty is in the eye of the beholder, so is a performance, and the answer to that question can only be found in the personal tastes of each viewer.

SOURCES
BOOKS
Everson, William K. *American Silent Film*. New York: De Capo Press, 1998.
Huff, Theodore. *Charlie Chaplin*. New York: Henry Schuman, 1951.
Karney, Robyn, and Robin Cross. *The Life and Times of Charlie Chaplin*. New York: Smithmark, 1992.
Milton, Joyce. *Tramp, The Life of Charlie Chaplin*. New York: Harper Collins, 1996.
Robinson, David. *Chaplin, His Life and Art*. New York: McGraw-Hill, 1985.
Spears, Jack. *Hollywood, The Golden Era*. New York: Castle Books, 1971.

OTHER
Brownlow, Kevin, and David Gill. *Unknown Chaplin* (documentary). Photoplay Productions, Ltd., 1983.

CHAPTER 5
The Divine Corinne Griffith
ɞ

It seemed the critics and the fan magazine writers were more taken with her beauty than her acting. One writer said she had the face of an Italian angel. Another called her the "Toast of Hollywood." One summed it up by saying, "There are pretty women, and there are beautiful women, and there are witty women. And then there is Corinne Griffith."

Corinne Griffith was born in Texarkana, Texas, on November 21, 1894. As with many stars, her birth year may vary depending on where it was published—for example, a date of 1898 was given by one fan magazine in 1925. She attended the local schools there and then went on to the Sacred Heart Convent in New Orleans, Louisiana, where she matriculated.

Griffith was a "popular society girl" in New Orleans, winning first prize in a Mardi Gras beauty contest. Afterwards, Vitagraph director Rolin Sturgeon encountered her at a society affair, where she "posed in tableaux and danced." He immediately offered her a movie contract. Although her parents were reluctant at first, they finally gave their consent, and her mother accompanied her to California.

The Door to Stardom

She made her first films in 1916, usually western two-reelers. She soon moved up to leading lady roles with established stars such as Earle Williams and Harry Morey and, by 1918, became the featured star of her own movies.

Griffith spent her first year working in California, but Vitagraph then moved her to New York, where she was introduced to the coldest weather she had ever experienced. While making *The Girl of Today* (1918), she was required to do location work on the ice blocks of the Hudson River, in the snow fields around Albany, and at the Ashokan Dam, the heart of New York's water supply. It was described as "the coldest winter since Washington crossed the Delaware," and, one day, Griffith finally collapsed on the verge of freezing. It was reportedly quite some time before she returned to work after a long illness.

In The Garden of Eden *(1928), Corinne Griffith is a poor Viennese girl who, with the help of an unidentified baroness, becomes a successful opera singer. Posing as a baroness's daughter, though, brings on the usual misunderstandings and love complications. With Griffith in this production still are Lowell Sherman and Maude George.*

From 1916 to 1922, Griffith made 35 features for Vitagraph. She began 1923 with one feature for Goldwyn and one for Selznick before signing with First National Pictures. From 1923 until 1930, she made 19 features for the company, straying only once when she made *The Garden of Eden* for United Artists in 1928. She is listed as executive producer of 11 of these films.

The Griffith Personality

Griffith took an active role in the making of her films and devoted herself totally to a film project once it began. She reportedly worked 10-hour days, as well as many evenings to confer on scripts, production details, casting, and more. She was one of the rare stars who would view the rushes of her films at the end of the day and have input into the cutting and titling.

It was pointed out by at least one contemporary writer that Griffith would not smoke, swear or wear make-up "in person." One of the most famous of the fan magazine writers, Adele Rogers St. Johns, said, "[S]he is innocence personified . . . no one would be apt to tell a risqué story in front of Corinne

Griffith," adding, "furthermore, she is reserved. In a land where last names are forgotten overnight, she is still 'Miss' Griffith." Another description for her was "calm and poised."

Griffith was also considered the most astute businesswoman in the industry this side of Mary Pickford. The fact that she was a calm individual complemented her business acumen. This was evident, in at least one instance that was recounted, as she arrived at an appointed hour to close a $200,000 deal "without so much as disturbing the dog that yawned on her arm or removing her fawn-gray gloves." A 1927 article quoted "an old financier of Beverly Hills" as saying, "What a brain that girl has!" noting that she had amassed half a million dollars in real estate while still in her twenties.

Griffith was always careful with her money and never yearned for the extravagances of most stars. During the four years she spent at Vitagraph in New York, she lived at the Hotel des Artistes, which was also the home of such stars as Mae Murray, Dorothy Dalton, and director George Fitzmaurice. When she signed with First National and moved to California, she did buy a large home, but with none of the excesses that one would expect of a wealthy star.

A Box-Office Attraction

Looking at Griffith's film output, one can see a steady succession of popular films that received notice in the fan magazines and were successful for the star, although none stands out as an enduring classic. Nevertheless, her popularity was consistently high from her first starring roles in 1918 to her last. In 1924, *Film Daily* conducted a poll of exhibitors to determine the top box-office attractions. Silent film fans today can gain some sense of her one-time popularity in that Griffith tied for sixth place with Rudolph Valentino in that 1924 poll.

A 1928 article on fan mail provides an unusual indicator of Griffith's popularity. The magazine noted, "Of all the stars in pictures, probably none is the namesake of so many babies as Corinne Griffith. Never a Griffith mail arrives but what there very likely will be news of another Corinne. 'And,' says Miss Griffith, 'it's a thing of which I'm very proud.'"

The fan magazines, however, most often focused their stories on her exceptional beauty, an assessment on which her public agreed. In 1924, *Photoplay* magazine asked their readers to select the most beautiful actresses on the screen. Griffith placed fourth behind Mary Pickford, Pola Negri, and Norma Talmadge. The article described her as "beautiful as a hot house flower. An orchid, robed in cloth of silver and glimmering chiffon."

Virtually every movie reviewer or interviewer paid homage to Griffith's beauty. One reviewer said, "In general, she is simply the insistently beautiful, willowy creature born to drive men cuckoo."

In a 1923, St. Johns said, "Her physical charms are too obvious to mention. In the old days, her little, slender feet, and her lovely hands—have you ever noticed her hands?—and her white teeth and her soft hair would have been the subject of poems. And, in passing, do you know she's the only woman in a long time whose hands any man has mentioned to me? In the old days, indeed, she would have been a belle and a toast."

When *Variety* reviewed Griffith's *The Divine Lady* (1929), the writer only gave her moderate praise for her acting, but added, "In general, she is simply the insistently beautiful, willowy creature born to drive men cuckoo."

In the mid-twenties, Griffith's height was 5 feet 4 inches. Her weight was listed as 120 pounds, and she had blue eyes and brown hair. As a matter of fact, in an earlier fan magazine article, she asked the interviewer to make sure her readers knew that her hair was naturally brown. Apparently, this genuineness was important to her.

Corinne Griffith was wed to Vitagraph director Webster Campbell from 1920–1923, and to producer Walter Morosco from 1924–1934. She was a far more private person than most stars and was much more interested in her work life than her social life. She would sometimes be referred to as "aloof," but apparently not in a negative way. She was well liked, particularly by the writers for the fan magazines, who heaped praise upon her in every way, often attributing her manners and hospitality to her Southern background. For example, one writer noted that Griffith offered her chair when she arrived for the interview, and, when viewing the day's rushes, preferred to sit on a bench instead of a comfortable chair so she could "sit with the boys" and "talk about the picture." The interviewer closed her article with: "And that's what Corinne Griffith suggests—whether she's going thru a scene in the studio or talking with you in her dressing room—she is the essence of the Old South with its ideals, its petty sentiments and its romance—ever and always the gentlewoman."

Apparently, though, Griffith was not without some of the typical star temperament. Colleen Moore said that Griffith complained often that First National gave Moore the lion's share of publicity. Also, when the studio provided Moore with a new bungalow, Griffith "caused such a commotion" that they had to build one for her as well. Moore said they planted a hedge between the two bungalows that gossipers referred to as "the spite fence." Despite this, Moore claimed that she and Griffith were "great friends" and that "we had nothing whatsoever to be jealous of each other about." She did add, however, that it irked Griffith to see Moore's movies making more money than hers.

Griffith never appeared onstage as so many actors had prior to entering the movies, even if she yearned for such an experience. In a 1921 interview, she admitted that she would love to star in a stage play, adding that she favored light comedy over melodrama. She even went so far as to get permission from Vitagraph for time off to do a Broadway play and made all the arrangements, including taking dance lessons, before deciding she couldn't do both stage and film work.

The Divine Lady

Griffith is photographed in costume for her last silent film, The Divine Lady *(1929), the story of the romance between Lady Hamilton and British naval hero Admiral Horatio Nelson.*

Griffith's final silent film was *The Divine Lady* (1929), a historical drama about the lives of Lady Emma Hamilton and Admiral Nelson. Anthony Slide claims *The Divine Lady* surpasses *Sunrise* (1928) in "the blending of German expressionism and technical virtuosity" and is therefore a more fitting example of silent film at its best at the close of the era. Slide also noted the "brilliant romanticism" of the film, adding that *The Divine Lady* was "exemplary of the best in direction, scripting, and cinematography, and, above all, is dominated by a lyrical performance from its star." Slide's assessment is supported by the fact that *The Divine Lady* was among the first films to receive Academy Awards for photography and direction. *Variety* opined that the movie has "sumptuous production, splendid acting, beautiful sets, costumes and photography," but the story is "spasmodic, episodic and anemic." Nevertheless, the success of the film was doomed by the onset of sound. To make matters worse, First National released Griffith's first talkie, *Saturday's Children*, just two months after the release of *The Divine Lady*—and although it included sound effects and a song, it failed to make a profit for the studio.

Griffith's career with First National ended with two talkies in 1930—*Lilies of the Field* and *Back Pay*. Of *Lilies of the Field*, *Time*'s resident critic wrote, "Pretty Corinne Griffith talks through her nose in her first sound film." The *New York Times* said, "Corinne Griffith in *Lilies of the Field* is probably the saddest person on the screen. Her voice is sad, her manner is tear-drenched, her gestures are those of despair, and the onlookers' reaction to all this sorrowful business is decidedly negative." The *Times'* review for *Back Pay* a few months later wasn't any better, with the reviewer commenting that the story had "no manner of suspense to relieve the quiescent performances of some of the players and only Miss Griffith's tired voice to listen to most of the time."

After these two films, Griffith released First National from her contract on the condition that she receive her full salary. She reportedly commented, "Why should I go on until I am playing mother roles? I have plenty of money. I want to improve my mind. Most of the time you'll find me bobbing around in Europe."

Griffith essentially finished her film career with a 1932 feature in England for Paramount-British entitled *Lily Christine*. She also had a cameo in producer-director Hugo Haas's *Paradise Alley*, which was released in 1962.

Life After Movies

In 1936, she married Boston Braves (later to become the Washington Redskins) owner George Marshall. They divorced in 1958. While married to Marshall, Griffith began her writing career with an article for the *Saturday Evening Post* about her experiences as a football fan. This was expanded into a book the following year entitled *My Life with the Redskins*. She authored several more books in the coming years, including *Papa's Delicate Condition* (1952), *Eggs I Have Known* (1955), *Hollywood Stories* (1962), *This You Won't Believe* (1972) and *I'm Lucky—At Cards* (1974). *Papa's Delicate Condition* was made into a motion picture in 1963, starring Jackie Gleason.

In the late 1950s, Griffith was the chairperson of The Committee for Honoring Motion Picture Stars, which sponsored a bronze statuary to be erected in Beverly Hills, honoring some of the community's most famous residents— Rudolph Valentino, Douglas Fairbanks, Tom Mix, Will Rogers. Griffith did not include herself among the honorees.

Her final marriage was in 1965 at the age of 71 to a realtor (one source says he was a Broadway actor) named Dan Scholl, 33 years her junior. They separated after six weeks and, following a messy and much-publicized court battle, were divorced.

Griffith lived her later years in comfort at her Beverly Hills mansion. She was one of the wealthiest women in the world when she passed away July 13, 1979, leaving an estate of $150 million.

Although Griffith starred in 58 feature films between 1916 and 1932, it appears that only about 10 survive. Two of her titles that have received excellent quality releases on DVD are *The Garden of Eden* (1928) and *The Divine Lady* (1929). The copy in circulation of *The Black Oxen* (1924), an especially good film, is missing the final reel. However, George Eastman House in Rochester, New York, and Gosfilmofond of Russia reportedly have complete copies.

The seven or so other surviving Griffith features have not, as of this writing, been made available to the home movie market.

Hopefully, more films featuring the talented and beautiful Corinne Griffith will be rediscovered and released on DVD. Fans could then see firsthand why she was consistently listed among the top 10 stars of the twenties.

SOURCES
PERIODICALS
Back Pay review. *New York Times*, May 31, 1930.
Bodeen, DeWitt. "Corinne Griffith: The Orchid Lady of the Screen," *Films in Review* (November 1975).
Bruce, Betsy. "Corinne Herself," *Motion Picture Magazine* (March 1920).
Craig, Marion. "Frapped in Flatbush," *Photoplay* (January 1919).
The Divine Lady review, *Variety*, March 27, 1929.
Evans, Delight. "The Girl on the Cover," *Photoplay* (January 1922).
Fletcher, Adele Whitely. "Instead of the Orchid . . .," *Motion Picture Classic* (March 1921).
Larkin, Mark. "What Happens to Fan Mail?" *Photoplay* (August 1928).
Lilies of the Field review, *New York Times*, February 22, 1930.
Lilies of the Field review, *Time Magazine* (March 10, 1930).
"*Photoplay* Readers Choose the Eight Most Beautiful Stars of the Screen," *Photoplay* (May 1924).
Schallert, Edwin. "The Age of Corinne," *Picture Play* (April 1924).
St. Johns, Adele Rogers. "Why Men Go Crazy About Corinne Griffith," *Photoplay* (December 1923).

BOOKS
Moore, Colleen. *Silent Star: Colleen Moore Talks About Her Hollywood*. Garden City, NY: Doubleday & Co., 1968.
Slide, Anthony. *Silent Players*. Lexington, KY: The University Press of Kentucky, 2002.

CHAPTER 6
The Tragic Flugrath Sisters: Edna, Viola and Shirley
எ

Hard to believe, and equally hard to understand, but all three sisters, within a span of eight years, experienced the same tragic loss in their lives.

The family name is Flugrath. However, only one of the three sisters did not adopt a stage name and that was Edna. Sister Leonie changed her name to Shirley Mason shortly after she went into motion pictures, and the most famous of the three sisters, Virginia, changed her name to Viola Dana early on in her movie career.

A Mother's Dreams

Edna was the oldest. She was born in 1893. Viola was born in 1897, and younger sister Shirley was born in 1901. The girls' mother had dreams of her daughters being actresses and enthusiastically sought stage work for them. "My mother was possessed to make actresses of us," Viola said, and, knowing the value of being able to dance, she saw to it that they had lessons at a young age. Most of their childhood was spent performing with touring companies, at Coney Island, Elks Clubs, or anywhere else employment could be found.

Since the Flugraths lived near the Edison studios, it was only natural that their mother would seek out jobs for them there. Viola was the first to gain employment in the movies. She was 13 years old, and, before long, little sister Shirley was tagging along. Later, when a role called for a blonde, Viola suggested older sister Edna, and soon, she, too, was acting in motion pictures. Viola said she continued to do stage work, though, and, when the season ended, she would go to Edison.

John Collins and Marriage

While at Edison, Viola met director John Collins. He fell in love with the young actress, and when she was 16, they were married. "Johnny gave me my first position in pictures," Viola said. "He was always my hero, and he used to tell me that he fell in love with me that very first day." Viola was adept at comedy, but at this time—and with her previous stage experience—she said she

Viola Dana, born Virginia Flugrath, was the most popular of the three Flugrath sisters. She was only 16 when she married director John Collins and was a widow by the time she was 21.

had never considered being a comedienne. However, it was Johnny who convinced her to try. The film was *Opportunity* (1918), and it proved to be such as hit that Metro immediately put her into more comedies. Collins had come to Edison in 1904 and took on a variety of jobs, including that of handyman, until he was finally promoted to director. After marrying Viola, he became her director and wrote many of her films.

An interviewer in 1919 asked Viola if she "realized what she was doing" when she married so young. Viola said, "Oh, yes, of course I did. You see, I had been asked to marry a very wealthy man much my senior. It meant a carefree life, no necessity for earning a living or shouldering responsibilities. But there was John Collins . . . I thought it over a great deal, and finally I said to Shirley, 'I believe it will be best for me to marry John, then we can just grow up together. . . I'm not afraid of the money end of it. John is clever and I am willing to work hard, so I am sure we will make good.'"

Under his guidance, she became one of Edison's top stars, and Collins's films were, according to William K. Everson, some of the best to come out of the Edison studio: "Despite extremely perceptive and laudatory reviews for his films of 1914-1918, he is an ignored and unknown figure to most American historians." He goes on to note that Collins's lack of recognition is due in part to the perception that no directorial talent ever came out of the Edison studios: "Collins' films show that not only were we wrong about him, but that it is quite possible that other directors of his caliber lie buried with the unseen Edison films."

In 1916, Collins moved to Metro and took his wife with him. Metro was founded by a group of "exchange men" with capital amounting to $300,000. (Louis B. Mayer was secretary, but he left the company in 1918.) The purpose was to control movie productions for exchanges. (Metro was successful in the ensuing years, and, of course, along with Mayer, was a part of the triumvirate known as Metro-Goldwyn-Mayer beginning in 1924.)

The husband-wife team was a winning combination at Metro during the latter half of the teens, with Collins directing Dana in 17 consecutive features from 1916–1918. Dana always credited her husband for the success she experienced in her career during those years.

Edna In England

In the meantime, Edna had left Edison with director Harold Shaw in late 1913 when he went to England to set up the first British film company. The couple was especially successful in the UK. Edna had 14 shorts and two feature films released in 1914 under the directorship of Shaw (as well as two more shorts *not* directed by Shaw). They made seven features in 1915, but then went to South Africa to make films for the African Film Company—and, at this point, their output reduced considerably. There were only a couple of releases in 1916, one short in 1917, and one feature in 1918. Oddly, there were none in 1919, and then they were back in England. Sometime during the years in South Africa, Edna married Shaw. But, in 1920, they were back in full swing in England with four features that year, two more in 1921, and one in 1922, before returning to America.

Edna chose to keep her birth name of Flugrath; however, most of her movie career was spent in England with her husband, director Harold Shaw.

Shaw was a director, an actor, and a writer. He began acting at the Edison studios in 1909, and a few years later, he directed his first film. Some sources state that Shaw directed, starred in, and wrote the adaptation for *Winning of a Continent* in 1924, which co-starred Edna. However, this is just the alternate title of *De Voortrekkers*, which was made and released in South Africa in 1917.

Love at the Edison Studio

Shirley also found love at the Edison studio. When she was 13, she met Bernard Durning, who was eight years her senior. Because of her diminutive size and young age, she was asked to be the waving arm from a smoking wreck. However, after some minutes of waving, she became faint from the smoke, and Durning had to rescue her. That was the beginning of a romance that culminated with their marriage in 1916 when she was 16 years old.

Durning, too, was a director and actor. He directed Shirley in her first feature, *The Unwritten Code* in 1919 for Edison, and in the last film he ever directed, *The Eleventh Hour* (1923) for Fox.

All Were Taken Too Soon

Viola was the first of the sisters to lose her husband unexpectedly. They had been married almost five years when Collins was called up to go to war. World War I was in its last days, but standing in Pennsylvania Station, Viola said goodbye to her husband, who was leaving for training camp. The next day he was home again with a fever of 104. He died five days later, one of thousands

Shirley Mason, born Leonie Flugrath, was the youngest of the three sisters. She, too, married at 16 years of age and was a widow by the time she was 22.

of casualties of the Spanish flu pandemic of 1918. Although Viola became ill with the flu as well, she overcame it and returned to California, where she would star in light comedies, but without her beloved John's guiding hand. At just 21, she was a widow.

Bernard and Shirley's marriage was a happy one. He was making films back East, and he and Shirley were both content there. Then, in 1923, Bernard became ill. A short time later, he was gone, too, having contracted typhoid fever, a disease that is usually spread through contaminated food or water. So, at only 22 years of age, Shirley was also a widow. Viola, in Hollywood, called her sister in New York.

"I'm all right, Vi," Shirley said.

"I know, Shirley, dear. Remember, I went through the same thing."

Shaw was the eldest of the three husbands. Born in 1877, he was 16 years older than Edna. Their marriage lasted the longest of the three sisters—almost 11 years. During that time, the two had had many memorable experiences, although not always in comfortable or safe conditions. They had stayed in London during the German air raids, went "hobnobbing" with the Bolsheviks in Russia, stole bread in revolt of the Germans in Berlin, and had filmed the unrest between the Boers and Blacks during their time in Africa. The Shaws returned to America in 1923.

Edna had only one more film credit, *The Social Code*, a Metro picture starring her sister Viola.

Edna retired from pictures after that and was contentedly operating a beauty shop in Hollywood in the mid-twenties. One day, word came that Shaw had been injured in a two-car collision. She rushed to his side, but he had already died. At 33, Edna was now a widow like her sisters.

Viola and Ormer

As if this wasn't enough sadness for the Flugrath sisters, Viola was to experience one more tragic loss of a loved one only two years after losing her husband.

The incident has been recounted in Kevin Brownlow and David Gill's superb 1980 documentary *Hollywood: A Celebration of American Silent Film* and the accompanying book, *Hollywood, The Pioneers*. Viola was engaged to aviator Omar Locklear, who was popular among the Hollywood crowd and had taken many of them on flights. His skill at aerial acrobatics made him perfect movie material, and, in 1920, while engaged to Viola, he was making *The Skywayman* for Fox.

Viola was in attendance one evening when the filming called for night-flying scenes over oil fields in the Los Angeles area. Locklear was to take his plane into a tailspin, heading dangerously toward the ground. Sunlight arcs were directed at the plane so it would show up against the night sky. The blinding lights were to be shut off just as Locklear reached the level of the oil wells, indicating that he should straighten out the plane. However, whoever was in charge never took the lights off him, and he crashed.

Sixty years later, Brownlow questioned her about the crash for his 1980 documentary. However, Viola could only speak briefly about the event before emotion took over, and she refused to talk about it any more.

After the death of her husband and prior to the death of Locklear, Viola and Shirley were interviewed in 1919. Viola expressed great wisdom, which, no doubt, contributed to her ability to persevere.

"For a while, I couldn't laugh much, but now we laugh all the time, don't we Shirley?" she said.

"Yes," replied her sister.

"Perhaps we are just silly," commented Viola, "then, perhaps we are just wise, and we get the best we can out of life, determined not to let sorrow or unhappiness spoil these precious years.'"

Both Shirley and Viola continued to make films until 1929. Edna died at 72 in 1966, Shirley at 78 in 1979, and Viola at 90 in 1987. Maybe the fact that they experienced the same tragedy made them that much closer . . . and stronger.

SOURCES
PERIODICALS

Carr, Harry. "The Star That Refused to Twinkle." *Motion Picture Magazine* (December 1924).

Evans, Nelson. "A Kinema Kewpie." *Motion Picture Magazine* (September 1919).

Gateson, Elizabeth. "Vivacious Vivid Viola." *Motion Picture Classic* (October 1919).

Howe, Herbert. "They Go on Smiling. *Photoplay* (June 1926).

James, Arthur. "The Girl Who Never Grew Up." *Picture Play* (July 1918).

Tully, Jim. "The Girl Who Kept Step." *Photoplay* (January 1926).

BOOKS

Brownlow, Kevin, and John Kobal. *Hollywood, The Pioneers*. New York: Alfred A. Knopf, 1979.

Everson, William K. *American Silent Film*. New York: Oxford University Press, 1978.

OTHER

Brownlow, Kevin, and David Gill. *Hollywood: A Celebration of American Silent Film* (documentary). Photoplay Productions, Ltd., 1980.

CHAPTER 7
"Heaven Flower Beauty" Francelia Billington
✌

She sits in a metal dining chair reading a newspaper outside the inn surrounded by the gorgeous snow-capped Tyrolean Alps. Out of the corner of her eye, she catches the movement of the immaculately uniformed
and monocled Austrian officer, but only glances to the right, not turning
her head. Suddenly, he touches her shoulder, silently asking her to lean
forward as he places a large, fluffy pillow behind her. She opens her mouth
slightly as if she is about to protest but does not. Hurriedly, he then lifts
her feet and places a stool under them. Again, she looks incredulously
at his presumptuousness. Finally, he places a wrap across her legs, bows
from the waist and salutes. At first, she looks at him blankly, but a slight
turning of the corners of the mouth shows that she is humored by this
uninvited attention to her comfort. Then, as the officer remains bowed,
she suddenly throws her head to the side in an accepting laugh. As she
continues to smile, charmingly but coyly, he pulls up a chair beside her.*

From Texas to Kalem

The above is a scene from *Blind Husbands* (1919), with Erich von Stroheim
as the Austrian officer, and Francelia Billington as the beautiful Mrs. Armstrong.
He continues to pursue Billington, who is on vacation with her doctor/hus-
band, throughout the film. The uncertainty of whether he will succeed in his
seduction is what keeps the viewer interested—but it is Billington who keeps
the viewer entranced.

Francelia Billington was born to musicians Adelaide Bueter and James Billington in Dallas, Texas, on February 1, 1895. She was raised on a ranch, providing her with a familiarity with horses, something that served her well in a
movie career that would include many westerns. She attended a convent,
and, at an early age, began taking part in plays there. When she was 10 years
old, she moved to New Orleans and continued her interest in outdoor activities, becoming quite accomplished at swimming, diving, and rowing. When she

FRANCELIA BILLINGTON

Director George Melford (The Sheik) and his wife were friends of the Billington family. It was he who convinced 17-year-old Francelia to come to the Kalem studio for a screen test.

moved to Los Angeles, she learned to drive a car, a skill that also proved valuable to her career.

It is not known how, or when, she arrived in Los Angeles, but Kalem director George Melford and his wife were friends of the Billington family there. Both joined Kalem as actors, but Melford was just beginning a much more prestigious career as a director at this time.

As Billington recalled, "Mrs. Melford was always trying to get me to go over to the studio for a test. But I considered being in movies a sort of disgrace and wouldn't go." One day, when she was visiting the Melfords, George announced that Alice Joyce was leaving Kalem, and he didn't have a leading lady. He turned to Francelia and said, "You look a bit like Alice Joyce; come over to the studio tomorrow for a test." Billington admitted, "You might imagine I would have been delighted, but I wasn't."

Nevertheless, her mother insisted she go to the studio the following day, and when Billington learned that she would be playing opposite the famous Carlyle Blackwell and getting $35 a week, she agreed. However, she was still embarrassed about appearing in movies. "Naturally, I got over that and began to like the work for its own sake." But, after several features at Kalem, she moved to Reliance-Majestic the next year.

In Front of or Behind the Camera

As a child on a ranch in Texas, Billington had developed "an obsession of interest" in photography. "My father gave me a small camera almost as soon as I was able to hold it, so keen was my desire to own a 'clicker,' as I used to call it. I was a camera fiend before I was 10 years old."

Billington said that because she lived on a ranch, it was necessary that she depend on her own resources for amusement—and she learned to notice things that "city children" usually don't notice. "I photographed everything on that ranch that I could level the camera at," she said. "Even when I was at school, I took pictures with the faithfulness of an aspirant for prizes. When I finished school, I fitted up a dark room where I could develop and print the pictures."

Billington admitted she was proud, not so much of her abilities in front of the camera, but behind the camera. "Almost any day at the studio it is possible to see a brown-haired, gray-eyed, olive-skinned girl of remarkable grace and extreme prettiness standing in back of one of the big cameras, turning a crank as she keeps close watch on the scene that a group of players are enacting," one interviewer reported. "Sometimes [Christy] Cabanne, the director, turns to her with a question concerning the placing of some player. Usually her criticism is accepted, for the director has found that Francelia Billington has an exceptionally quick eye for picture effects, and, as a result, he is permitting her to develop her talent in this line as well as in her own posing for the films."

Steps to Von Stroheim

Billington left Majestic in 1915, and, after working on an uncompleted movie with Nell Shipman for the Palo Alto Film Corporation, she went to Universal. She stayed there until 1917 when she moved to American and made 12 successive films in 1917–1918 as leading lady to William Russell, under the direction of Edward Sloman. Amazingly, she had made 11 of these features all in one year.

Billington's film output slowed down with only five total films in 1918 and 1919, but one of those was to be the most significant film of her career, Erich von Stroheim's directorial debut, *Blind Husbands*. The film was a big gamble on the part of Universal head Carl Laemmle, and the negative cost ran nearly five times what he had originally been budgeted for the film. However, unlike future films under von Stroheim's direction, this one was completed in a reasonable amount of time, about two months between April and June of 1919.

Francelia Billington's most memorable role was in Erich von Stroheim's Blind Husbands
*(1919). She is the married woman who is the object of an Austrian officer's affections—played,
of course, by von Stroheim.*

Although her performance brought praise from the critics, the Fates had
no great roles waiting for Billington, and she continued in a mix of undistinguished melodramas, westerns, and actions films.

Rex, Ormer, and Tom

1919 brought the first of two associations with Rex Ingram in *The Day She
Paid*. The movie, which was based on a short story by Fanny Hurst, began to
show some of the genius that would soon assure Ingram's place among the
great directors. In it, Billington plays a mother who sacrifices her own reputation to save her daughter's. The movie received positive reviews, but this was
prior to Ingram's great success with *The Four Horsemen of the Apocalypse*
(1921) and brought no significant recognition to the director or the actress. Billington made only one other film that year, an insignificant action film entitled
The Great Air Robbery with stunt pilot-turned-actor Ormer Locklear. (Locklear
would die tragically the following year in a flying mishap while filming *The Skywayman*: See Chapter 6 on the Flugrath sisters.)

Her first film of 1920 was a western with Tom Mix entitled *Desert Love* (also in the cast was Francelia's future husband, Lester Cuneo). Later that year, she returned once again to Rex Ingram's directorship with *Hearts Are Trumps*. In her previous film with Ingram, she had been in the lead role, but this time, that belonged to the beautiful Alice Terry. (Terry was not only the star of future Ingram films—she also became the director's wife.) Reviews were favorable, but once again the film did nothing to bring Billington special recognition, especially now that she was moving more and more to secondary roles or low-budget pictures. She finished the year with one more Tom Mix western, *The Terror*.

Japanese Fans

In a 1920 interview, Billington noted that she had a big following in Japan—although she didn't know why. "I think they must be partial to blondes, not having any of them in that country." She said that two-thirds of her fan mail came from Japan, and each letter included some type of gift. She said each letter is filled with "extravagant praise for my work and flowery compliments for my 'heaven flower beauty,' as they call it." She went on to say, "Recently I won the popularity contest over there, and since then the whole studio force has joked me about my collection of Japanese 'fans.'"

Cuneo, Marriage, and Steady Work

It was also during 1920 that Billington married actor Lester Cuneo, who was seven years older than she, having been born in 1888 in Chicago. In 1910, he entered pictures by way of the Selig Polyscope Company; from there, he would go on to work for a variety of companies in a mixture of roles before going overseas during World War I. He returned in 1918 and continued with his film career, most often cast as a heavy. Cuneo soon began gravitating toward westerns. His six-one, 180-pound frame and good looks were well-suited for the role of a western hero. In 1921, he organized Lester Cuneo Productions, and his wife began co-starring with him in a series of western melodramas.

Billington appeared in at least 11 features, mostly under the Capital Films banner, with her husband between 1921 and 1925. There were a few other features mixed in during that time, including *High Gear Jeffrey* (1921), with William Russell; *The Truant Husband* (1921), with Mahlon Hamilton; *Blue Blazes* (1922), with Pete Morrison; *Restless Souls* (1922), with Earle Williams; *What a Wife Learned* (1923), with John Bowers; and *White Sin* (1924), with Madge Bellamy. *White Sin* is one of her films that still exists, and although it's a secondary role

The variety of elegant clothes Billington wore in The White Sin *(1924), starring Madge Bellamy, only enhanced her beauty. She plays a wealthy lady who employs Bellamy, comforting her when she becomes the victim of a trick marriage.*

to that of Madge Bellamy, Billington's presence adds much to the film. She is dressed exquisitely and exudes beauty and grace.

At least one of the Cuneo-Billington features is available for home viewing—*Blazing Arrows* (1922). It should also be noted that the features Billington made without her husband during this period were for a variety of companies, including Palmer Photoplay, Vitagraph, Rockett, Universal, and Ince.

Billington and Cuneo had two children: Jack, born in 1923, and Francelia, born in 1924. Jack, who became a chemistry teacher at Los Angeles High School, died on February 14, 2000; his sister passed away in 2018, at the age of 94.

Divorce and Suicide

Cuneo and Billington made their last two features together in 1925, but apparently the marriage was on the rocks well before that. The March 1924 issue of *Screenland* magazine reported, "Check this up on your divorce calendar: Francelia Billington is suing Lester Cuneo for divorce, alleging that Lester was the bootlegger's best customer." Their divorce was finalized in November of 1925.

Billington married western star Lester Cuneo in 1920, and, over the next five years, co-starred with him in 11 of his features, this being a scene from Blazing Arrows *(1922).*

One can assume that when he formed Lester Cuneo Productions in 1921, his star was on the rise, and, reportedly, these first features were well made and a hit with fans. And then, for whatever reason, Cuneo was back to supporting roles in 1922. He was given a second chance for starring status with a series for independent producer Ward Lascelle in 1923. According to Kalton C. Lahue, this was a series "he never should have filmed. . . these features disappointed exhibitors and fans alike with their woefully weak story lines and inept direction."

Cuneo was reportedly despondent over the poor reception of his films and his divorce from Billington. He committed suicide by shooting himself on November 2, 1925, supposedly two days after his divorce from Billington became final.

The Last Films

Billington's film output after this is sparse, and, as a matter of fact, one 1926 fan magazine listed her among a group of "Stars of Yesterday." She made *Tex* in 1926 with Ruth Mix, worked again with former leading man William Russell in *A Rough Shod Fighter* in 1927, then was absent from the screen until 1930 when she appeared in *The Mounted Stranger* with Hoot Gibson for Universal. She only appears onscreen twice for two short scenes as the mother of Gibson's love interest, and both are full-length shots of her, with no close-ups. It is not intended to be a glamorous part, and her dark, unkempt hair, dowdy frontier dress, and thin appearance certainly do not recall the beauty that was so apparent only a few years earlier. This was to be the last film of her career.

Her health was declining, and, although always slender, one can only guess at whether her thin, frail-looking body in *The Mounted Stranger* may have been due to early stages of the tuberculosis that would soon take her life. A short four years later, on November 24, 1934, Billington passed away from the disease in Glendale, California. According to author Billy Doyle, "A brief obituary appeared in the Glendale paper, but there were no obituaries in the trade papers. The actress' death went unnoticed by the film industry and public."

There's no question that Billington was a stunning beauty and a fine actress. She was hardly the only beautiful, talented actress whose star didn't shine as brightly as it should have, and explanations are usually moot. Many unknown reasons could have contributed to the course—good or bad, personal or professional. It is gratifying, though, that some of her work remains, and those films provide ample evidence of a serenely charming, lovely, and talented—albeit neglected—actress who graced the screen all those years ago.

SOURCES

PERIODICALS
Marshall, Eunice, and Helen Lee. "The Listening Post." *Screenland* (March 1924).
Squier, Emma-Lindsay. "Milady of the Fan." *Motion Picture Classic* (April–May 1920).
Synon, Katherine. "Francelia Billington Who Can Play Both Ends of a Camera Against the Middle." *Photoplay* (December 1914).

BOOKS
Doyle, Billy. *The Ultimate Director of Silent Screen Performers*. Metuchen, NJ, and London: Scarecrow Press, 1995.
Katchmer, George A. *A Biographical Dictionary of Silent Western Actors and Actresses*. Jefferson, NC: McFarland, 2002.
Lahue, Kalton C. *Winners of the West*. New York: A. S. Barnes & Co., 1970.

CHAPTER 8
Harold Lockwood—A Tribute
❧

The results of *Motion Picture Magazine*'s "Motion Picture Hall of Fame," published in December 1918, listed the top six stars in order as Mary Pickford, Marguerite Clark, Douglas Fairbanks, Harold Lockwood, William S. Hart, and Wallace Reid. Sadly, by the time this issue was in the hands of its readers, Harold Lockwood was dead.

From Horses to Theatre

Born April 12, 1887, in Newark, New Jersey, Harold Lockwood quickly developed his athletic skills, excelling at swimming, track and football; he was also an expert horseman. At some point he also developed an interest in the theatre, attending plays as often as possible. As a result, the teenaged Lockwood was delighted when he and his family moved to Manhattan.

He was able to get some occasional employment on the stage in extra roles, but his father urged him to attend business college, which he did. After a brief period as a dry goods salesman, he convinced his father that he could only be happy acting and spent the next seven years working regularly in musical comedy, vaudeville, and stock.

He soon married a fellow actress, and on June 3, 1908, Alma and Harold Lockwood's only child, William, was born.

Introduction to Movies

In 1911, Lockwood was returning from a tour in a Frohman and Shubert production. At the urging of Archie MacArthur of *Moving Picture World*, Lockwood took a letter of introduction to Edwin S. Porter at his Rex Company. Porter had made his reputation as the director of such seminal films as *The Life of An American Fireman* (1902) and *The Great Train Robbery* (1903) at the Edison studio. Immediately recognizing this handsome young man's potential, the director placed him in leading roles in a few one-reelers (which were virtually all that was being produced at this early date). After only a few months, Lockwood moved to Nestor, which also had headquarters in New York. In the

A fan magazine poll in 1918 listed Lockwood as one of the six most popular stars of the day. Unfortunately, he was taken by the Spanish influenza epidemic that same year, believed to have been contracted while he was selling Liberty Bonds for the war effort.

latter part of 1911 when Nestor opened a studio in California, Lockwood went with the troupe.

In the spring of 1912, Lockwood made the move to Thomas Ince's 101 Ranch, playing leads in westerns and Civil War stories. After nine months, he signed with Selig, where he was guaranteed regular leading man status. His tenure with Selig contributed to his experience and popularity, as well as being very profitable, with Lockwood playing a variety of roles in everything from comedies to dramas and costume romances to action melodramas. In *The Millionaire Vagabonds* (1912), he was part of a comedic group of rich men who become "knights of the road." This was his first film after moving from 101-Bison to Selig. Another example of his work with Selig was *Two Men and a Woman* (1913), in which he was a rich banker in a love triangle that included his wife and another man. *Margarita and the Mission Funds* (1913) was a romance of Old Mexico, while in *The Tie of the Blood* (1913), he was "Deer Foot," an Indian brave. All of these were either one or two-reelers, the common length for a film at the time. These were churned out quickly, with Lockwood participating in 35 films in his first full year with Selig.

By this time, Porter had moved to Famous Players, and when he needed a leading man for an upcoming Pickford feature he was directing. Porter was able to gain Lockwood's release from Selig and co-starred him in two features with Pickford, *Hearts Adrift* (1914) and *Tess of the Storm Country* (1914). *Hearts Adrift* was only four reels, but it qualified as a feature and, due to the popularity of Mary Pickford, boosted his career substantially.

Because of his success in the Pickford films, Porter recommended to Adolph Zukor that he hire Lockwood. He was cast for a third time with Pickford, in *Such a Little Queen* (1914). His work with "America's Sweetheart" no doubt solidified the producer's confidence in Lockwood because, after a few more shorts, he was cast in features, not necessarily as the star in the beginning, but that was to come.

The Lockwood-Allison Team

With Famous Players-Lasky, Lockwood had his first co-starring role with May Allison, a pairing that proved to be more popular with the moviegoing public than the established team of Francis X. Bushman and Beverly Bayne at Essanay.

The first of these was *David Harum*, released in 1915. In this story, Lockwood plays a poor but honest clerk who loves the local schoolteacher. There were four more features after *David Harum*, three of which starred Lockwood, although without Allison.

However, American Flying "A" director Thomas Ricketts saw potential in the Lockwood-Allison team and hired them from Zukor to star in a series that caught fire with the public. The first of these features was *The Secretary of Frivolous Affairs*, released in the summer of 1915. The story has Allison hired by a wealthy lady as her social secretary. However, her main responsibility is to keep her son and daughter from entering into undesirable marriages. Of course, Lockwood is the frivolous, polo-playing son. American ran a two-page ad in *Motion Picture News* to promote the film, with exhibitors exclaiming, "Harold Lockwood and May Allison! They are stars of the greatest magnitude in filmdom's firmament!"

Their fourth pairing was in *The House of a Thousand Scandals* (1915), in which the owner of a rich estate (Lockwood) falls in love with a poor farm girl (Allison). One of several titles in 1916 is *The Gamble*. In that one, a farmer (Lockwood) neglects his wife (Allison) for his farm. The team made comedies as well. In *The River of Romance*, released in mid-1916, Lockwood's rich uncle forces him to go out and make his own money for a valuable vase he broke—so he gets a job operating a ferry. A passenger (Allison) finds herself attracted to the young man, but she is convinced that the police are looking for him. In the end, she finds the man she plans to marry is not a thief, but an heir to a fortune.

A 1917 article in *Motion Picture Magazine* entitled, "On Location with Harold Lockwood and May Allison," recounts the writer's two days of tagging along behind the famous couple around Monterey, California, during the filming of *Pidgin Island*, their final feature released in 1916. Rather than relating some insight into the filming, the writer instead recounts a pleasant drive up the coast with the couple as they passed the time taking pictures, sightseeing, fishing, hiking, and picnicking. Of course, the inevitable "mishaps" that occurred add charm to the story, with Lockwood changing a flat tire and later getting drenched by an unexpected wave.

This is obviously journalistic fluff, but it indicates the popularity of the couple and how fans were eager for tidbits about the stars' offscreen activities.

In all, Lockwood and Allison made 22 consecutive features between 1915 and 1917, so it was natural that the media would link the two actors romantically. However, that was not the case. Lockwood had been estranged from his wife for quite some time, but his love for his son prevented him from bringing a sudden end to the marriage. In 1915, he and Alma were briefly reconciled, but the relationship was an on-again, off-again affair until they were finally divorced, very quietly, in 1917. Lockwood's personal life was always beyond reproach, and, during the times he and his wife were not living together, he was living with his mother.

Although Lockwood and Allison made 22 pictures together, only the first 14 were made by American Flying "A." In April 1916, the couple began making pictures for Fred J. Balshofer's Yorke-Metro. Their popularity continued to rise, as did their salaries. Lockwood admitted that he was more interested in the pay-

From 1915–1917, Harold Lockwood and May Allison co-starred in 22 consecutive films together, making them the most popular romantic film couple on the screen.

check than performing for the sake of art. He also said that working during the daytime hours and the opportunities to shoot outdoors placed filmmaking far above the stage.

Despite the popularity of the Lockwood-Allison pairing, Balshofer decided the couple was becoming too expensive as a team and that each could carry a picture without the other. That was the end of one of the cinema's most popular romantic couples. They never again appeared together on the screen.

Lockwood's popularity did not wane, however. He was co-starred with such popular actresses as Carmel Myers, Ann Little, Vera Sisson, Pauline Curley, Martha Mansfield, Rubye de Remer, and Bessie Eyton, and the audiences still flocked to see his pictures.

An Actor and a Writer

In June 1918, *Motion Picture Magazine* began offering a monthly column by Lockwood entitled "Funny Happenings in the Studio and on Lockwood." The actor drew on personal experiences that made moviemaking appear to be lighthearted and fun. He tells of the prop man who was ordered to quickly get a safe for an upcoming scene. It wasn't until the next day that everyone learned he had removed the safe from the studio owner's office! In another story, he tells of the cook who mistook the actor's cold crème for lard. He noted that the cast and crew wondered about the "remarkable" taste of the food.

Lockwood continued to work under Balshofer's direction into 1918. He was also active in the Liberty Loan drives of the time, doing what he could to help out on the home front as the war raged in Europe. Although stars such as Mary Pickford, Douglas Fairbanks, Charlie Chaplin, and William S. Hart are the best-remembered stars for their bond-selling efforts, one fan magazine said Lockwood was an "ardent worker for the Fourth Liberty Loan" and said his "sale of bonds at the *Morning Telegraph* booth was the greatest stimulus that booth had during the whole campaign." Mabel Normand was also in the booth, selling bonds.

Reports stated that men flocked to see Normand, and the women flocked to see Lockwood.

This was also when the Spanish influenza was taking lives throughout the country. It is believed that Lockwood's work in the *Morning Telegraph* booth brought him into contact with the deadly disease.

The Final Days

It was early October 1918, and he had just begun work in Manhattan on an espionage-aviation film entitled *The Yellow Dove*. Lockwood became sick with what was initially believed to be "la grippe," but which later turned out to be influenza. On October 19, 1918, he died of complications from pneumonia. He was just 31 years old. His funeral was held at Campbell's Funeral Parlor on Broadway and 66th Street, and he was buried at Woodlawn Cemetery. The following January, *Photoplay* published a full-page tribute to Lockwood. It reads, in part:

> In his profession, he was duly modest, a steady worker, and consistently progressive in the art of acting . . . Away from the studio, Lockwood was a clean, wholesome, worthy young American citizen in the very best sense of the term.

Motion Picture Magazine also published a full-page tribute, stating:

> Harold Lockwood, a man of sterling worth, a sincere worker, a lovable playfellow, a promising star, died at the Hotel Woodward, New York City, on Saturday, October 19, from pneumonia brought on by the Spanish influenza . . . One of the most obvious reasons for the success of Harold Lockwood was his unqualified willingness to place his own little whims entirely out of consideration and give first place in his thoughts to the making of successful pictures.

The tribute goes on to refer to the "bigness, the simplicity, the light-heartedness and the lovability of the man. Harold Lockwood has passed on to a larger field, but his memory will always be cherished in motion picture circles."

Lockwood's ex-wife, Alma, announced a few months after Lockwood's death that she would contest his will that had bequeathed $45,000 to his mother, his son, and a friend. However, a lack of future reports seems to indicate she did not follow through on this. In the ensuing years, she tried unsuccessfully to establish an acting career. She also remarried in 1919.

The End of the Road *(1915), starring Harold Lockwood and May Allison, is a story of a young Northerner who falls in love with a girl of the Carolina pines. The couple's eighth film together, it is replete with counterfeiting and moonshining.*

Lockwood's son, William, who was only 10 when his father died, changed his name to Harold Lockwood, Jr., and worked briefly as an actor in the late 1920s. He also showed up in a couple of extra parts in movies in the 1950s. He passed away in 1996.

May Allison continued a successful career throughout the twenties, although she never made what would be called a "big" picture. She voluntarily called it quits in 1927. She was married a total of four times, apparently living a comfortable life until she died in 1989.

As for Lockwood's career on film, only a handful of films survive. This, sadly, helps understand why a star who once rivaled Mary Pickford and Douglas Fairbanks in popularity is all but forgotten today.

In his obituary in *Motion Picture Magazine*, Lockwood was quoted regarding his untiring ambition as an actor.

> The art of pleasing people is an art great enough to tempt any man's ambition. It is big enough to be worthwhile, without any thought of doing more than brightening the playtime of the great public. It is really a very large contract for one to fill and fill adequately, and I, for one, realize how great is the task.

SOURCES

PERIODICALS

"Harold Lockwood Is Dead," *Motion Picture Magazine* (January 1919).

Harold Lockwood obituary, *Photoplay* (January 1919).

Lockwood, Harold. "How I Got In." *Motion Picture Magazine* (September 1917).

"The Motion Picture Hall of Fame." *Motion Picture Magazine* (December 1918).

Zeidman, Bennie. "On Location with Harold Lockwood and May Allison." *Motion Picture Magazine* (March 1917).

OTHER

"Harold Lockwood." The Internet Movie Database. IMDb.com

"May Allison." The Internet Movie Database. IMDb.com

The American Films Institute Catalog of Feature Films. AFI.com.

CHAPTER 9
The Lubin Manufacturing Company: Its Rise, Its Reign, Its Requiem
❧

The Lubin Manufacturing Company operated studios throughout the country during its heyday. The one in Philadelphia was the most modern, state-of-the-art studio of its time. At its peak, the company owned a chain of more than 100 theatres along the East Coast; it manufactured and sold motion picture cameras and projectors; it employed more than two thousand actors, writers, directors, and technicians; and it was turning out more than a film a day. Despite this, the Lubin Company suffered possibly the swiftest decline and dissolution in motion picture history.

Sigmund "Pop" Lubin, the founder of one of the most successful film companies of the industry's first 20 years.

Its Rise

Born in 1851, Siegmund (sometimes spelled "Sigmund") "Pop" Lubin was a German-Jewish immigrant who came to the United States in 1876. He was a traveling peddler, did some gold prospecting, and was known for his storytelling ability, which led to his being offered a contract as a vaudeville comedian. He finally settled in Philadelphia, where he opened an optical shop. It was his knowledge of lenses that led to an interest in photography and then to the design and development of his own motion picture projector. It was this optical shop that soon became the home of "S. Lubin: World's Largest Manufacturer of Life Movies." The company's logo was a logo representing the Liberty Bell and accompanied by the slogan, "Clear as a Bell," emphasizing the quality of its films.

Lubin began producing films in 1896, and his output before the turn of the century was no better or worse than that being turned out by other film companies of the day. For example, one short film showed Lubin's two daughters in a pillow fight. Another was of a horse eating hay.

In 1897, he employed two Pennsylvania railway men to re-enact the Corbett-Fitzsimmons fight, reading an account of the fight for the "actors" to follow accordingly. His recreations of prizefights proved to be quite popular; they were filmed on the roof of a building the producer rented in the red-light district of Philadelphia. He would give spectators one dollar each to bet on the fight in return for their appearance in these films. It was not unusual to have a few hundred spectators on the roof, shouting and screaming, followed by a raid from the Philadelphia Fire Department—which only added a sense of realism to his films.

Moviemaking was not Lubin's only enterprise. He also manufactured and sold a patented projector he called the Cineograph. In 1899, he became an exhibitor in Philadelphia, constructing what was perhaps the first theatre built solely for the exhibition of motion pictures. Soon, he had over 100 theatres all along the East Coast.

In 1898, Edison filed suit against Lubin for copyright infringement. As a result, he returned to Germany, but was back in a short time producing pictures once again. Edison's claims of copyright infringement led to a 10-year battle that Edison waged not only against Lubin, but many other film companies.

During this time, quite a few tactics were used to disrupt filming, and Edison wasn't beyond sending out thugs to bring a stop to a day's shooting. One of Lubin's favorite tricks to deal with these situations was to set up a fake film crew. While they were taking the thugs on a merry chase, the real film company would be in some other location, completing their day's work.

To make matters worse, Lubin, like many other filmmakers of his day, was not exactly ethical in his practices. For example, he was known to remake someone else's film scene for scene and shot for shot. In 1903, Edwin S. Porter had directed *The Great Train Robbery* for Edison. Immediately afterwards, Lubin produced *The Bold Bank Robbery*, which had a suspiciously similar storyline.

However, the legal troubles with Edison came to an end in 1909 when the Motion Picture Patents Company (MPPC) was formed with Edison and each of the companies he claimed were infringing on his copyrights—Biograph, Vita-graph, Essanay, Selig, and Lubin. The companies agreed to pay Edison a roy-alty, and Edison acknowledged the legality of their various patents. Also, all parties agreed to pay royalties to the owners of the various patents for the use of their devices. The "Trust," as it was called, survived until an anti-trust suit brought the MPPC to an end in 1916.

Its Reign

In 1910, Lubin built the most modern, up-to-date studio in the world. The glassed-in structure boasted editing rooms, laboratories, machine shops where the cameras and projectors were made, and the largest artificially lit stage in the world with one of the world's most powerful indoor lighting systems. The studio permitted five film crews to work at once. Located in Philadelphia and known as Lubinville, the studio turned out films that were known for their pro-duction values, technical sophistication, and sharp images.

A visitor to the studio in 1916 made note of the many stars as they arrived that morning: Ethel Clayton, Billie Reeves, Octavio Handworth, Richard Buhler, Jack Pratt, Vinnie Burns, Tom Moore, E. K. Lincoln, and others. The visitor also took note of the several stages in the huge, glassed-in studio building, all

Lubin's large glassed-in studio in Philadelphia was built in 1910. It was one of the most modern, up-to-date studios in the world, with editing rooms, laboratories, machine shops to build cameras and projectors, and stages to allow five crews to film at once.

operating at once—and the brightness of the Klieg lights that tended to alter colors. Most notable perhaps was a drawing room set in a soft-toned purple, which photographed well on the Orthochromatic stock then in use; it registered onscreen as a "French gray."

It surprised the visitor that, in filming a silent movie, there were a multitude of sounds accompanying the shootings on the stages—shrieks, bombs exploding, glass breaking, falling walls, etc. It was explained, however, that the sounds that would naturally accompany the action were necessary to elicit proper performances from the actors.

Two years after the studio was built in Philadelphia, Lubin purchased a 500-acre estate in Betzwood, near historic Valley Forge, which was the home of brewer John Betz. He transformed this estate into a studio and lot that was renowned for its scenic beauty. The $2 million complex was outfitted with state-of-the-art technology that included air-conditioned, automated labs.

The Betzwood studio provided locations for virtually any kind of story. Westerns were a popular product of the Lubin Company, and the grounds of the estate were perfect for filming these "Eastern Westerns." Lubin even hired real cowboys who lived on the grounds of the estate. One of his most famous productions, *The Battle of Shiloh* (1913), was filmed at the Betzwood location. The Betz home provided an ideal backdrop for a European mansion and storylines involving "the wealthy." The estate also included four complete farms all filled with livestock, a deer park, and a two-mile stretch of the Schuylkill River.

But Lubin expanded beyond the East Coast and had studios throughout the country, though none was nearly so large as Lubinville in Philadelphia and the Betzwood studio. He even owned a studio in Berlin. These were employing some individuals whose names are among the most famous in motion picture history: Arthur Johnson, Florence Lawrence, Ethel Clayton, Lottie Briscoe, Rosemary Theby, Ormi Hawley, Edwin Carewe, Constance Talmadge, and many others. Harry Myers, who is best remembered as the drunken millionaire in Charlie Chaplin's *City Lights* (1931), was a leading director and scriptwriter for the company. Frank Borzage, who later became one of Hollywood's most prestigious directors, started as an actor with Lubin.

Ethel Clayton was one of the company's most popular stars during the teens. Her first appearance in a movie for Lubin was *When the Earth Trembled* in 1912. She and House Peters co-starred in one of Lubin's last productions, the 1916 feature *The Great Divide*. Future director Henry King made his acting debut in Lubin films at the Los Angeles studio. At the Jacksonville, Florida, studio in 1913, a young bystander named Oliver "Babe" Hardy was given his first chance at acting and continued honing his craft with the Lubin company for the next two years.

An unusual actor known as Romaine Fielding was Lubin's leading male star for a time and made films in the Southwest that became popular for their psychological implications. The authenticity of the westerns he made for Lubin earned him the reputation as "The Man Who Put 'Real' in Realism." He made history when he wrote, produced, directed, and played the only two roles in a film entitled *The Toll of Fear* (1913), itself a film of daring subject matter and innovative treatment.

Its Requiem

The beginning of the end for the Lubin Manufacturing Company came on June 13, 1914, when a massive film vault explosion destroyed the master film negatives for all of Lubin's films. Two months later, World War I broke out, drying up Lubin's and other filmmakers' foreign market.

He joined in the formation of VLSE—a distribution group that included Vitagraph, Lubin, Selig, and Essanay, but this partnership barely lasted a year. An indication of Lubin's growing financial difficulties was the sale of the controlling interest in his company to Vitagraph after the demise of the VLSE.

Then, the dissolution of the Motion Picture Patents Company in 1915 caused Lubin to lose millions of dollars, adversely affecting his health.

The downhill spiral continued, and on September 1, 1917, the Lubin Manufacturing Company closed its doors forever. Various publications advertised a liquidation sale of "real estate, machinery, and equipment of the Lubin Manufacturing Company in Philadelphia, September 10–14, 1917."

Lubin spent the last years of his life tinkering with radios. He ended up back in his original optical shop in Philadelphia, where he also dabbled in optical and photographic work. The world lost one of its greatest film pioneers on September 11, 1923, when "Pop" Lubin passed away at his home in Ventnor, New Jersey.

SOURCES

PERIODICALS

Motion Picture News (September 8, 1917).

Roy, Marie. "A Visit to the Lubin Studio," *Motion Picture Magazine* (April 1916).

BOOKS

Eckhardt, Joseph P. *The King of the Movies: Film Pioneer Siegmund Lubin.* Vancouver, BC: Fairleigh Dickinson University Press, 1998.

Slide, Anthony. *The New Historical Dictionary of the American Film Industry.* Lanham, MD, and London: The Scarecrow Press, 2001.

INTERNET

"Lubin Manufacturing Company," Wikipedia.com.

"VLSE Incorporated," Wikipedia.com.

OTHER

The History of the Lubin Manufacturing Company documentary. Prism Productions, 1985.

CHAPTER 10
The Silk Hat Comedian: Raymond Griffith
☙

Raymond Griffith began in films in 1915 as an actor, a gag man, a scenario writer— or whatever else was required of him; however, it was his comedies of the mid-twenties that brought him the greatest fame as the "Silk Hat Comedian."

A Child of the Stage

Griffith was born in Boston, Massachusetts, on January 23, 1895, to theatrical parents. He made his debut on the stage at 15 months. At seven years of age, he played *Little Lord Fauntleroy*, and at eight he was playing a female part in *Ten Nights in a Barroom*.

As a young boy, Griffith lost his voice playing a part in *The Witching Hour*. According to *Photoplay*, "His part required that he scream out each night at the threat of a beating. On the fatal night, he ran and cowered, as the direction demanded. The audience heard a piercing shriek from the boy as he cringed before the whip. That was all. The terror on the boy's face was the terror of realism; he was stricken dumb. He could not speak a line after that scream. He has never spoken a line from the stage since then. His recovery was so gradual that he could not speak above a whisper for years, and he has never recovered the full carrying power which the stage demands."

With the loss of his voice went his stage career, and Griffith finally joined a circus doing trapeze work, bareback riding, working as a clown, and at any other job required of him. He also worked as a dancer, a dance instructor at the Grand Central Palace in New York, a vaudeville performer, and toured Europe with a group of French mimes. Additionally, he served a tour of duty in the U. S. Navy.

One source claims that in 1914, after being discharged from the navy, Griffith went west to California where he had a friend working with Vitagraph. Griffith was reportedly on the set to visit his friend when the director asked him if he'd like to play a Mexican bandit for $3 a day. This was the beginning of his film career, although Albert E. Smith, who co-founded Vitagraph with J.

Stuart Blackton, did not list Griffith among the Vitagraph players in his 1952 autobiography.

Another source states that he ended up in California during his vaudeville days and decided to try the movies. This source said his first job was with Kalem in 1915.

Comedy and Drama

It is documented, however, that he was working for L-KO as early as 1915. He left L-KO in the spring of 1916 and went to work for Sennett. Since his appearances in Sennett comedies during the next year are rather sparse, it is assumed he may have also been working as a scenario writer/gag man. Griffith worked for Sennett until 1917 (except for a brief stint with Fox) when Sennett left Triangle. But Griffith continued to work for Triangle as an actor, a gagman, and a scenarist.

Around this time, he was drafted, but was released because of his vocal limitations. By the end of 1918, Griffith was working for Sennett again, gradually favoring story preparation to acting.

From June of 1921 until the fall of 1922, Griffith left Sennett and joined director Marshall "Mickey" Neilan's unit as an actor. In late 1922 or early 1923, he signed a contract with Goldwyn. His first picture for the new company was *Red Lights* (1923), a mystery-melodrama co-starring Marie Prevost.

A review of one of the Goldwyn features, *The Day of Faith*, is a good example of how, with his return to acting, Griffith was beginning to be noticed, even when appearing in a mediocre film: "*The Day of Faith* succeeds only in being a preposterous story of character development . . . What interesting moments it offers are found in a few character sketches, one of them capably played by Raymond Griffith as a hard-boiled newspaperman."

Although not considered in the same league as Chaplin, Keaton, and Lloyd, Raymond Griffith (shown in his trademark tux and top hat), nevertheless made some of the most delightful comedies of the silent era.

Another of Griffith's films during this period was *The White Tiger* (1923), directed by Tod Browning. This film, which is available for viewing today, casts Griffith as Roy Donovan, also known as "The Kid." Griffith plays a fine dramatic role as a con artist working in conjunction with his sister (Priscilla Dean); however, because they were separated at an early age, they have no idea they are related. Also unbeknown to the other, they are each looking for the man responsible for their father's death. The third part of their con artist team (Wallace Beery) is—no surprise here—the very man they are looking for! Griffith appeared in only two more films for Goldwyn before signing a contract with Famous Players-Lasky in late 1923 or early 1924.

A Unique Style

Griffith was establishing a unique style of acting during this period, not strictly comedic and not strictly dramatic. In 1991, historian Davide Turconi had this to say concerning the evolution.

> As for Griffith's Goldwyn period, however, it is worth mentioning that he introduced certain changes to the films in which he appeared between 1922 and 1923 that clearly reflect his earlier experience with Lehrman (L-KO) and Sennett. In the films produced by Goldwyn, Griffith does not portray explicitly comic characters. They are shady figures, or detectives or journalists, whose portrayal is enlivened by frequent comic touches, sometimes reaching slapstick levels and giving rise to farcical scenes. According to some people, it was this very peculiarity that got him the contract with Famous Players.

During 1924, Griffith made five features for Famous Players, the first being *Changing Husbands*, directed by Cecil B. DeMille and co-starring Leatrice Joy. His second feature was *The Dawn of Tomorrow. Movie Weekly* panned the film as "bunk ad infinitum" and said of Griffith's co-star Jacqueline Logan, "Acting is out." However, in the midst of all this criticism, the same review said, "Raymond Griffith, as the crook, gives a fine, interesting and convincing performance. His portrayal is sleuthy, without being of vicious nature. You can readily believe that a 'sweet young thing' like Glad [Logan's character] would fall for his caveman tactics."

The Comedy Genius Begins

His final feature that year was *Open All Night*, starring Adolphe Menjou and Viola Dana. This film, also available for viewing, casts Griffith as Igor Romano, an ex-New York floorwalker who is in France to absorb some "atmosphere" in preparation as becoming the next movie sheik. Throughout the film, he is slightly tipsy—a part he plays well—and, of course, he is dressed in his usual top hat and tux, a costume with which he had already become identified.

Griffith has many enjoyable comedic scenes in the movie, which range from subtle humor to mild slapstick. In one, he is trying to eat a plateful of food, but his fork and knife keep getting tangled up in his cape, a dilemma that Griffith milks for quite a few laughs. He finally decides to get up, take his hat and cape off, and hang them up. However, when he sits back down, the plate is gone—someone has taken it! Unflustered, he removes the napkin from his collar, dabs the corners of his mouth as if he has finished a hearty meal, and lights an after-dinner cigarette.

At the end of the movie, he is walking down a street when he sees a man wearing a sandwich board that advertises, "Valentino Returns to the Screen!" As Griffith alternates between a forced smile and deep concern over his lost opportunity to be the next movie sheik, two gendarmes who apparently know of his aspirations, ask him, "What will you do now?" Griffith hands one end of his cane to each of them to hold in a horizontal position. He then leaps over the cane, flashes a "Fairbanksian" grin and answers simply, "Doug!" He then dashes off, only to fall down a flight of stairs.

His first film of 1925 was the Bebe Daniels feature *Miss Bluebeard*. In this, Robert Frazer is Larry Charters, a wealthy composer who has a string of young ladies at his door. Griffith plays his lazy friend, Bertie Bird, whose only ambition in life is to sleep. When one of Charter's girlfriends comes in, demanding his attentions, Bertie is lying on the sofa, hidden from view, and is very much annoyed at having his nap interrupted. After chiding Charters about one of his other girlfriends, the girl tells him to kiss her, and she will behave. She closes her eyes and puckers, but Charters is reluctant. So, Bertie leans over, gives her a peck, and lies back down on the sofa. The girl is delighted thinking that Charters has kissed her and tells him to do it again. Again, when Charters hesitates, Bertie leans over to kiss her, she grabs him around the neck and they both fall to the floor. Of course, the girl is not at all pleased when she realizes the true identity of her Romeo.

Two pictures later, Griffith co-starred with Betty Compson in one of his best comedies, *Paths to Paradise*. This film, which is also available for viewing, brought Griffith some of his highest praise. His performance received a positive review in the *New York Times*, and *Screenland* magazine went so far as to say that Griffith would soon be Chaplin's top rival. Perfectly cast as a debonair con man, Griffith keeps the laughs coming nonstop so that the film moves along at a sprightly pace.

His Best Comedy

1924 and 1925 were Griffith's most productive years, with 15 features during that period. However, he hadn't reached his peak yet, as many consider his best comedy to be *Hands Up!* (1926). Set during the Civil War, Griffith portrays a Confederate spy. His mission is to keep the gold of one Silas Woodstock (Mack Swain) out of Union hands. During his mission, he tangles with Indians, evades a firing squad, the Union army, and the affections of both of Woodstock's daughters (Marian Nixon and Virginia Lee Corbin). Walter Kerr wrote, "*Hands Up!* contains some work that is daring for its period, certainly, and some that is masterfully delicate, the work of an inventive, unaggressive, amiably iconoclastic intelligence."

Because it is a Civil War film, the inevitable comparison between *Hands Up!* and Buster Keaton's *The General* (1927) is often made. Although Kerr affirms that,

Many regard Griffith's Hands Up! *(1926) as his best comedy. In this Civil War story, he is a Southern spy on a mission to keep Mack Swain's gold from falling into Union hands. However, he doesn't plan on Swain's two lovely daughters, Marian Nixon and Virginia Lee Corbin (pictured in the lobby card), falling in love with him.*

of the two films, *The General* is the masterpiece, he takes exception to a quote in the Stanley Kauffman-Bruce Henstell anthology *American Film Criticism*, which states, "*The General* was voted one of the 10 best films of all time. *Hands Up!* is deservedly forgotten." According to Kerr, "[T]hey have gone too far. . . 'deservedly forgotten' is surely the wrong phrase for what has happened to *Hands Up!* 'Ignobly forgotten' might be better."

His next film, *Wet Paint* (1926), brought him more high praise from the critics. *Pictures* magazine said, "Griffith takes the very slender plot and clothes it with comedy both subtle and slapstick, but laughable withal. In many respects, it is the best thing he had done—certain sketches compare favorably with Chaplin's work."

Griffith made another well-reviewed film in 1926, and two that were not-so-well-received in 1927. Reportedly, Griffith and Famous Players severed ties by "mutual consent."

In January 1928, Griffith married Bertha Mann, a stage and film actress, and they spent most of the first half of the year in Europe. Griffith made no films in 1928, although several projects were said to be in the works, including one with Howard Hughes and another with Louis Wolheim. In 1929, Griffith, despite his vocal limitations, made two sound two-reelers.

His Screen Farewell

Griffith was to appear in films only once more, but he did it with style. His appearance in the 1930 anti-war film *All Quiet on the Western Front* brought him praise from many sources. In the film, Griffith plays a French soldier who has been wounded by a German soldier (Lew Ayres). Because of his wounds, he cannot speak above a whisper. The two spend the night in a foxhole together as the French soldier slowly dies. Although this was only a short sequence in the movie, Griffith's last appearance on film turned out to be one of his most memorable.

Griffith did not act before the camera again, but he did continue to work in films as a production supervisor and associate producer on at least 55 films, from 1931 to 1940.

Newspaper reports say that on November 25, 1957, he was at a Masquers Club in Hollywood dining with friends when he collapsed from a heart attack. He was pronounced dead at the scene. Some sources claim that he choked to death. This may be from the fact that some newspaper reports said he began choking and collapsed, but, nevertheless, attributed his death to a heart attack. Griffith was 62 years old.

SOURCES

PERIODICALS

The Day of Faith review. *Motion Picture Classic* (March 1924).

The Dawn of Tomorrow review. *Movie Weekly* (April 19, 1924).

Howe, Herbert. "He's the Whole Show." *Photoplay* (May 1925).

Turconi, Davide. "Another Griffith." *Griffithiana* (October 1991).

Wet Paint review. *Pictures Magazine* (August 1926).

BOOKS

Kerr, Walter. *Silent Clowns*. New York: Alfred A. Knopf, 1975.

CHAPTER 11
"Garbo: The Official Dream Princess of the Silent Drama Department"
સ્જી

After seeing her in only two films—*Torrent* (1926) and *The Temptress* (1926)—critic Robert Sherwood, who was well acquainted with the many beautiful stars of Hollywood, dubbed Greta Garbo "the official Dream Princess of the Silent Drama Department of *Life* [magazine]."

Sherwood was "taken," "enamored," "smitten," or, in his own words, "knocked for a loop" by this heavenly creature who had suddenly graced movie screens across America. *Torrent* failed to leave a deep impression, and *The Temptress* had "shortcomings," in his opinion. "She may not be the best actress on the screen," he said, adding, "I am powerless to formulate an opinion on her dramatic technique"—yet he affirmed, "[T]here is no room for an argument as to the efficacy of her allure."

Why So Mesmerizing?

Sherwood's experience seems to align with others' first encounters with Garbo on the screen—an allure, possibly even a bewitching as the final credits roll marking that first rendezvous with Sherwood's "dream princess"—not the most original or descriptive term for someone with the eloquence of this respected critic—but, no doubt, he, like so many others, was at a loss for words to describe this star who seemed to have fallen from the heavens.

So, why were moviegoers so mesmerized when this newcomer from Sweden suddenly appeared on American movie screens for the last three or four years of the silent era, not just in the emotional or poignant scenes, but doing *anything*—slowly raising her eyes to look into the camera—glancing to the side in a haughty manner—looking lovingly into her leading man's eyes? Why are her movies so loved by so many, especially when seen in an obviously mediocre story that would no doubt be forgotten had anyone else been in the lead? Why is her beauty so unique and appealing? Why is it that she can be photographed from any angle, with any expression, with any style of dress or hair—

Greta Garbo's first film in the U.S. was Torrent *(1926) co-starring Ricardo Cortez. The picture was a hit, and one reviewer said (in what can only be called an understatement) that Garbo was "the find of the year."*

and her beauty is no less remarkable? Why are photographs of her so much more than just a picture—they are more akin to works of art—too other-worldly to be real?

Author Gary Carey also saw her beauty in an artistic sense: "One can't discuss Garbo without touching on her beauty because it is the cornerstone of many of her performances. She is herself a work of art."

"To watch her face is like contemplating a masterwork—it becomes an experience that strikes both the heart and mind," biographer John Bainbridge quoted from an anonymous source. However, Bainbridge goes on to make some insightful comments regarding Garbo's beauty. Quoting others who espoused, "She is as beautiful as the aurora borealis," or "It needs a work of fiction to invent a face to approach hers," or "Garbo manages, because she is a supremely beautiful woman, to make beauty look like a mark of religion," and he concludes, "Garbo, like any other thing of beauty, is indescribable."

The Eye of the Beholder

The impact of her beauty, though, is also evident to Bainbridge. As he noted, "Garbo has probably had a greater influence on the appearance of women today than any other person." Even though Bainbridge wrote this in 1955, it is still an astounding statement. He points out that if one looks at pre-Garbo photographs of stars such as Joan Crawford, Tallulah Bankhead, Katharine Hepburn, Marlene Dietrich and others, their "portraits show a collection of rather plump and perky young women with short, fuzzy bobbed hair, thick eyebrows, fussy make-up and wearing expressions that were either fatuous or coy. In their post-Garbo portraits, the same young women look startlingly alike—their hair is now worn in the long, plain page-boy style, their eyebrows are mere pencil lines, their eyelashes have been artificially lengthened, their cheeks look as if they are being determinedly sucked in, their make-up is of the simplest, and their expressions are uniformly languorous and inscrutable."

Consider the year of 1926, when Garbo made her American debut in *Torrent* and *The Temptress*. Compare the Garbo of these films with other stars and their movies of the same year: Dolores Del Rio in *What Price Glory*; Joan Crawford in *Tramp, Tramp, Tramp*; Clara Bow in *Kid Boots*; Jobyna Ralston in *For Heaven's Sake*; Eleanor Boardman in *Tell It to the Marines*; Sally O'Neil in *Battling Butler*; Mary Brian in *Brown of Harvard*; Laura La Plante in *Skinner's Dress Suit*; Marie Prevost in *Up in Mabel's Room*—the list could go on and on. Without a doubt, there is a prescience of the "look" moviegoers would see in their leading ladies in the years to come.

Those Eyes

In analyzing her beauty, the feature that has by far received the most attention is her eyes. Writers, searching for adjectives to describe them, have struggled with such words as *haunting*, *sad*, *quizzical*, *languorous*, *melancholy*, and *omniscient*. Her eyes were blue, but are more accurately described by others as an "unforgettable blue," indicating the uniqueness that belongs to every aspect about Garbo. Bainbridge described her eyes as "arresting," an excellent description of what one feels, especially when she is shown for the first time in each of her silent films.

Consider her reveal in *The Temptress* (1926), when she is wearing just enough of a mask to be discreet. However, later, in the garden, when leading man Antonio Moreno asks her to remove the mask, she reaches behind to unclasp it, and then the camera moves behind her so the viewer can only see Moreno's face. His expression changes from grinning merriment to one of awe. Director Fred Niblo has her looking down and then slowly raising her eyes to look at Moreno. Moreno exclaims (via an intertitle), "You are—beautiful!"

In *Flesh and the Devil* (1927), John Gilbert is an Austrian officer greeting his family at the train station when he happens to look over and see a beautiful woman disembarking from the train. The viewer can only see her from Gilbert's somewhat distant vantage point, but the camera follows her as she walks quickly to a waiting carriage. She drops a bouquet of flowers, and Gilbert rushes over to pick them up. He holds them for a moment, unblinking, unmoving—gazing on her exquisite beauty, and then, for the first time, her face is seen in a close-up, making it easy to empathize with his character's reaction.

Love (1929) gives the best example of this. Gilbert, as a Russian officer, happens upon Garbo, who is stranded in her sleigh during a heavy snowstorm. She wears a hat and veil, so, of course, he is unable to see her face. Being chivalrous, he takes her to the closest inn. She sits on a bench by the fire, and he turns his back as he continues chatting. We see her lift the veil first, then, still chatting, Gilbert turns and sees her face for the first time. Stunned by her beauty, he stops talking and can only stare as if momentarily paralyzed.

As noted, one cannot write of Garbo's beauty without mentioning those eyes—eyes which adjectives seem inadequate to describe. However, the Garbo eyes were so much a part of her superb acting ability. Sherwood may have been "powerless to formulate an opinion on her dramatic technique"—which could be because he was unable to get past her incredible beauty, or maybe it was because he had only seen two of her films. But her acting, like her beauty, was somewhat of an anachronism for the silent era. Always restrained, always underplayed, her eyes said more than any number of animated gestures could.

. . . And She Could Act

Just as they were at a loss to adequately describe her beauty, writers also searched for adjectives to describe Garbo's eyes, using such terms as "haunting," "languorous," "omniscient" and "arresting."

Screenwriter Frances Marion said, "It was always fascinating to watch Garbo; her economy of gesture, constant changing of moods revealed by her luminous eyes that never played the little physical tricks used by so many actresses." Director Clarence Brown (*Flesh and the Devil* and *Woman of Affairs*) said, "Garbo had something behind the eyes that you couldn't see until you photographed it in close-up. You could see thought. If she had to look at one person with jealousy, and another with love, she didn't have to change her expression. You could see it in her eyes as she looked from one to the other. And nobody else has been able to do that on the screen. Garbo did it without the command of the English language."

Garbo as an actress has been compared to Bernhardt or Duse, something that at least on one occasion caused her great embarrassment. At a party, someone commented that her recent role in *Camille* (1936) was finer than Duse's. She immediately got up from her chair and left the party. One guest recalled, "Her face was white as chalk. She valued the compliment, of course, but her very great modesty made hearing it unendurable agony."

In her article on Garbo, Louise Brooks commented:

She's so perfect that people say she can't act. People would much rather see someone like Peter Sellers performing than see real acting, which is intangible. People are pretty good judges of dancing, because they've all tried to dance a little. They recognize a technique. They're judges of singing, because they've tried to sing, and they recognize a technique. So they must have some visible technique in order to judge acting, and there isn't any. Acting is completely a personal reaction. That is why I get so inflamed when people tell me Garbo can't act. She is SO great.

It is a tribute to Garbo's acting greatness that her technique was so different, so unique to the period of cinema history in which she arrived. It is no wonder that with the combination of beauty and acting being so unconventional for the time, so prescient (maybe not so much prescient as the one who set the standard), and all so beguiling to the picturegoer, she swept the world off its collective feet. It is also a tribute to her greatness that she transitioned so effortlessly from silent film to sound—without changing her technique or worrying about adapting to the new medium. Garbo was already perfect for it—and who else was so perfect in both media?

Works of Art

Garbo's silent films are works of art, in a sense. No, she wasn't given the best stories; instead she was given the popular novels of the day—basically soap operas with elegant backgrounds. However, silent film fans must be thankful that she was a part of a studio such as MGM, where quality was revered and expected. Therefore, although the stories themselves may not be masterpieces, the visual experience alone makes them an aesthetic gratification equal to the viewing of a great painting. Add to that the beauty of emotion and motion—Garbo moving across the screen, expressing joy or sadness, smiling, gazing with her impenetrable eyes—and the viewer has an artistic experience that touches the heart and moves the spirit.

Biographer Barry Paris explained:

> For the denizens of the first half of the twentieth century, when such images still counted, Garbo *was* the moviegoing experience — theory and practice alike. Some quirk of Nature and Art created a face, a personality, and an erotic presence unprecedented in history . . . Garbo was an anomaly, not a mystery. She is something to be experienced rather than adored, but people did both.

One needs only to look at the sheer presence of Garbo in the 20th century and the fact that her presence continues just as memorably in the 21st century. The number of books on Garbo is remarkable. Her films still attract large audiences on television and in theatres. Her image is constantly being reproduced and sold. With the arrival of her 100th birthday in 2005, there were special remembrances and the release of films that have never been available for the home video market. In the 1960s, Clarence Brown declared that Garbo and Rudolph Valentino were the only two stars who would endure through posterity. One may argue that others should be included on the list, but no one can deny that Garbo, certainly, will endure.

SOURCES

BOOKS

Bainbridge, John. *Garbo*. Garden City, NY: Doubleday and Co., 1955.

Brooks, Louise. *Lulu in Hollywood*. New York: Alfred A. Knopf, 1982.

Brownlow, Kevin. *The Parade's Gone By*. New York: Bonanza Books, 1968.

Carey, Gary. *Cukor & Co.* Boston: New York Graphic Society, 1971.

Marion, Frances. *Off with Their Heads: A Serio-comic Tale of Hollywood*. New York: The MacMillan Company, 1972.

Paris, Barry. *Garbo*. Chicago: University of Minnesota Press, 1994.

Swenson, Karen. *Greta Garbo: A Life Apart*. New York: Charles Scribner's Sons, 1997.

CHAPTER 12
The Reluctant Star: Nils Asther

‹›

Nils Asther was like his fellow Swede Greta Garbo in many ways—stardom wasn't important to him, although acting in something that satisfied him was. He didn't seek publicity, choosing instead to be alone. He is mainly remembered for the two films he made with Garbo—*Wild Orchids* and *The Single Standard*, both in 1929. However, Asther was a talented actor, and, without a doubt, those two films, as well as others he made, would not have been the same without his unique contributions.

Asther was born in Hellerup, near Copenhagen, Denmark, on January 17, 1897. His parents were Swedish with the last name of Andersson, but his father later changed it to Asther. His mother was Andersson's second wife, and he had a half-brother, Gunnar, from his father's first marriage, with whom he did not get along. Friends from the stage were frequent visitors to the Asthers' home, which fueled Nils's desire to be a performer. During these years, he was a loner who attended school only reluctantly. He preferred to spend his time alone, reading.

One source said his father owned factories, newspapers, and bank stock, and that he expected his son to succeed him in the business world or to enter the diplomatic profession. However, in his mid-teens, he decided he wanted to be on the stage. When his father forbade him to do so, Asther left home to pursue his dream, and his father disowned him.

Pursuing His Dream

In Copenhagen, one of Sweden's best-known actors, Aage Hertel of the Royal Danish Theatre, took him under his wing. After six months in Copenhagen, Asther had to return home to finish school because he was only 15 years old. However, another source said he spent the next two or three years acting in films in Copenhagen, Berlin, and Paris.

At any rate, in 1916, when he was 19, he went to Stockholm, where he met director Mauritz Stiller. He was offered a screen test for a lead in a film but lost the part to Lars Hanson. Stiller felt sorry for Asther, though, and wrote a small

Nils Asther is mainly remembered for the two silent films he made with Greta Garbo; however, he also had a distinguished career in sound films both in the U.S. and Europe.

part in the film for him. His film debut, then, was in *Vingarna* (1916), coincidentally, as a movie-struck young man. Receiving little work in Sweden, he went to Denmark in 1917; while there, he made two films. Finally, by this time, he was financially stable enough to return to Sweden so he could train for his original dream of acting on the stage. He eventually made his stage debut under the direction of Per Lindberg at the Lorensbergsteatern in Gothenburg.

Later, while he was acting at the Royal Dramatic Theatre in Stockholm, he was offered a role in a German film, *Das Geheimnis der Herzogin* (1923). Over the next few years, he acted in German, Swedish, and Danish films, but spent most of that time working in Berlin, where he became a popular film star. His fame was noticed by American producers, and he was soon fielding offers to come to Hollywood. He chose Paramount. However, Joseph Schenck wanted him for United Artists and immediately bought out his contract.

The Duncan Sisters and a Smash Hit

Asther was frustrated at having to wait so long for a role to come along, but he was eventually cast in *Topsy and Eva* (1927) with the Duncan Sisters (Vivian and Rosetta). A more substantial role followed in *Sorrell and Son* (also 1927), directed by Herbert Brenon. It was a smash hit.

Asther began 1928 by appearing in the DeMille Pictures production *The Blue Danube* (directed by Paul Sloane), *The Cardboard Lover* with Marion Davies (Cosmopolitan Pictures), *The Cossacks* with John Gilbert (MGM), and *Dream of Love* with Joan Crawford (MGM). It was his next two films, however, that seemed to ensure his future as a true star. He was selected to play the young romantic interest opposite Loretta Young in Lon Chaney's *Laugh, Clown, Laugh* (1928), followed by *Loves of an Actress* with Pola Negri for Paramount.

Around this time an article appeared in *Photoplay* magazine entitled, "Will Nils Asther Retire?" Apparently threatening to quit movies due to his frustration with America's rushed filmmaking techniques (he made seven features in 1928 alone), he stated his desire to "live in the country with his writing and reading." He was also quoted as saying: "Work to me is like some people's religion. It is my god. I forget everything when I am working. Yet, I cannot do my best going in such a hurry from one leading man to another. If a story is interesting—all right. But to become a star or a famous leading man, to have to take every part that they give me—*No!*" He went on, "I feel I am wasting my time! Life is too short. There is so much to be accomplished. I would like to play in one big picture—a character part—to show the American people what it is I want to accomplish. I don't care about fan letters, publicity. I would like to play with Von Stroheim. He would have much to teach me."

He had, however, found a perfect home for his talents at MGM, and his final film of 1928 proved to be one of his most popular—*Our Dancing Daughters*, the second time he was paired with Joan Crawford. Although Crawford and John Mack Brown are the true leads in the story, Asther has an excellent part as Norman, who becomes jealous and angry when his wife, Beatrice (Dorothy Sebastian), continues to party with her hard-drinking friends.

Starring Garbo and Asther

It was in his next film that his true talents came to the fore and he was recognized as a star. Cast opposite Greta Garbo in *Wild Orchids*, he had a meaty role as the tempting Javanese Prince De Gace. Adapted from a story aptly entitled *Heat* by John Colton, John Sterling (Lewis Stone) is an inattentive husband to his much younger wife, played by Garbo. At one point, she tries to arouse his interest by donning a seductive Balinese costume, only to be told, "You look silly, dear—take off all that junk and go to bed." Asther is forward and brash in his attempts to entice Garbo into an illicit relationship, virtually under the nose of her husband—and, due to her husband's lack of interest, the viewer is left to surmise whether she will succumb. Asther's character is at once held in our contempt for his lascivious behavior, yet not totally relegated to the role of villain because of her husband's obvious lack of attention. *Photoplay* said, "Here is a role that will push the young Swedish actor up close to stardom. To it he lends something of the charm and poise of Valentino." The reviewer's comparison to Valentino is on target, although Asther exuded a sophistication that was never associated with the Sheik. Then again, Asther would never come close to Valentino in terms of onscreen charisma.

Asther gave an outstanding performance in Wild Orchids *(1929) as a Javanese prince trying to seduce Garbo while hosting her and her older husband, played by Lewis Stone, in his home.*

Asther and Garbo had known each other in Sweden, and finding themselves relatively new to a foreign land, they obviously spent a great deal of time together visiting a friend's ranch outside Hollywood, where they could relax and ride horses together, go climbing, and swim in Lake Arrowhead. This friendship was especially helpful when Garbo's beloved mentor, Mauritz Stiller (who had come with her to America), died suddenly during production.

Wild Orchids was a huge success for MGM, so Asther and Garbo were quickly paired in another feature, *The Single Standard* (1929). In that, Garbo is unaccepting of the double standard that exists regarding the expected behavior of men and women. When a handsome artist (Asther) comes along and invites her to go with him on a long cruise, she does so regardless of the scandal she may ignite. However, after cruising around the world for many months, he tires of her and says their relationship must end. Devastated, she goes home and concedes to the unending pleas of the boyish John Mack Brown to marry him. One day, Asther, her true love, returns, begging her to come back to him. In a situation not unlike the one in *Wild Orchids*, Garbo must choose between the safe, unexciting life she agreed to when she married, or be swept away by the captivating and impetuous artist.

Although the interplay between Garbo and Asther is sexy and compelling, the *Variety* reviewer was unimpressed with Asther's performance, noting, "Nils Asther, with his black hair and John-like mustache, while doing a good job, does not lend the sailor-artist-boxer role the Gilbertine touch."

Tired of Being Just a Screen Lover

Asther, like Garbo, was never taken with being a star. He had a fair amount of contempt for Hollywood, a fact that is discernable in interviews. "Like Garbo, I have been given many labels by the newspapers," he said. "'Very nearly as handsome as Valentino' . . . 'the masculine version of that mysterious fascination with Garbo's.' [But] I am tired of being just a screen lover, and I hope someday to get a chance to be myself. I am rather like Greta in that I like to be alone. I love peace and quiet. Hollywood is really no place for me. I stagnate here . . . I only feel awake when the air is fresh and crisp as in my native Scandinavia. I believe it is because Garbo is from Sweden, that she feels the same."

Although Asther had made two silent films in 1929, this was the watershed year for the industry's transition from silence to sound. With an accent that would limit his acting opportunities in the new medium, Asther returned to Germany where he made *The Wrath of the Seas* (1929). However, the next year he was back at MGM for his first foray into the new medium of talkies, not as a leading man, but as an unlucky rival for the affections of Caribbean beauty Raquel Torres. Asther's character in *The Sea Bat* (1930) is killed by the rival and thus began his career in sound films. It was also in 1930 that he married Vivian Duncan of the Duncan Sisters, with whom he had co-starred in his first American film. The couple had a daughter, Evelyn, in 1931, but the marriage only lasted two years, ending in divorce in 1932.

After an absence from the screen of two years, Asther landed a good part in *But the Flesh is Weak* (1932), starring Robert Montgomery. This marked the beginning of a new path, one that would last for the rest of his film career: no longer a star, but an actor with sufficient roles to keep him busy and financially stable.

Steady, Starless Work

One exception to the secondary roles he was being given came in 1933. It became his most memorable performance in a sound film—the title character in *The Bitter Tea of General Yen*. Barbara Stanwyck stars as American missionary Megan Davis, who goes to Shanghai during the Chinese Civil War. When she is separated from her fiancé and injured, it is General Yen who saves her.

In time, the general grows fond of Megan. When he is about to execute his mistress, Mah-Li, for betrayal of classified information, Megan successfully intervenes. Once again, as in *Wild Orchids*, the temptation of our heroine to surrender to the advances of the so-called "villain" is ever present, yet she keeps her virtue intact. Nevertheless, when his empire is lost and his death imminent, Megan remains by his side.

The film was the initial program for Radio City Music Hall when it opened on January 11, 1933. Asther received praise for his portrayal, and the film went on to be named one of the 10 best pictures of the year.

Asther was offered a film deal in England in 1934. Planning to appear in one film and return, he ended up staying for five films during a five-and-a-half-year sojourn. He returned to Hollywood and continued to find work in lower-budget films, such as *The Man Who Lost Himself* (1941), with Brian Aherne and Kay Francis; *Dr. Kildare's Wedding Day* (1941), with Lew Ayres (who had also starred with Greta Garbo in her last silent, *The Kiss*); *Sweater Girl* (1942), with Eddie Bracken and June Priesser; *Night Monster* (1942), with Bela Lugosi; *Bluebeard* (1944), with John Carradine and Jean Parker; *Son of Lassie* (1945), with Peter Lawford; and even an uncredited part in Cecil B. DeMille's *Samson and Delilah* (1949), with Hedy Lamarr and Victor Mature. His nineteen films during the 1940s were scattered among a variety of studios—major ones like MGM, Universal, and Paramount—but also "poverty row" outfits, such as PRC, Monogram, and Republic.

His last American film was *That Man from Tangier*, a Spanish-American production shot in 1950 but not shown in the U. S. until 1953. From that point on, he began to find work in TV and the theatre. His longtime desire to be on the stage was realized once again in 1953 when he made his Broadway debut in *The Strong Are Lonely* playing "a blunt, swashbuckling Dutch trader." The show only lasted seven performances.

In 1958, he went back to Sweden and made some films and appeared on the Swedish stage in 1961. His last film was made in Denmark in 1963, entitled *Gudrun* (American title: *Suddenly, A Woman!*). Asther remained in Sweden for the rest of his life, never remarrying after his divorce from Duncan in 1933 (which is alleged to have been "a marriage of convenience" to help divert the stigma of his homosexuality). He spent much of his time becoming an accomplished artist with several exhibitions to his credit. On October 13, 1981, he died at the age of 84, in a hospital outside Stockholm, Sweden.

SOURCES

PERIODICALS

Biery, Ruth. "Will Nils Asther Retire?" *Photoplay* (October 1928).

Lundquist, Gunnar. "Nils Asther." *Films in Review* (August/September 1979).

Picture Show (October 1935).

Wild Orchids review. *Photoplay* (March 1929).

BOOKS

Card, James. *Seductive Cinema: The Art of Silent Film*. New York: Alfred A. Knopf, 1994.

Conway, Michael, et al. *The Films of Greta Garbo*. New York: Cadillac Publishing Co., Inc., 1974.

Katz, Ephraim. *The Film Encyclopedia*. New York: Thomas Y. Crowell, Publishers, 1979.

The New York Times Film Reviews: 1913-1931. New York: The New York Times and Arno Press, 1970.

Paris, Barry. *Garbo*. Chicago: University of Minnesota Press, 2002.

Ragan, David. *Who's Who in Hollywood: 1900–1976*. New York: Arlington House Publishers, 1976.

Swenson, Karen. *Greta Garbo: A Life Apart*. New York: Charles A. Scribner's Sons, 1997.

Variety *Film Reviews: 1926–1929*. New York and London: R.R. Bowker Company, 1983.

Variety *Obituaries: 1980–1983*. New York and London: Garland Publishing, Inc., 1988.

Vieira, Mark A. *Greta Garbo: A Cinematic Legacy*. New York and London: Harry N. Abrams, Inc., 2005.

OTHER

The American Film Institute Catalog of Feature Films. AFI.com.

CHAPTER 13
The Mysterious Death of Olive Thomas
ᴇᴏ

She never appeared in a picture that qualified as a silent screen classic. Of course, the point could be debatable since so little of her work is available for review. So, sadly enough, she is remembered today for being married to Jack Pickford and for dying under mysterious circumstances at the young age of 25.

Clerk, Model, Ziegfeld Girl, Movie Star

Oliva Duffy was born in Charleroi, Pennsylvania, on October 20, 1894. Supposedly an extended visit to an aunt in New York opened the door for her to pose for such famous artists as Harrison Fisher and Howard Chandler Christy. Fisher introduced her to Florenz Ziegfeld (she claimed in a 1919 magazine article that she simply went to Ziegfeld and asked for a job without an introduction) and that led to wide acclaim on Broadway for Olive Thomas. (The name Thomas came from a 1911 marriage to a clerk in a department store where she worked. That marriage ended in divorce in 1915.)

Not surprisingly, her notoriety with Ziegfeld led to a movie contract with the International Film Company in 1916. It was in March of that same year that she met Jack Pickford at a dance at Nat Goodwin's on the Santa Monica pier. Screenwriter Frances Marion remembered, "I had seen her [Thomas] often at the Pickford home, for she was engaged to Mary's brother, Jack. Two innocent-looking children, they were the gayest, wildest brats who ever stirred the stardust on Broadway. Both were talented, but they were much more interested in playing the roulette of life than in concentrating on their careers."

A year after they met, Thomas commented in an interview, "Jack is a beautiful dancer. He danced his way into my heart. We knew each other for eight months before our marriage, and most of that time we gave to dancing. We got along so well on the dance floor that we just naturally decided that we would be able to get along together for the rest of our lives." They were married in October 1916.

Thomas would continue to make pictures, signing with Triangle Film Corporation in 1917. She and Jack would often be parted by their careers, and although their marriage was rocky at times, they appeared to spend as much

Before entering films, Olive Thomas posed for some of the most famous artists of the day, appeared in the Ziegfeld Follies, *and performed on Broadway. It was inevitable that her beauty and talent would one day lead to a place in the movies.*

time together as possible. In May 1918, Pickford joined the Navy. It was generally believed that Pickford enlisted to impress Thomas because he feared the marriage was "on the rocks."

Scandal

It wasn't long before Jack Pickford found himself at the center of a scandal. He allegedly served as a "go-between" for a Lt. Benjamin Davis, who arranged safe assignments for "bluebloods" who wanted to be "far away from shot and shell." Davis was court-martialed and found guilty. Pickford, because he testified for the prosecution, was dishonorably discharged, although it is presumed that Mary and/or her mother, Charlotte, arranged to have the word "dishonorable" removed from his discharge.

A Second Honeymoon and Tragedy

After more than a year together in California, making pictures, with the usual occasional separations brought about by going on location (for example, Thomas was on location in Louisiana between January–March 1920), Pickford and Thomas sailed from New York for Paris on August 12, 1920. Upon arrival, they checked in at the Hotel Ritz for what was planned as a second honeymoon, designed to save what, by then, had become a failing marriage.

While there, they immersed themselves in the nightlife. They explored various clubs with other American friends in the Montmartre, an area rampant with drugs and bootleg alcohol. One speakeasy they frequented was representative of this kind of atmosphere—The Dead Rat.

During the day, Thomas was being fitted for clothes for upcoming films. Jack left for London on August 25 to be fitted for suits for his own films, returning to Paris on September 5. That night, they went out on the town, returning to their rooms between 3 and 4 a.m. Shortly afterward, it was reported that Thomas took mercury bichloride tablets and mixed them in a glass of alcohol. This was a corrosive substance that was used as a disinfectant, but also used externally to treat syphilis. Within a couple of hours, Pickford called downstairs to say that his wife had taken an overdose of medicine and needed a doctor. A doctor arrived in 10 minutes to find Thomas, writhing in pain.

A prevailing theory is that the mercury bichloride was prescribed to Pickford for his venereal disease. This is supported by the fact that Pickford's doctor had admitted to prescribing the medicine for him in 1917 as a treatment for syphilis.

Pickford was quoted as saying he was in bed when he heard Thomas shriek from the bathroom, "Oh, my God!" He rushed in and caught her in his arms. She had swallowed a lethal dose.

Jack Pickford and Olive Thomas were married in 1916. However, Thomas would die before they could celebrate their fourth anniversary.

Mary Pickford biographer Eileen Whitfield said the couple had gone to bed after an evening of visiting "the bistros of Montmartre." A half-hour later, Thomas was unable to go to sleep and reached for sleeping pills in the dark, mistakenly grasping a bottle of bichloride of mercury. "Jack woke to Olive's screams as the pills burned through her throat and stomach. Or perhaps it was a maid who came to Olive's rescue. Another story has it that "Jack had slipped out for a last-minute round of drugs," she said.

Another version of the story, albeit not as popular, is that Thomas, who was known to be impetuous, took the pills to commit suicide, possibly after a row with her husband. Whatever happened that night, Thomas suffered for another four days before she passed away on September 10, the substance having burned through her vocal cords and blinded her.

The Parisian police conducted an investigation, and an autopsy was performed. The ruling was that Thomas had ingested the poison accidentally.

Unanswered Questions and Rumors

Director Marshall Neilan was quoted as saying he believed Thomas's death was a suicide. Mary Pickford and Douglas Fairbanks's biographer Booten Herndon said, "Ugly rumors were whispered on both sides of the Atlantic; one was that she had committed suicide because Jack had given her syphilis; another theory is that he had poisoned her for her various infidelities." Newspapers of the day were quick to report rumors of Thomas's heroin addiction and venereal disease as well as her husband's infidelities.

Another rumor was that Pickford had murdered Thomas for her money, but, as Whitfield observed, that theory "didn't hold water with those who knew him. After all, when Jack was broke, he had only to call his mother or older sister." Biographer Scott Eyman noted, "Jack—and undoubtedly Mary—tried to recoup the public relations disaster by renouncing any share of Thomas' small $36,875 estate, but it was too late."

No matter, the whole affair was an ugly one, with a dark pall surrounding the death of a talented and beautiful young woman who should be remembered for better things. Of course, the investigation resulted in a finding of "accidental death," but time has not left her death with such an easy conclusion.

Pickford brought his wife's body home, and, on September 24, a funeral was held at St. Thomas Episcopal Church in New York. Over four thousand people were in attendance, and it was described as "chaotic." Her body was interred in a crypt at Woodlawn Cemetery in the Bronx.

One week after her funeral, Thomas's final film, *Everybody's Sweetheart*, was released, giving fans one last time to see the lovely actress on the screen.

After Her Passing

Pickford, with his sister's help, was back making movies shortly after Thomas's death. In 1922, he made one movie, which was financed by Mary Pickford. Also that year, he married another former Ziegfeld girl, Marilyn Miller, a marriage that ended in 1927. In 1930, he once again married a former Ziegfeld girl, this time ending in divorce in 1932. In and out of hospitals for several years (the claims were usually a nervous breakdown or exhaustion), Pickford died on January 3, 1933, at 36 years of age.

For several years, it appeared the only Olive Thomas feature that was available on home video was *Love's Prisoner* (1919). Then, in 2005, Milestone Films released *The Flapper* (1920), along with a documentary on Thomas entitled *Everybody's Sweetheart*. In recent years, other Olive Thomas films such as *An Even Break* (1917), *Broadway Arizona* (1917), *Betty Takes a Hand* (1918), and *Out Yonder* (1919) have surfaced, but, at the time of this writing, none have been released commercially.

What a loss it is that no more of her work is available on home video, and what a greater loss that she died so young at the dawn of the next and greater stage of the silent movie era. Without a doubt, her beauty and charm would have been well suited for the post–World War I audiences. What her career could have been is now left only to conjecture.

SOURCES

BOOKS

Eyman, Scott. *Mary Pickford, America's Sweetheart*. New York: Donald I. Fine, Inc., 1990.

Foster, Charles. *Stardust and Shadows*. Toronto: Dundurn Press, 2000.

Herndon, Booten. *Mary Pickford and Douglas Fairbanks*. New York: W.W. Norton and Company, Inc., 1977.

Marion, Frances. *Off with Their Heads*. New York: The MacMillan Company, 1972.

Whitfield, Eileen. *Pickford: The Woman Who Made Hollywood.* Lexington, KY: The University Press of
    Kentucky, 1997.

OTHER

Everybody's Sweetheart documentary. Timeline Films. 2004.

CHAPTER 14
Pickford's Patriotism
❧

Since Uncle Sam started measuring his sons for uniforms and set in motion his gigantic fighting machine, various persons prominent in the public eye have devoted much of their own time to help brighten up the lives of the boys in khaki who have set about the job of 'kanning the Kaiser.' Conspicuous among those whose activities have attracted considerable attention is none other than our own Mary Pickford, known throughout the land as 'America's Sweetheart. (Peter Gridley Smith in *Photo-Play Journal*, December 1917)

The Little American

Yes, Pickford was the epitome of "The Little American" (although she was born in Canada) during World War I, and, because of her sensational popularity at the time, she was the perfect proponent for the war effort.

When the war in Europe began in1914, Pickford held forth the same pacifist sentiment as most of the country at that time—remain neutral! She verbalized her stance in a newspaper column, which Frances Marion "ghost wrote" for her, entitled "Daily Talks."

Woodrow Wilson was re-elected president in 1916 on a promise to keep the nation out of the war in Europe, and Hollywood followed suit with pacifist-themed films, such as Thomas Ince's *Civilization* (1915), Alla Nazimova's *War Brides* (1916), and even D.W. Griffith's *Intolerance* (1916).

However, with the sinking of the *Lusitania* in 1915, public sentiment began to slowly swing in the other direction. "Preparedness" was the catchword. Vitagraph's *The Battle Cry of Peace* in 1915 was unashamedly pro-war in its sentiments and showed Americans being invaded by "Hun-like" armies. When the United States entered the war in 1917, Hollywood jumped on the bandwagon and began making a flurry of pro-war films. Columnist Louella Parsons commented, "[T]hese film plays have been raising the temperature of the Allies' patriotism to blood heat." Actually, Hollywood was prohibited, in a roundabout way, from making pacifist-themed films with the passing of the Espionage Act of 1917, which banned "disloyal acts."

Pickford had performed for soldiers for the first time as a child on the stage during the Boer War. She thrilled at the sight of the young men in uniform, and early in the war effort, she began to offer her services as a morale booster whenever possible.

Pickford biographer Eileen Whitfield said, "She seemed to be everywhere at once, speaking through megaphones, posing for posters, collecting cigarettes to send to the doughboys, leading a marine band through San Francisco, and sending her photograph to decorate the trenches."

At one point, Pickford, with the help of Douglas Fairbanks, was collecting toys from all the Hollywood stars to send to the children in Belgium. She was very visible and active during this time—the Navy named her their "Little Sister." There were photographs of her kissing the American flag. She also helped raise money for the Red Cross by signing the receipts for those who gave money.

Formally Adopted

Pickford's adoption of a Battalion took place at Camp Kearney in 1917. In a speech, Pickford said, "I shall take each of my 600 sons under my wing, and I intend to see to it that they receive the little luxuries which they cannot otherwise obtain, including plenty of tobacco and candy." Pickford was referred to as these soldiers' "godmother," and they were known as "Mary Pickford's Fighting Six Hundred." True to her word, she saw to it that they had a steady supply of tobacco, chewing gum, and candy. When they shipped out to France, it was noted, "[E]ach man in 'Mary's Six Hundred' will wear a locket about his neck containing a miniature of his petite protector."

One report read, "It was a great day for Mary and the 143rd when she came to Camp Kearney near San Diego, California, and reviewed her troops. She is the first woman to have that honor. Mary's regiment belongs to the 'Sunshine' Division, which is also known as 'He-Men.' She had lunch with the officers; she gave her regiment 1,200 Smileage Books; she was guest of honor at the regimental ball at Coronado and led the grand march with Colonel Funeuf. She also received the honorary title of 'Colonel'—and the band played 'Her Name was Mary' and 'Mary is a Grand Old Name.'"

A 1918 *Photoplay* article entitled, "Colonel Mary of the 143rd Field Artillery, U.S.A.," reads:

Recently Colonel Pickford's regiment took a long hike from its encampment and training quarters in San Diego County to Los Angeles. It was three days en route, and the ranchers' wives along the dusty way fed it and bedded it and coddled it to the point of almost making it a pageant instead of a march. At the edge of Los Angeles were a score or so of newspapermen, Eastern correspondents, and cameramen from the news weeklies. But Colonel Pickford was not one of these. She had gone far out into the ranch country and did not meet her boys but arrived with them. Previously, she had paid them a visit or so at their official home, Camp Kearney.

One story relates how Mary saw posters appealing for "smokees" for the soldiers, and that she was moved to do something personally about this need. First, she obtained copies of the poster and had them displayed all about the studio. Then she made personal visits to everyone in the studio, requesting cigarettes. From those who didn't have cigarettes, she was given money to buy some. This developed into a routine where Mary made the rounds of the studio each week, soliciting the cigarettes, and each week she had a case of tobacco sent off to the boys at the front. Other luminaries of the screen found it impossible to turn Mary down when she came asking for their help. When she decided to have a Christmas party in September, complete with decorated tree and all, she asked her fellow stars to bring gifts to put under the tree. The following day, Christmas presents were on their way to the boys overseas.

Entertaining the Troops

A group of soldiers, identified only as "the boys of Battery A," stopped by the studio for a visit. Mary welcomed them with open arms. Upon learning that they were on a recruiting mission, she asked if they would like her help. Soon, she was in the streets of Los Angeles with the soldiers, and, in a short time, they had met their quota for new recruits.

The Lasky Home Guard was formed in Hollywood, which was made up of Famous Players-Lasky studio employees. Heading up this "regiment" was none other than director Cecil B. DeMille, who was appointed their "captain." His brother, William, and movie idol Wallace Reid were also in the Lasky Guard. The "regiment" could often be seen marching down Hollywood Boulevard and spent their Sunday afternoons drilling with prop rifles and uniforms.

In 1918, the governor of California reviewed the Lasky Guard, and Mary had the opportunity to present them with their colors, a silk flag with hand-embroidered stars that she had commissioned.

According to Colleen Moore, Pickford organized a benefit performance at the Grand Opera House, which raised $40,000 to buy ambulances as gifts

from the motion picture stars. However, the war ended before all the money was spent, leaving $27,000 in the treasury. Through Mary's efforts, this became the seed money for the realization of a dream she had—the Motion Picture Home, that famous memorial to Hollywood's willingness to care for its own.

War-Themed Movies

Two of Mary's features during this period deal with war and made the most of the pervasive sentiment of the time that all Germans were barbarians who raped and pillaged wherever they went. *The Little American*, directed by the Lasky Guard's captain Cecil B. DeMille, was released on July 2, 1917. It cast Mary as Angela Moore, whose German-born sweetheart, Karl Von Austreim (Jack Holt), must return to his homeland at the outbreak of the war. Angela is called to France to care for her dying aunt and is caught up in the fighting. She is captured by the Germans, very nearly raped and almost killed by a firing squad. The film also gives a graphic depiction of the sinking of a ship called the *Veritania*, an obvious reference to the *Lusitania*. Almost as a throwback to America's original

The 143rd California Field Artillery, stationed at Camp Kearney near San Diego, was "adopted" by Mary Pickford when the United States entered World War I. From that point on, she was given the honorary titled of "Colonel Mary."

Pickford worked diligently to support her "adopted" soldiers, hosting them at the studio, giving them books and ensuring they had a steady supply of chewing gum, candy, and cigarettes. Each soldier was also provided a locket to wear with a photo of Pickford inside.

desire to stay out of the war, one of the titles has Mary proclaiming, "I stopped being neutral and became a human being."

Her lover, who is now in the German army, is influenced by the war (some say the movie implies his change is due to genetics) and becomes one of these barbarous soldiers. When his unit commandeers the home where Mary is, he threatens to rape her until he realizes who she is. Suddenly, it dawns on him what a "beast" he has become, and he is immediately redeemed. Of course, they survive the war and live happily ever after.

Commenting on *The Little American*, Pickford biographer Scott Eyman said, "[It] is a film of little distinction, filled with the rape fantasies that were de rigueur for these sort of films . . . De Mille achieves a lurid, if unlikely, melodramatic splendor when he has his beastly Huns say things like 'Where are the pretty girls, Fritz?' Worse, the Germans force Mary to undergo the second-worst degradation: taking the muddy boots off a German general sporting a Kaiser Wilhelm mustache."

Although *The Little American* may have been "a film of little distinction," it showed respectable profits of somewhere between $130,000 and $150,000, giving a clear indication of the public's fervor at the time.

Johanna Enlists was released September 29, 1918, and, although war related, this was a comedy-drama about a regiment of soldiers located on her father's farm, which, subsequently, more than fulfilled Johanna's dream of having a beau. Two of the soldiers fall in love with her, one ending up in a court martial due to "fighting" over her. However, she finally marries a third soldier, whom she meets at the court martial.

Despite being a comedy-drama, this film, too, has its moment to preach. Within the film is newsreel footage of Mary's troops and "Colonel Mary Pickford" in uniform, charging, "Don't come back 'til you've taken the germ out of Germany!"

Mary was also in a couple of patriotic shorts during the war. One was entitled *100% American*. In this film, she is a poor girl named Mayme, who walks two miles instead of taking the streetcar so she can use her nickel to buy bonds. Mary also headed a cast of stars who appeared in the 1917 propaganda short *War Relief*.

The Liberty Loan Drives

Of course, most attention is given to Mary's work in the Liberty Loan drives in 1918, possibly because she and Douglas Fairbanks were secretly courting during this time. Although the romance had started well before she, Fairbanks, Charlie Chaplin, and Marie Dressler commenced the tour, this afforded her and Fairbanks their first opportunity to be alone together.

The foursome began in Washington and moved on to New York. This first opportunity for the crowds to see the biggest names on the movie screen proved to be the perfect formula for raising money for the war effort. However, it wasn't just "appearing" alone that did it. Little Mary was highly adept at rousing the passions of the masses and proved to be an extremely capable speechmaker, proclaiming, "We are at war with beasts! Every bond you buy is a nail in the Kaiser's coffin," and "This is not a time for 50-50 citizenship!"

After New York, the foursome split and went in different directions as they continued selling bonds. Mary went to the Midwest, and, when all was said and done, she had outsold each of the other three. She participated in other bonds tours that year and could be found near the end of the war, making personal appearances in theatres, and telling of her experiences as she visited wounded soldiers in the hospitals.

A True Patriot

Although there is no doubt that Mary's patriotism and sincerity in these war efforts were genuine, it also provided a great boost to her career. The Loan Drives alone were a public relations dream come true. As Whitfield noted, "By November [1918], when the armistice was reached, Little Mary had also reached apotheosis."

She had endeared herself to her public, not only as she had been doing for years on the screen, but in real life, exuding qualities that were respected and admired. In tribute to Pickford's patriotic efforts, *Photo-Play Journal* commented, "And thus, although unable to herself shoulder a gun in the cause of democracy, 'Our Mary' is doing everything possible to help those to whom this duty is entrusted. Many a son of Uncle Sam 'over there' will silently thank America's motion picture queen whose heart is as big as her popularity and wish her greater success as a reward for her attention to their welfare."

SOURCES

PERIODICALS

"Colonel Mary of the 143rd." *Photoplay* (May 1918).

"Colonel Mary of the 143rd Field Artillery, U.S.A." *Photoplay* (September 1918).

Parsons, Louella. "Propaganda!" *Photoplay* (September 1918).

Smith, Peter Gridley. "Mary Pickford in the Midst of Christmas Spirit." *Photo-Play Journal* (December 1917).

BOOKS

Eyman, Scott. *Mary Pickford, America's Sweetheart*. New York: Donald I. Fine, Inc., 1990.

Whitfield, Eileen. *Pickford, The Woman Who Made Hollywood*. Lexington, KY: The University Press of Kentucky, 1997.

CHAPTER 15
Pretty, Funny Ladies
&

All silent film fans have their list of favorite two-reel silent comedies and comedians who starred in them. It may be an early Chaplin, Lloyd, Keaton, or Langdon before each entered feature films exclusively. Some may prefer those who specialized almost entirely in two-reelers, such as Charley Chase, Lloyd Hamilton, Laurel & Hardy, Charlie Bowers, Lupino Lane, or a host of others. But one must consider how much different those favorite two-reel comedies would be if the female lead were a different person or someone not quite so "perfect" for the part.

A silent film fan would not likely say, "I want to see that comedy because it has Sybil Seely in it!" or "Anything with Anita Garvin is going to be good!" Yet, these two, along with many other beautiful ladies of the silent era, added much to these comedies, not only through their beauty, but their comedic timing, their expressive features, and their ability to "play off of" these comedy geniuses.

Just as there are hundreds of wonderful silent two-reelers to enjoy today, there are dozens of beautiful co-stars who have graced these films and added so much to their enjoyment. Below are just a few.

Marion Byron in *A Pair of Tights* (1929)

Marion Byron is remembered mainly for two things—she was Buster Keaton's leading lady in *Steamboat Bill, Jr.* (1928), a role she filled to perfection—and for her appearance in Hal Roach shorts during the late twenties.

Byron was born in 1911. She toured as a chorus girl and had roles in several stage plays on the West Coast. She was a latecomer to the silent era, entering films in 1926, at only 15 years of age. It was immediately after *Steamboat Bill, Jr.* that she began her tenure with Roach.

Byron was a delightful addition to many of that studio's two-reelers. She was a petite, dark-haired beauty with an attractive figure. However, her most memorable feature were her large, expressive eyes, a trait put to good use in *A Pair of Tights*.

Stan Laurel wants a kiss from the pretty Marion Byron under the mistletoe, but Oliver Hardy seems to be insisting that he go first. Producer Hal Roach teamed Byron and Anita Garvin in hopes of creating a "female Laurel and Hardy." Unfortunately, the experiment only lasted for three films.

Roach envisioned cashing in on Laurel and Hardy's popularity with a female version of the team. Byron, at 4'11," was matched with the leggy Anita Garvin, who was 5'6." In their first two films together, Byron was outfitted in an ill-fitting garb reminiscent of the comedy queens of the teens. Thankfully, in their third—and by far the best—outing, she was dressed prettily in a typical short, late-twenties dress.

A Pair of Tights has four leads—Garvin, Byron, Edgar Kennedy, and Stu Erwin. Erwin comes to pick up girlfriend Byron and brings along a blind date (Kennedy) for Garvin. The two girls, especially Garvin, could not care less about their dates. Starving, with nothing to eat in their apartment, the girls just want someone to take them out to a restaurant for a nice meal. However, the two tightwads (hence the title *A Pair of Tights*) do everything they can to avoid spending money on a big meal and figure getting some ice cream cones will spoil the girls' appetites.

Marion is elected to go inside the store and get the ice cream while Anita and the boys circle the block (there's no place to park). However, each time she comes out of the door holding the four ice cream cones, she runs into trouble. The first time, she encounters a playful pup who keeps jumping up on her to get to the ice cream. She tries her best to "shoo" him away but holding two cones in each hand severely restricts her defenses. Byron turns her back to the dog, trying to push him away with her posterior, to no avail. She tries kicking at the dog, but he keeps coming back. The whole sequence is a beautiful comedic ballet, and Byron is excellent throughout.

More troubles are encountered in this sequence, including a lengthy run-in with Roach's ubiquitous rotten kid, Spec O'Donnell.

Probably the most hilarious part comes when Marion lays the cones of ice cream down in a car seat while she pulls up her falling hose. While her back is turned, a very dignified, well-dressed lady (Elinor Vanderveer) gets in the car and sits on them. When Marion turns around, she sees the expression on the lady's face and realizes what has happened. Marion turns to face the camera, eyes wide in disbelief and hand to mouth as she utters "Oh, my!"—very funny bit made all the funnier by Byron's reaction.

To see Byron at her best, this film is a "must-see." *Steamboat Bill, Jr.* is required viewing, as well.

Anita Garvin in *From Soup to Nuts* (1928)

Anita Garvin was born in 1906, and by 1919, she was a Mack Sennett Bathing Beauty. She also worked in the *Ziegfeld Follies* and made comedy films at Christie, Century, Educational, and Fox. In the early twenties she worked for Joe Rock's short-lived Standard Cinema Corporation, and this is where her lasting friendship with Stan Laurel began.

Byron's co-star in *A Pair of Tights* is certainly no less enjoyable to watch in that film; however, Garvin has another film in which her role is equally signifi-

One of Anita Garvin's most delightful performances is in Laurel and Hardy's two-reeler From Soup to Nuts *(1928). Garvin proved to be a great asset to the Hal Roach studios, appearing with Laurel and Hardy and other Roach comedians well into the sound era.*

cant to the plot but gives her more opportunity to get the laughs—something she does with skill and style.

In *From Soups to Nuts* (1928), Laurel and Hardy have been hired as butlers for the wealthy Mrs. Culpepper (Garvin), who is ignorant of the social graces but wants to impress her snobbish friends with a dinner party. Of course, Laurel and Hardy bring in a gag-filled two-reel comedy with many memorable moments, but Garvin makes an equal contribution to the enjoyment of the film and has her own special moments, as well.

For example, everyone who's seen the film remembers her attempts to chase down a cherry that has fallen from the dessert dish to her plate with a very small spoon. Laurel and Hardy were masters at taking a simple gag and milking it for laughs. Garvin shows that she is equally adept as she spends several minutes of screen time trying to get the little cherry from the plate to her mouth, without success. This "chase" is complicated by an uncooperative tiara that keeps falling down over her eyes. Just as she is about to put the cherry into her mouth, the tiara falls over her eyes and causes her to lose it again. Another time, she succeeds in getting the cherry on the spoon, assumes a very satisfied expression at her accomplishment, and then is given a congratulatory slap on the back from Laurel, causing the cherry to leap from the spoon AND the tiara to fall back down over her eyes!

To select the best film to feature Laurel & Hardy and Garvin is a difficult task since she shines brightly in each of her films with the comedy duo, both silent and sound.

Her forté was her expressions of exasperation and anger with teeth clenched and lips held tightly as she uttered whatever venomous words were appropriate to the situation. Garvin was funny and a joy to watch, but still an extremely attractive lady through it all.

Sybil Seely in *One Week* (1920)

Pretty, dark-haired Sybil Seely was, according to author Jim Kline, "one of Keaton's favorite and most charming leading ladies"—and charming she was.

Seely was born in 1902 to a vaudeville family who had a swimming act. So, it's not surprising that she got her start as a Bathing Beauty with Mack Sennett. It was Buster Keaton's director who suggested Seely, having worked with her while he was as Sennett.

Pretty Sybil Seely was one of Buster Keaton's favorite supporting actresses. They are pictured above in a scene from One Week *(1920), a hilarious two-reeler about some newlyweds' disaster-filled attempts to put together a prefab house.*

She joined Buster Keaton's company in 1920, appearing in only five of his shorts and none of his features—and this certainly was Keaton's and silent film fans' loss. But she added considerably to the films in which she did appear—much more so than Virginia Fox, who took Seely's place in eight of Keaton's shorts.

Seely is appropriately cast and effectively counterbalances Keaton's antics in every film in which she appeared, but, for some reason, her first with the deadpan comedian, *One Week*, is considerably more charming than the rest.

Maybe this has to do with the fact that, in this two-reeler, Buster and Sybil are newlyweds who work, hand-in-hand, to construct their new prefab house. Almost graciously, Sybil stands by her man and suffers each mishap and set-back with pragmatic acceptance—unruffled and ready to move on to the next task at hand.

Seely wasn't above joining in some of the risky or messy slapstick, either. In one tricky gag that makes the viewer's heart leap, she is sitting in the unfinished window opening downstairs while Buster is in the window upstairs, dangling their feet outside. Suddenly, the entire wall flips, and we find Sybil upstairs and Buster down. The fact that she held on is amazing. Of course, the wall eventually falls, and there's Sybil hanging on from another, second-story wall.

As for messy, we see her in a quick gag preparing a meal for the two of them. She punches the cardboard top on the bottle and milk spews all in her face and everywhere, eliciting a shocked look from the comedienne.

Her most memorable scene in the movie is meant to tease the male viewers and does so successfully. We see Seely in a bathtub, scrubbing away. The camera is positioned so the side of the old box-shaped tub comes just high enough to modestly reveal Seely from her bare shoulders up. Suddenly, she drops the soap on the floor. Now, the viewer quickly thinks, "How is she going to get the soap without getting out of the tub and completely revealing herself?" As she looks toward the camera, we see an unknown hand (obviously Buster's) come from the side of the frame and cover the lens. When the hand is removed, Seely is back in the tub, scrubbing away with the soap. But the most adorable "cap" to the scene comes when she looks straight into the camera and gives a flippant little laugh as if to say, "Fooled you, didn't I?"

Seely's performances are marked by their restraint while providing enough energy and presence so that she's not just a fixture in the films. She's also one of Keaton's most attractive leading ladies, and it's really a shame that he didn't use her in at least one of his features (too bad he didn't use Seely instead of Natalie Talmadge for *Our Hospitality*!).

After her all-too-brief stay with Buster, she moved to Fox Comedies, but retired when she married screenwriter Jules Furthman, her last film being made in 1922.

Phyllis Haver in *The Balloonatic* (1923)

Phyllis Haver only made one film with Buster Keaton, The Balloonatic *(1923). Eleanor Keaton (his widow) said of the comedy, "[It] is the only one of the 19 independent shorts in which the interplay between Buster and his leading lady is wholly successful."*

Why Phyllis Haver appeared in only one Buster Keaton short is a mystery—and a shame! However, her one appearance in *The Balloonatic* was a most fortunate pairing as the two could have easily made a series of films together. It's a pairing that brings to mind the Harold Lloyd-Bebe Daniels matchup and how well they "clicked."

Phyllis Haver was born in 1899 in Kansas, but she and her mother moved to Los Angeles when she was only four years old. She met Marie Prevost when she was nine, and the two became best friends, attending school together.

In 1916, she auditioned for Mack Sennett on a whim, becoming, along with Gloria Swanson, one of the two most famous Sennett Bathing Beauties.

The Balloonatic (1923) (see *the photo in Chapter* 3) is a collection of some of Keaton's best outdoor gags, all built around the sportsman's life at a mountain stream. By coincidence, he meets Haver there: she has come to enjoy the outdoors herself, with a bit of fishing and swimming.

Each of Keaton's encounters with Haver is a sheer delight, and it's hard to imagine anyone else in the part. After a short sequence showing her fishing, we are treated to a view of the lovely Haver in a bathing suit, standing on a rock, stretching back and about to dive into the stream. She dives right on top of Keaton, who, through one of his many mishaps, is being swept down the swiftly moving mountain stream. When Haver regains her composure after the collision and realizes who this is (Buster came out on the losing end earlier in the film when he tried to kiss Haver in a tunnel of love), she begins a verbal attack on him, and he wisely beats an immediate retreat.

This love-hate relationship is carried throughout the film, and we are teased with the possibility that she may warm up to Buster at some point. The opportunity arises when Phyllis is backed against a hillside by a bull and shouts for Buster's help. Of course, his attempts to help are useless, and Phyllis takes the bull by the horns (literally!) and throws him down, much to Buster's amazement. She runs to a safer location, regains her composure, and then looks for Buster—and she doesn't look happy! She shouts to him, stomping her foot and pointing to the ground, demanding that he, "Come here!" Buster will have no part of this bull-wrestling female and once again retreats—but Phyllis persists, demanding that he *"Come here!"* She eventually runs after him, but Buster keeps running in the opposite direction. In this sequence, Haver is both cute and feisty, making the scene all the more hilarious and enjoyable.

The viewer is treated to at least one medium close-up of Haver in *The Balloonatic*, which, as in so many "vignettes" in the short comedies of the silent era, contributes nothing to the plot. However, it does give a chance to show just how beautiful and expressive she was. She has just prepared a cup of hot coffee, puts it to her mouth, and almost scalds herself. She jerks the cup away, and a big puff of steam emits from her lips. She rounds out her mouth, runs her tongue around the lips to assess the damage, and then blows hard with a "Whew!" Very cute, indeed!

The fact that Keaton used Haver only once (the pairing with Keaton was a nice contrast to the dark-haired Seely and Fox) is certainly odd since they played so well together, but the fact that Haver's role was much different than the other female leads in Keaton's shorts was unusual, too. Haver is a dominant figure in the film, equal to, and in some instances much stronger than, Keaton's character. Keaton retracts from her anger as he would a male nemesis in his films—his perennial nemesis, big Joe Roberts, for example. Keep in mind, too, there are no other roles in this film (that is unusual in itself). The whole film is carried by Keaton and Haver alone, and—certainly with much credit given to Haver—it is one of his best shorts.

Keaton's widow, Eleanor, with co-author Jeffrey Vance, commented in their Keaton biography that *The Balloonatic* "is the only one of the 19 independent shorts in which the interplay between Buster and his leading lady is wholly successful."

After *The Balloonatic*, Haver went on to make 39 features before leaving films in 1930. Often the star of the film, she also played supporting roles. She is at her comedic best in the Christie feature *The Nervous Wreck* (1926), opposite Harrison Ford. Possibly the stand-out performance of her career was as

Roxie Hart in the first filming of *Chicago* (1927). She was also leading lady to Lon Chaney in his first talkie, *Thunder* (1930), but, unfortunately, the majority of this film is lost.

Ruth Hiatt in *Saturday Afternoon* (1926)

Ruth Hiatt was born in 1906. Prior to coming to Mack Sennett Studios in 1925, she had been a leading lady for Lloyd Hamilton and had worked for Jack White Comedies, for whom she was variously paired with comedians Lige Conley, Cliff Bowes, and Lee Moran. While she was at Sennett, she was the co-star, along with Raymond McKee, of Sennett's foray into domestic comedies, a series entitled *The Smith Family*, which was filmed from 1926 to 1929.

Harry Langdon made some great shorts while he was with Mack Sennett, and *Saturday Afternoon* is one of the best—and of his four co-stars in the film (Vernon Dent, Alice Ward, Peggy Montgomery, and Ruth Hiatt), petite, dark-haired, wide-eyed Ruth Hiatt by far contributes the most to the film. She is pert, cute, lively, simply adorable, and absolutely perfect for the part.

Vernon convinces Harry to join him on a Saturday afternoon double date with Ruth and Peggy. The only trouble is . . . Harry's married! Of course, all sorts of mishaps occur, turning the date into a disaster, but Hiatt's chance to shine is in the first half of the film—and shine she does!

After Vernon has introduced Harry to the girls, he pulls his little friend aside and tries to convince him to go out with them. Vernon gives an apt description of Hiatt when he tells Harry, "The little one with the swell lamps is dyin' to meet you." As they walk home, Hiatt is full of life and exceedingly playful. Literally skipping down the street, she holds Harry's hand and swings their arms high in the air, grabs his lunch box and takes it away, pushes his hat to one side and pulls his overalls strap down — all of which is very annoying to the bashful Harry. At one point, she weaves her arm through his, then twists her body around and in front of him while still holding on so she's looking right into his face. All of this playfulness is so cute, we wonder how Harry can resist.

Hiatt is superb at little nuances and bits that add so much to her character. For example, as they stand in front of her house, she straightens Harry's collar and hat, and gives him a kiss by touching her hand to her lips and then to his. She then scampers up to her front porch, turns to give a final, admiring look at her newfound date, and runs into the house. Later, when she comes back outside to retrieve her dog which has chased after Harry, she stands in the middle of the street looking over at him, smiles lovingly, and, with a heaving of the chest, throws two kisses his way and again scampers back into the house.

Pretty Ruth Hiatt had worked with Lloyd Hamilton and other comedians before Mack Sennett teamed her with Harry Langdon in the two-reeler Saturday Afternoon *(1926). Hiatt adds much to the film as Langdon's date—and an excellent venue for her beauty and charm.*

Hiatt's loveliness is displayed well in the few seconds of film highlighted by a beautiful, full-face close-up. She looks up at Harry, flutters her large, lovely eyes at him, then smiles one of the prettiest smiles of any silent movie starlet.

Hiatt did co-star in one of Langdon's features, *His First Flame* (1927), but because her part is so limited, *Saturday Afternoon* provides a much better venue for her beauty and talent.

Hiatt worked with Lloyd Hamilton again in some of his talkie comedies; she also played small bits in movies until the mid-1930s, but nothing could compare with those joyous moments as the little one with the "swell lamps."

Viola Richard in *Limousine Love* (1928)

Viola Richard was a lovely comedienne on the Hal Roach lot, and her most memorable performance was in Charley Chase's Limousine Love *(1928).*

Viola Richard was born in 1904 in Ontario, Canada. Her family relocated to the U.S. in 1910. How she ended up at Hal Roach studios is a mystery, but she was suddenly appearing in comedies there after one film, her very first, entitled *Exclusive Rights* (1926), for B. P. Schulberg.

Richard is another of those dark-haired beauties who seemed to have been so plentiful at the Hal Roach lot. Of course, just as the other ladies who supported the silent era's multitude of zanies, she had to be able to convey a wide range of emotions with her facial expressions—surprise, fear, embarrassment, frustration, anxiety, anger, relief, joy, and that constantly called-upon false smile. Oddly enough, in Charley Chase's two-reel gem, *Limousine Love*, it was necessary for Richard to display each of these emotions—and JUST with her face! Would you like to know why? Well, for about 90 percent of her screen time she is naked—so, obviously, her face is going to be ALL the viewer sees!

Limousine Love is one of the all-time favorite two-reel comedies for silent film buffs. The main reason, no doubt, is that it's one of Charley Chase's best comedies, and certainly he is one of the comic geniuses of the silent era.

Another reason is the great storyline. The gag writers came up with a "pip" (one of Chase's favorite words) of a script that is hard to beat.

The story begins when Richard overturns her car in a water-filled ditch. Although unhurt, her clothes are drenched. She finds an abandoned touring car on the country road, jumps in the back seat, pulls down the shades, undresses, and hangs her clothes outside the window on a makeshift clothesline to dry. It turns out that the car belongs to Charley, who ran out of gas on the way to his wedding. He returns with a can of gas, fills up the car, jumps in, and hurriedly drives off. As he pulls away, Richard's clothes are lost in a water-filled culvert, and Charley must modestly help the young lady get some clothes while getting to his wedding on time AND keeping the whole affair from his fiancée. Hitchhiker Edgar Kennedy adds to the fun as he assists Charley with his dilemma.

As noted, Richard is called upon to give a variety of reactions to the incidents in the story while she is seen only from the neck up. When Charley goes to retrieve her clothes, he returns only with an elastic garter. Tapping on the back window, Viola's head pops up in front of the shade. From behind the glass, she sees the tiny garter, and her mouth opens wide in disbelief. Then the expression turns to a "What am I gonna do?" look before disappearing behind the shade again.

In one of the more hilarious sequences, Charley is stopped by a cop looking for rumrunners. Charley tries his best to wrestle the cop and keep him from looking in the back seat, but his efforts are in vain. The cop finally opens the back door but sees nothing out of the ordinary. Charley looks tentatively into the back seat himself, and there is Richard completely covered with a newspaper up to her neck, looking as if she's simply checking up on the latest news. All the viewer sees is the newspaper and a smile (albeit a nervous smile). The look Richard gives is just what one would expect from someone in this same predicament—that is, IF anyone in the world was EVER in such a predicament!

Throughout the film, as events are taking place outside the car, there are close-up glimpses of Richard's face to show her reaction to the ongoing series of near misses that keep her from getting some clothes. Each time, the gag is enhanced by Richard's reactions—each perfectly suited for what's going on around her.

Richard only made 19 films from 1926 to 1935, and with the exception of her very first, they are all shorts.

And a Few Others

Another Hal Roach comedienne deserving of recognition for her contributions and the special beauty is Edna Marion. A petite, blonde beauty with big, dark eyes, a small mouth, and a somewhat prominent nose, she was perfect as the younger girl, more innocent than the characters Richard or Garvin would play. She figures very prominently in *Limousine Love* as Chase's fiancée and does an admirable job of being frustrated with Chase's silly behavior as he attempts to keep her from finding out about the naked lady in his back seat.

Marion was used often by Chase in his comedies during the 1926–1927 period, and silent movie fans should also remember her as the young daughter in Laurel and Hardy's *Sugar Daddies* (1927). Another chance to see Richard and Marion together is in Laurel and Hardy's *Should Married Men Go Home?* (1928). Both are given the perfect opportunity to display their beauty in their cute 1920s sports outfits on a golf course. Naturally, this being a Laurel and Hardy film, before it's over, they are both seen at their messiest after being caught up in one of the team's melees in a mudhole.

A seemingly overlooked—although one of the liveliest—comic leading ladies was Martha Sleeper, particularly in the Charley Chase two-reelers. Sleeper was one of the few supporting players who could be just as funny as the star. And if there ever was a co-star who would "take one for the team," it was Sleeper. The department store "sheets sale" melee in *Fluttering Hearts* (1927) can only be described as "wild," and should be required viewing. Possibly, the top of the list belongs to the comedy gem *Bad Boy* (1925), with Chase and Sleeper doing a choreographed dance in a tough dancehall. Amazingly, Sleeper was only between 15 and 17 years old when she was working in these comedies.

It's okay to have a favorite comedian, and it's okay to have a favorite short or two that may be watched over and over and recommended to anyone who hasn't seen them. But the leading ladies should neither be overlooked nor forgotten. They may not be remembered as well or get the mention in history books that leading ladies in feature comedies receive, but when thinking about favorite two-reelers . . . weren't these ladies great?

SOURCES
BOOKS

Keaton, Eleanor, and Jeffrey Vance. *Buster Keaton Remembered*. New York: Harry N. Abrams, Inc., 2001.

Kline, Jim. *The Complete Films of Buster Keaton*. New York: Citadel Press, 1993.

Massa, Steve. *Slapstick Divas: The Women of Silent Comedy*. Albany, GA: BearManor Media, 2017.

CHAPTER 16
The Dapper Reginald Denny
☙

The screen is crowded with Americans trying to act like Englishmen, but Reg is the only Englishman we know of who tries to act like an American and gets away with it. His comedies are both typically American and very funny.

— *Motion Picture Magazine*

Stage and Travel

Reginald Denny was born Reginald Leigh Dugmore in 1891 in Richmond, Surrey, England, to a long-established theatrical family: his father was the actor and opera singer W. H. Denny. Reginald first appeared on the stage at age seven, but left school at 16 to pursue a theatrical career in earnest. In 1911, he came to America as a part of *The Quaker Girl* cast. He returned to England in 1912, and, in the ensuing years, performed in India, Australia, and the Orient. He married Irene "Renee" Haisman, a British musical comedy star, and returned to the United States in 1914. He toured until 1917 when he went to New York to enlist with the Royal Flying Corps. Stationed in Hastings, England, the war ended before he completed his training.

Denny returned to America and immediately went to Chicago, where he performed onstage. Upon notification that his wife had suffered a nervous breakdown, he rushed back to New York to be at her side. Biographer George A. Katchmer relates that the actor was told his wife needed surgery to save her life. However, Denny had no money and needed to raise $1,000 for the surgery. He contacted everyone he knew in New York but received no help. As a last resort, he went into the offices of theatrical producer Morris Gest. Although he had never met Gest, the producer apparently knew Denny from his stage work. The office boy went into Gest's private office and returned in a few minutes with an envelope and informed Denny that the producer could not see him. When he opened the envelope, Denny was surprised to find that it contained a check for $1,000.

First Films and Fame

Reginald Denny never relied on prop mustaches or ill-fitting clothes for his comedy. Although an Englishman, Denny was at his peak portraying the average American husband in films such as Skinner's Dress Suit *(1926).*

Fort Lee, New Jersey, was still a popular place for film companies, and Denny applied for work with the World Film Corporation there in 1919. He appeared in two films for the company: *Bringing Up Betty* (1919) and *The Oakdale Affair* (1919), both starring Evelyn Greely. He returned to the stage, however, and even performed with the great John Barrymore in *Richard III*.

The combination of popular stage work and these first two films opened the door for more movie offers. At Paramount, he supported some of the more popular stars of the day, including Ethel Clayton, Richard Barthelmess, and Elsie Ferguson. Denny had made 12 features—in supporting roles only—before being offered a role in a series that was to bring him some much-needed recognition.

Denny earned the title of brigade heavyweight boxing champion while in service, and that, along with being over six feet tall and possessing an excellent physique, no doubt contributed to his starring role in a series of two-reelers called *The Leather Pushers*. The first two entries in the series were made independently by Denny and director Harry Pollard, but their money ran out. Fortunately, Carl Laemmle saw promise in the actor and the series, and it was picked up for an additional 22 entries by Universal. It was a gamble for Laemmle because no one thought a series about prize fighting would be popular. They were wrong.

Universal then sent Denny out to California to star in a series of two-reelers about the Northwest Mounted Police. His inexperience with riding a horse, however, stymied his first attempts. He was thrown, resulting in a broken ankle. After two entries, Universal brought an end to the series. Denny finished up

The Leather Pushers series at this time and was cast in a couple of features, one of which was *The Abysmal Brute* (1923), the Jack London story about a backwoods boy who becomes a boxer. At Denny's insistence, some light comedy was injected into the otherwise "hokey" story, and it became a hit.

A Serious Performer with a Funny Streak

Denny had found his niche in light comedy. His droll sense of humor and his chiseled matinee idol looks gave him a romantic edge. With this new approach, he appeared in such films as *Sporting Youth* (1924), his second outing with Laura La Plante, a cute, perky young lady with a distinctive blonde hairdo (she and Denny had previously worked together in the 1923 Hoot Gibson western *The Thrill Chaser*; *The Reckless Age* (1924), with Ruth Dwyer; *The Fast Worker*, also with La Plante; *Oh, Doctor!* (1925), with Mary Astor; and *California Straight Ahead* (1925), with Gertrude Olmsted. All totaled, he did 10 feature comedies for Universal between 1923 and 1925—films that added greatly to his popularity and the studio's coffers.

After crashing his honeymoon trailer in California Straight Ahead *(1927), Denny rushes from the hospital to his wedding in a commandeered ambulance, but just as he arrives, the entire wedding party comes out only to see a deranged woman clinging to him and claiming Denny is her long-lost lover.*

However, with the release of *Skinner's Dress Suit* in 1926, Denny hit his peak. Everything about this film worked. It marked the fourth time he was teamed with La Plante, who complemented Denny's style of comedy perfectly. Author and historian Richard Koszarski praised *Skinner's Dress Suit*, noting that it "confidently displays a sophisticated style unknown only two years earlier."

A Happy Family

One reason for the success of the Denny comedies may be the camaraderie he enjoyed while making these films for Universal. According to Kevin Brownlow, "With cameraman Arthur Todd, and some supporting players who appeared often enough to warrant the term stock company, the Reginald Denny company grew very close." The biggest asset for Denny, however, was director William A. Seiter, who understood Denny's comedic talents perfectly. "Seiter is a vital part of Denny's career, because he appreciated his talents and brought them out to their fullest advantage," Brownlow said. In discussing his favorite director with Brownlow, Denny said, "We never had an argument, never a cross word, and we always brought the picture in within budget."

Although Denny was making big bucks for Universal at this time, his demands for his own unit were never granted. The happy "family" he had known in such films as *Skinner's Dress Suit* was soon to dissolve as Universal had Seiter direct only the solo films of Laura La Plante. Denny would make three more films with Seiter: *The Cheerful Fraud* (1927), with Gertrude Olmsted; *Out All Night* (1927), with Marian Nixon; and *Good Morning, Judge* (1927), with Mary Nolan.

Instead of Seiter, he was now assigned Harry Pollard (his director from *The Leather Pushers* series and the feature *California Straight Ahead*) and Harold Lloyd's former director Fred Newmeyer for several of his subsequent films. However, his ideas about comedy differed from both directors, and he clashed with them often. "Pollard didn't have the real comedy touch," said Denny. "He didn't have Bill Seiter's ability. Pollard was all for the broad comedy, and I was for the lighter. We just couldn't agree."

Clash with Laemmle

The making of *That's My Daddy* (1928), with Barbara Kent, is a good example of the problems Denny began to encounter. He had written this story, and Newmeyer was brought in to direct. But when the inevitable conflicts arose, Denny ended up directing the film and writing the intertitles himself. Universal tried to keep the sneak preview from him, but he managed to see it anyway. When he did, he was furious! According to Denny, in addition to several cuts

Skinner's Dress Suit (1926) is considered a classic, but it displays a totally different type of comedy than was typical for the time. The underplayed style finds its humor in situations, not physical comedy—a style that is more akin to the situation comedies of the television era.

with which he disagreed, "They had gagged it up with silly titles and ruined it. It was vile."

Denny went to Carl Laemmle and demanded he be given the negative, threatening to quit if he did not. The dapper comedian eventually got his way and restored the cuts and rewrote the titles. Despite some negative reviews, the movie was a hit, and Laemmle sheepishly admitted to Denny that he had been wrong—surely a rare event among movie moguls!

Another major event in Denny's life was his divorce from Haisman in 1928. He wed aspiring actress Isobel Steiffel that same year. She was 21 at the time, and Denny was 37. The couple had three children in a happy marriage that lasted until Denny's death.

And Away from Work . . .

Denny liked fast cars, boating, fishing, and hunting. One article said that he was seldom seen around the movie colony—he was more likely to be found in the mountains, in Mexico, or cruising off the California coast in his yacht. He even bought an airplane, but his flying was put to an end as too much of a risk for one of Universal's top comedians.

In February 1926, Denny and friends set out on his 32-foot yacht and were caught in a storm. The group was not heard from for four days—and the consensus was that they could not have survived the storm. However, after experiencing four days of worry, the family received a message that Denny's party had docked at Ensenada, Mexico.

In January 1927, newspapers reported that Denny was stricken with appendicitis while working on a picture, and peritonitis had set in—the same infection that had killed Rudolph Valentino the year before. Fortunately, Denny managed to survive this deadly attack.

Denny Crosses Over to Sound

Denny's last two years at Universal were undistinguished. In 1929, he made one silent and two part-talking features. His first full talkie was *One Hysterical Night*, with Nora Lane. His last feature for Universal was *Embarrassing Moments* (1930), with Merna Kennedy. Neither of these films was especially liked by the public.

Because Denny was English, the coming of sound brought about some changes in his career. Rather than leading roles as "the frustrated average American husband," he was given supporting roles as "the affable Englishman." Nevertheless, he was extremely active during the next four decades, appearing in such classics as *Kiki* (1931), with Mary Pickford; *Parlor, Bedroom and Bath* (1931), starring Buster Keaton and Charlotte Greenwood; *Private Lives* (1931), with Norma Shearer; *The Barbarian* (1933), starring Ramon Novarro; *The Little Minister* (1934), with Katharine Hepburn; *The Lost Patrol* (1934), starring Victor McLaglen; *Of Human Bondage* (1934), co-starring Leslie Howard and Bette Davis; Greta Garbo's *Anna Karenina* (1935); and *Romeo and Juliet* (1937), with Leslie Howard and Norma Shearer in the title roles.

Between 1937 and 1939, Denny made a string of Bulldog Drummond mysteries, not as the title character, but as Drummond's friend Algy Longworth. He also continued with such classics as David O. Selznick's *Rebecca* (1940), directed by Alfred Hitchcock and starring Laurence Olivier and Joan Fontaine; *Seven Sinners* (1940), starring Marlene Dietrich; *Sherlock Holmes and the Voice of Terror* (1942), with fellow Brits Basil Rathbone and Nigel Bruce; *Tangier* (1946), starring Maria Montez; the Bob Hope comedy *My Favorite Brunette* (1947); Danny Kaye's *The Secret Life of Walter Mitty* (1947); *Mr. Blandings Builds His Dream House* (1948) starring Cary Grant and Myrna Loy; *Abbott and Costello Meet Dr. Jekyll and Mr. Hyde* (1953), featuring Boris Karloff; and Michael Todd's

Around the World in 80 Days (1956), starring David Niven and supported by an international, all-star cast.

Denny worked almost to the end of his life. His last appearances on film were *Cat Ballou* (1965), with Jane Fonda and Lee Marvin; *Assault on a Queen* (1966) starring Frank Sinatra; and *Batman* (1966) starring Adam West and Burt Ward.

Although he adopted America and made his home in California, Reginald Denny passed away in the town of his birth. He suffered a stroke while he and his wife were visiting his sister in Surrey, and he died on June 16, 1967. Denny's body was flown back to his America. He rests next to Isobel at Forest Lawn Hollywood Hills.

Only Slightly Below the Masters

Creating and maintaining an awareness of the unique artistry of silent era comedians has been, at best, a struggle. The big four—Chaplin, Keaton, Lloyd, and Langdon (Laurel and Hardy are considered a team and in a class by themselves)—have enjoyed firm revivals. The second tier of comedians, such as Charley Chase, Raymond Griffith, Roscoe "Fatty" Arbuckle, Lupino Lane, Max Linder, Larry Semon, and Ben Turpin are slowly becoming known again, especially due to the availability of their silent films on home video and the Internet. Reginald Denny is part of this group, and, as Kevin Brownlow put it, he is "on a level only slightly below that of the masters," but typically not given the credit he is due. It is unfortunate that none of his films had received a "restoration" for the home video market until 2020, when a three-feature set was released. Hopefully more will be released.

Denny's comedy was real and charming, and, certainly, much more subtle (he didn't need to rely upon a gimmick or a "look") than any of the four "masters." His unique style was "individual enough to withstand such searing competition," Brownlow noted. Denny deserves renewed attention, and the wonderful work he did during the silent era is proof enough.

SOURCES
PERIODICALS
"Critically Ill." *The Times Union.* January 28, 1927.
Motion Picture Magazine (January 1928).
"Movie Star and Party Declared Safe in Harbor." *The World* (Coos Bay, OR), February 5, 1926.

BOOKS

Brownlow, Kevin. *The Parade's Gone By*. New York: Bonanza Books, 1968.

Katchmer, George A. *Eighty Silent Film Stars: Biographies and Filmographies of the Obscure to the Well-Known*. Jefferson, NC: McFarland, 1991.

Koszarski, Richard. *An Evening's Entertainment: The Age of the Silent Feature Picture, 1915-1928*. Berkeley and Los Angeles: University of California Press, 1994.

CHAPTER 17
Stuntmen: Risking Their Lives to Thrill Moviegoers
❧

Buddy Mason, Gene Perkins, Harvey Parry, Al Wilson, Dick Grace. These are not names that were well known to moviegoers of the teens and twenties; they were, however, well known to those behind the scenes in the industry. These were the stuntmen, those who risked their lives to bring audiences the action and thrills for which the films of that era were so famous.

Actors, Not Stunt Men

In the early days of filmmaking, there was no cadre of professional stuntmen from which to draw. Dangerous scenes were shot by the actors and actresses themselves. Pearl White, the serial queen, was famous for doing her own stunts. Tom Mix performed his stunts from the time he entered films in 1914 all the way through the silent era. All of Mack Sennett's Keystone troupe were expected to take risks.

In his autobiography, Sennett relates several examples of the rough-and-tumble existence to which Keystone comedians had been subject. One such story concerns Hank Mann, referred to by Sennett as his "toughest" comedian. He described a stunt that Mann was doing with Roscoe "Fatty" Arbuckle and Al St. John involving a wagon and runaway horses.

> Al St. John was to jerk the pin from the singletree, and the horses were to pull Hank Mann off the wagon. St. John had trouble with the pin, sweating and bawling. This delayed the action until the horses had picked up too much speed for such a stunt. When Al did get the pin out, the horses cut loose like runaway ghosts and snatched Mr. Mann 30 feet through the air, like a kite, until the law of gravity remembered him.

> By this time, Mann and the horses were almost out of Los Angeles County, certainly at least three whoops and a loud holler out of camera range. Hank descended into a plowed field, chin first, and fur-

rowed a belly-whopping trench for 10 yards before, with considerable common sense, he let go the reins.

Actress Grace McHugh lost her life performing in a scene that should have been done by a stunt double, although she, herself, was considered an accomplished horsewoman. In 1914, while filming *Across the Border* for the short-lived Colorado Motion Picture Company, she was required to cross the Arkansas River on her horse. The horse stumbled, throwing her into the rapidly moving water. Cameraman Owen Carter tried to save her, but he and McHugh both lost their lives. McHugh was only 16 years old.

Circus Performers, Cowboys, Race Car Drivers, etc.

It wasn't long before stuntmen became a regular part of the movie scene, particularly in westerns. Regular job requirements included the ability to ride, rope, fight, jump from a speeding horse, and transfer from a horse to a stagecoach. They were quite often former circus performers, cowboys, and racecar drivers, or just daredevils willing to take risks to make a dollar. It was not a polished art, and many learned as they went, oftentimes with disastrous results.

While filming Charles Ray's *Percy* in 1925, a young stuntman named William Harbaugh from Virginia, along with another, more experienced stuntman, was being swept down the Colorado River near Yuma, Arizona. The locks had been opened to portray a flood scene for the picture. Harbaugh, being smaller and less experienced than his companion, had a rope tied to his waist for safety. Finally, the stuntmen neared the shore, the shot was finished, and the director was able to shout over the roar of the water, "Cut!" However, just as Harbaugh loosened the rope from his waist, an unexpected whirlpool swept him away. His body was found six weeks later, buried in silt.

Chick Morrison was considered one of the best horsemen on the West Coast and one of the most dependable stuntmen in westerns. He was asked to stage a fight between two horses in *Rex, the King of Wild Horses*, a 1924 Hal Roach production, which he did without incident or harm to either of the horses. However, shortly after the picture, he took an Arabian stallion from the Roach stables to teach him quick turns for an appearance in a polo game. The horse fell on him, and Morrison died from the injuries.

Cowboy star Fred Thomson, who, like Tom Mix, did most of his own stunts, broke his leg in two places filming a stunt for one of his movies in August 1924. A leap from his horse to the wheelhorse of a stagecoach went awry and laid the actor up for almost four months before he could go back to work.

Timing Is Everything

The most difficult stunts to "pull off" were those that required the coordination and precision timing of two men.

For a stuntman, failure to be perfectly in sync can lead to disaster. Buddy Mason, who had been hired to work on a serial, was asked to drive a motorcycle through a bridge's guardrail and onto the top of a moving train. Mason explained, "They had part of the roof of one of the freight cars cut out and covered with thin laths and cardboard. In the car, beneath the opening made in the roof, were mattresses for me to land on." Mason said the stunt would have transpired flawlessly, except that the engineers "got the speed bug." His motorcycle went half in the opening and half out. Mason slammed against the motorcycle's handlebars, then did a nosedive into the train car, missing the mattresses below. He ended up with a broken shoulder, five broken ribs, and a dislocated hip.

For another movie, "Speed" Osbourne was called on to race a motorcycle off a cliff. He wore a parachute, which he was to open when about 30 feet from takeoff. Cameraman J. B. Scott was filming the scene and described what happened: "About the time 'Speed' should have pulled the parachute, the motorcycle developed carburetor trouble. Instead of pulling the chute, the nut reached down and primed the carburetor. By the time he straightened up, he was out in the air. He crashed and busted himself all up. I was the first one to him, and his shinbones were sticking straight out through his boots. All he said was, 'Cut those damn boots off, will you, Scotty?'"

Richard Talmadge got his start showing Douglas Fairbanks how to do his stunts. In addition to performing stunts for other stars, he also became a popular star of his own films.

From Stuntman to Star

Although Douglas Fairbanks did many of his own stunts, it was Richard Talmadge who would often do the stunt first to show Fairbanks how it was done. Talmadge, a fair actor, was one of those who possessed both the athleticism and the "handsomeness" required for stardom.

One of Talmadge's starring vehicles, *The Prince of Pep* (1925), has been available for years on home video in abridged form. The film shows off some of his athletic prowess as he scales the sides of city apartment buildings, jumps from fire escape to fire escape, and generally seems like Douglas Fairbanks in motion. In one stunt, he leaps from a rooftop across an alleyway to a window of the next building, making it look almost *too* easy.

Another of his surviving features, *Let's Go* (1923), also in the Fairbanks mode, has Talmadge scaling a fire escape—he even does a somersault when jumping from one rooftop to another. The chase of the crooks is an exciting finale as he rides a buckboard at breakneck speed, falls through a roof, battles two crooks at once atop a large stack of hay bales, and crashes through fences to nab the criminals.

Talmadge made over 30 films in the silent era. He was originally from Germany and came to the U.S. in 1910 when he was 18. He retained his German accent all his life, which proved a detriment when sound films came in. Nevertheless, from 1914 to 1962, he has 62 credits, either doing the stunts himself or as stunt coordinator.

Another stuntman-turned-actor, Charles Hutchison, has several films available for home viewing today, including a 1926 serial entitled *Lightning Hutch*. Like Talmadge fans, Hutchison's following went to see his pictures for the stunts, not the storyline. For example, one scene requires him to jump from

This motorcycle stunt required Charles Hutchison to race toward a broken bridge and leap across just as an oncoming locomotive passes through.

atop a 125-foot grain elevator into a river. Another has him jumping from one building's roof to another, across a 14-foot alley and 80 feet from the ground. Yet another has him driving a motorcycle 70 mph across a bridge to make a leap across a 25-foot gap in the center. Still another has him swinging on a rope from one building into the window of another. Finally, he jumps from the wing of a hydroplane into the ocean, 70 feet below. One of his most popular stunts has him planting his back against a building and his feet against the adjacent building four feet away and then climbing upward in this position for several stories until he reaches the top.

Although there were no serious "disasters" to speak of in his career, Yakima Canutt, whom some consider the greatest stuntman of all time, must be mentioned. His heyday was really in the 1930s, when he was doubling for John Wayne and a host of other western and non-western stars. His expert horsemanship was in high demand during the silent era, as well, which made him a natural to star in a series of fine B-westerns that weren't designed to just be a showcase for a lot of stunt work, but, instead, were better than average, popular, and had solid storylines. His most famous claim to fame in the silent era was as the second unit coordinator for the chariot race in MGM's *Ben Hur* (1925). Canutt continued to work as a stuntman and/or second unit director well into the 1970s.

Trick Photography?

Trick photography was, indeed, used during the silent era, although it mostly involved forced perspective. For example, Harold Lloyd built a set for *Safety Last!* (1923) on top of another building, and, with the camera placed at the proper angle, it looked to the moviegoer as if he were really several stories off the ground. There were a few shots from above, or from a distance, that showed a climber on the side of a real building several stories high. But, in those shots, the climber is stuntman Harvey Parry, who routinely doubled for stars in the silent era.

Although such trickery was closely guarded from the public, fans were becoming increasingly aware of the ingenuity behind their favorite thrill scenes. And, because of this, stuntmen were rarely given credit for the risks they took as cynical moviegoers questioned even the most realistic-looking stunts.

Stunt pilot Dick Grace recalled going to the movies and viewing one of his stunts in which he made a dangerous transfer from a speeding automobile to an airplane. "I must admit that I probably received as much thrill as anyone in the theatre, for I alone knew that I had caught that rope ladder with three fingers and for seconds did not think that I was ever going to be able to gain the cockpit of the airplane," he said.

However, as the movie ended, he overheard two ladies talking about the stunt. "That certainly was clever photography," one of them remarked to the other. "I wonder if it was double exposed or whether they used a dummy." Grace remembered, "I sat rather limp, feeling keenly disappointed."

Apparently, Talmadge wanted to dispel such doubts in his movie *Let's Go*, so the producer introduces the movie with an opening intertitle that states, "The amazing athletic 'stunts' performed by Mr. Talmadge in this picture are *actual*, and are not achieved by means of 'doubles,' 'dummies,' or tricks of the camera."

Stunts in the Air: The Big Three

Coincidentally, airplanes and movies can claim to have experienced their "birth" in the same year—1903. This was the year that the Wright Brothers made their first successful flight at Kitty Hawk, and this was also the year Edison released Edwin S. Porter's *The Great Train Robbery*, generally credited with being the first story film and thereby serving as a "birth" of the movies as they are known today.

Movies and aviation also grew together. As movies became more sophisticated, so did airplanes. Considering the public's fascination with new inventions at the turn of the century, it was only natural that the two should come together. Although no one really knows when or how airplanes were first used in the movies, their comedic and thrill potentials were exploited early on. Mack Sennett, for one, used them many times, one of the first being *A Dash Through the Clouds* (1912) with Mabel Normand, made when they both were still working for Biograph. Later, under the Keystone banner, he continued using them for a combination of laughs and thrills in such films as *The Sky Pirate* (1914) and *Dizzy Heights and Daring Hearts* (1916). Much of the filming was faked, though, with airplanes only a few feet off the ground and wind machines creating a sense of movement.

Exhibitions, or air shows, were a big attraction around the Los Angeles area in the early part of the 20th century. In 1910, the world's second international air meet took place at Aviation Park, 15 miles from downtown Los Angeles, and, over a 10-day period, attracted thousands of spectators. Another airfield was located at Griffith Park, and then, according to stunt pilot historian H. Hugh Wynne, the first real "stunt flyers" appeared at Venice, California. Although an airfield was located there, it quickly became popular among the pilots inclined to acrobatics, because, being a resort area, there was always an available audience of several thousand beach patrons.

At first, these exhibitions were filmed for theatres much in the manner of a newsreel, but gradually, filmmakers began to call on actual pilots when the storyline required the use of an airplane. As Wynne noted, much of the movie "aviation activity was minor, and the aviators who maneuvered their machines for these early films were not yet motion picture stunt pilots. A takeoff, fly-by, and landing scene or two, mixed with close-ups of the actors in crude flying machine mock-ups, was the usual extent of motion picture flying."

The Schiller Aviation School was located at the Venice Flying Field, and one of the instructors, Thomas J. Hill, could likely be credited with performing the first real air stunts for motion pictures. During the summer of 1914, he performed dives and spirals for a film whose title has been lost to history, but Wynne said, "This appears to be the beginning of aviation stunts for motion picture purposes at the Venice Flying Field." A 1915 Mutual film entitled *Out of the Air* (a two-reeler starring Fred A. Turner and Seena Owen) supposedly showed the first airplane-to-train transfer performed by stuntman Charles Gaemon. However, Wynne said that the distinction of the first professional motion picture stunt pilot should go to Al Wilson.

Al Wilson was another aviation stuntman whose work for other stars soon led to his own starring pictures. He is considered to be the first real professional motion picture stunt pilot.

Al Wilson

Born in Kentucky, Wilson's family moved to Southern California when he was a young boy. When he was 18, he and a friend built an airplane using a four-cylinder motor. It wasn't the most professional creation and would only rise about 50 feet off the ground, but it *did* fly. When the many hard landings finally took their toll on the contraption, Wilson sold it to a motion picture company as a prop.

His contact with the film industry continued as he performed small tasks and even worked as a bit player.

He is also credited with constructing the first wind machines used by the movies from airplane propellers and automobile engines.

During this time, Wilson took a job in maintenance at the Schiller Aviation School, which also gave him the opportunity to begin learning how to be a pilot. He later moved to a flying school at Riverside, where he completed his training. Wilson returned to Venice, which was now named the Crawford-Saunders Field, and the American Aircraft Company hired him as their chief instructor. He developed his stunt-flying skills by performing acrobatic maneuvers that would "stimulate students." Wilson's brother, Herbert, built a two-seat monoplane at this time, which, with Al as the co-pilot, was rented to movie companies. This was the beginning of Al Wilson's motion picture stunt-flying career.

One of Wilson's students while at Venice was Cecil B. DeMille, who had hopes of becoming a pilot during the war. Although he became an accomplished pilot, the war ended before his dream was realized. However, this led to another opportunity for Wilson. When DeMille formed the Mercury Aviation Company, Wilson was named vice-president and general manager. The company offered flight instruction, sightseeing tours, charter flights, and more. Most importantly, motion picture prop masters went to Mercury when they needed airplanes and pilots.

Wilson didn't stay in this position long. Apparently missing the thrill of performing stunts, he resigned his post and returned to exhibition flying. At one point he formed a partnership with stuntman Frank Clarke and piloted one of two airplanes as Clarke performed a wing-to-wing transfer. The availability of the Wilson-Clarke team was advertised in the October 10, 1919, issue of *Billboard* magazine. Wilson was also known to perform his wing-walking acrobatics while stunt pilot Wally Timms (whom Wilson had trained back at Mercury Aviation) piloted the airplane.

One of his more spectacular stunts—one that brought him quite a bit of publicity—was a double airplane transfer in February 1920. It called for him to grab the landing gear of the airplane above and pull himself up. Then the first plane changed to the overhead position, and Wilson once again pulled himself up by the landing gear to the original airplane. While this was being done, there was the additional risk of being dangerously close to the whirring propeller.

Wilson continued working exhibition tours and doing movie work in the off-season. Around 1922, he signed a contract with Universal, but it is difficult to determine exactly how many, or which, films he may have contributed to as a stuntman.

In 1923 he was featured as an actor for the first time in the Fred Thomson 15-chapter serial *The Eagle's Talons*. Of course, he wasn't just hired to act. He also performed his stunts, one being a plane-to-train transfer. This was followed the same year with a role in the 15-chapter serial *The Ghost City*, starring Pete Morrison. One stunt in that film came close to disaster when Wilson was transferring from a car, traveling at 70 miles-per-hour, to a rope ladder dangling from an airplane overhead. However, when Wilson put his weight on the ladder, the plane settled, hitting Wilson on the ground. Although the initial inclination was to turn loose since he was already at ground level, he would have been injured even more severely at that speed had he let go. He held on, and the pilot pulled up, leaving Wilson with only some bumps and bruises.

After this, Wilson formed his own production company and began a series of thrillers for which he wrote the scripts, served as the star, and performed the stunts. In 1924, he made *The Air Hawk*, followed by *The Cloud Rider* and *Flyin' Thru* in 1925, and *The Flying Mail* in 1926. Each film followed a basic storyline:

This lobby card shows a scene from Al Wilson's 1925 film The Cloud Rider, *co-starring Virginia Lee Corbin (left) and Frank Rice (center). He would star in a dozen silents and one talkie before dying in an airplane crash.*

Wilson, as a Secret Service agent, works for the Air Mail Service or in some other "do-gooder" capacity—always saving the girl and everyone else from the villains. Of course, a variety of aerial stunts were performed to accomplish this, including changing the wheel of an airplane above him while standing on the wing of a plane below; making a plane-to-automobile transfer to capture the escaping heavy; and transferring from a speeding motorcycle to a rope ladder dangling from an airplane above.

Charles Lindbergh's solo crossing of the Atlantic in May 1927, which created a national obsession with aviation, coupled with the spectacular success of William Wellman's epic, *Wings*, which was released in August, was enough for filmmakers to realize what would sell at the box office. For some reason, Wilson got out of the producing business and was back with Universal in 1927. Could it be that the studio heads, also wanting to cash in on the aviation craze, enticed Wilson back to the fold? Whatever the reason, he was busy starring in a new series of films—*Three Miles Up* (which was released less than two months after *Wings*) and *Sky High Saunders* in 1927, followed by *The Air Patrol* in 1928.

Variety said the air stunts were the "only feature" of *Three Miles Up*. Two months later the publication criticized *Sky High Saunders*, saying, "The airplane stuff is okay and held attention. Otherwise, blotto." In January, *Variety* called *The Air Patrol* "fourth rate stuff." Obviously, Universal wasn't lavishing time and money on these productions (three such films were released within a four-month period), but in all fairness to the studio, Wilson wasn't hired because of his acting abilities.

One can only assume that, regardless of the reviews, the films were making money for Universal because Wilson starred in three more in 1928—*The Cloud Dodger*, *The Phantom Flyer*, and *Won in the Clouds*, followed by *The Sky Skidder* in 1929. In one of his films, Wilson almost lost his life when his plane caught fire. The fuel line broke, and he barely made it to the ground before the plane was consumed by flames.

Won in the Clouds is also available for viewing on home video and contains some of Wilson's most spectacular stunts. The opening title calls him "The World's Most Sensational Stunt Flyer," and this film shows why.

Early in the story, Wilson makes a transfer from the top of a speeding car to the wing of an airplane. Later, he saves his guide from being killed by the natives by hanging from a rope ladder on an airplane, swooping down, snatching the guide, and flying away as the two men hang high above the ground on the ladder.

The best stunt, appropriately, is saved for the climax. Wilson's girlfriend has been kidnapped by the heavy, who steals her away in his biplane. Wilson and his sidekick give chase. For this stunt, Wilson walks out on the top of the wing and grabs, after several unsuccessful tries, the wing of his rival's airplane. And that's not all. Once on the bottom wing of the biplane, he and the rival stage a fight that is not only realistic but extremely frightening. Wilson is hanging by one hand or by his legs a couple of times during the fight, and, yes, this is frightening because of some superb camera work that clearly shows the planes to be high above the ground, with no trick photography involved (outside of the a few close-ups that were staged at ground level).

Wilson was one of several pilots who worked on Howard Hughes's *Hell's Angels* beginning in 1929. It was a tragic accident on this shoot that had the most profound impact on Wilson up to this point in his career.

The scene called for a plane to be flown while "lamp black" was released, which resembles smoke coming from a damaged aircraft. Although several other pilots had refused to fly the plane because of its condition, Wilson volunteered. However, he insisted that he fly alone and release the lamp black by a control in the cockpit. A mechanic named Phil Jones, who wanted to earn some extra money, convinced the director that he should accompany Wilson in the plane and release the "lamp black."

Although the scene appeared to be progressing as planned, the plane went into a spin and began to fall apart. Wilson told the mechanic to bail out, and then bailed out himself. For some unknown reason, the mechanic stayed in the plane and was killed. Wilson said he yelled twice at Jones to bail, but perhaps he did not hear him. It's also possible that Jones had been knocked unconscious from being thrown around in the spinning plane, or even pinned by the centrifugal force. At the site of the crash, Jones was still in his place in the plane, parachute unopened.

There was an investigation for homicidal neglect, but no evidence was found to support the charge. Wilson did lose his license for a time, but it was restored. The criticism he received, especially from some of his peers, for not "saving" the mechanic affected him deeply. Although three planes were filming the scene, and all three pilots said Wilson should not be blamed, the fearless aviator gave up motion picture stunt flying to work as a pilot for Maddux Air Lines.

Like so many of his contemporaries, Wilson's luck ran out in 1932. He was appearing at the National Air Races in Cleveland, and his plane was drawn into the vortex of an Autogyro's blades. Both machines fell to the ground. The two occupants of the Autogyro escaped without serious injury. Wilson was taken to the hospital with lacerations, a crushed rib cage, and a fractured skull. He died a few days later, on September 5, 1932.

Ormer Locklear

Ormer Locklear was born on October 28, 1891, in Fort Worth, Texas, where he was working as a carpenter and mechanic when he joined the Army Air Corps in October 1917. While stationed at Barron Field in Texas, he began his wing-walking career. This reportedly occurred when military experts were trying to figure out how to mount a machine gun on the plane's wing without increasing the wind resistance, which made it difficult to maneuver. Locklear decided to prove the experts wrong and had another pilot take him up while he walked back and forth along the wing without affecting the airplane's performance. Another account states that, while flying with his instructor, he was unable to see some communication from the ground because the engine housing and wing were blocking his view. He needed to interpret the communication to pass his flight test, so he left the plane in the control of the flight instructor and climbed out on the wing to get a better look. His instructor was not pleased.

Locklear's stunts intensified—including making repairs while in mid-air. His wing walking became especially popular, not only with his fellow pilots but with his superiors as well.

Toward the end of the war, Locklear performed an even more spectacular stunt at the Fort Worth Army airfield to help recruit for the Air Service. While wing walking on one airplane several thousand feet in the air, he dropped from the undercarriage to the top wing of another airplane several feet below. "This was the first time in the world that anyone had transferred from one airplane to another while in flight, and it opened the way for many daring motion picture stunts of the 1920s," Wynne said.

Locklear never made it into battle and left the military in May 1919 to tour the country with his airplane stunts. Within a year, he was the most widely known stunt pilot in the world and was making as much as $3,000 a day. He was so popular that county fairs around the country were hosting "Locklear Days." Carl Laemmle was the first to realize the potential of a stunt-filled air adventure when a fantastic airplane stunt in Harry Houdini's *The Grim Game* (1919) proved to be the most popular portion of the film. Locklear was the obvious choice for a star, and *The Great Air Robbery* was released at the end of that same year, with Locklear playing the lead. In addition to performing his famous airplane-to-airplane transfer, he transferred from an airplane to a speeding car then back to the airplane just before the car crashes. The movie

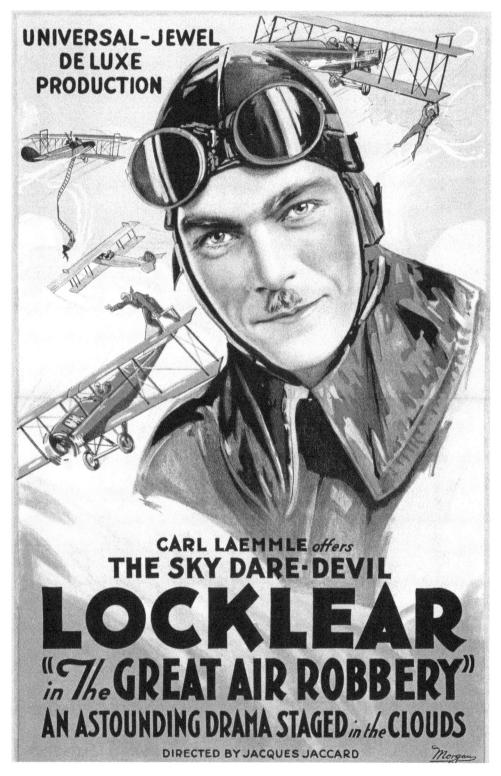

Ormer Locklear's first starring role was in The Great Air Robbery *(1919) and proved to be popular with audiences. He was killed while filming a stunt in his second picture,* The Skywayman *(1920).*

was a success and is generally credited as the first aviation feature film, opening the door for many more in the succeeding decade.

After completing his work on *The Great Air Robbery*, Locklear returned to exhibition flying. While on this tour, he met a young flyer named Dick Grace at the Minnesota State Fair, and it is this meeting with Locklear that resulted in Grace's decision to enter the movie business. As noted in the comments on Wilson, stunt pilots were becoming more in demand from the newsreels, which were becoming a regular part of a movie bill. Locklear, Wilson, and many other stunt pilots from the Venice area supplemented their earnings well as a result of these newsreels.

When the 1919 barnstorming season came to an end, Locklear returned to Fox for his second feature, *The Skywayman*, on which he started work in June 1920. There was a plane-to-plane transfer required in the film, but it was performed by another stuntman, Milton "Skeets" Elliott. A plane-to-train transfer was performed by Locklear, however, followed by a gun fight while he sat on the landing gear, and the villains raced away in their automobile.

Sadly, Locklear lost his life performing a second stunt for the film. He and Elliott were replicating a night-time fiery crash to the ground, but due to failed communication with those in control of the lights on the ground, he never pulled up, and both men lost their lives in the crash. (The accident is discussed in detail in Chapter 6 on the Flugrath sisters.)

Dick Grace

Dick Grace was born in Morris, Minnesota, January 10, 1898. His father was a judge, and he intended following in his footsteps by attending the University of Minnesota. When the war broke out, he joined the Naval Air Service, receiving his training in Pensacola, Florida. He served in France and Germany, but upon returning to the United States, he decided to forgo a law career for the more exciting vocation of barnstorming.

A chance meeting with Ormer Locklear at the Minnesota State Fair in 1919 gave him his first introduction to a Hollywood movie star (this was following Locklear's success with *The Great Air Robbery*), and by the summer of 1920, Grace was in Hollywood, working for Fox. Grace didn't initially start out as a stunt pilot but was soon performing virtually any stunt that came his way.

His first motion picture aviation stunt was in Tom Mix's *Sky High* (1920), and it almost proved to be Grace's last. He was to climb from the cockpit of a plane down an 18-foot rope and back up again, but he had to do it twice so filming could be done once from the ground and again from the air. When the cameraman decided he wasn't satisfied with the shot, Grace had to perform the

During his career, Dick Grace was said to have performed approximately 50 airplane crashes; he also broke more than 80 bones, once even breaking his neck.

stunt a third time. He was so fatigued by this time that he hardly made it back up the rope to the cockpit; he was also hindered from actually getting into the plane when a gun belt he was wearing caught on the fuselage. While still controlling the plane, pilot Bud Creeth leaned over the side and helped to pull Grace into the plane.

Contemporary publications state that Grace worked on another Mix film referred to as *Forest Ranger*, however, no reference can be found to this film. It is most likely the working title for the 1923 Fox feature *Eyes of the Forest*, which stars Mix as a pilot. In this film, Grace perfectly executes a plane crash into a barn. However, when he and cameraman Norman Devoe went up for some stock aerial shots, the engine died, and they were forced to make a crash landing. Fortunately, neither man was injured.

Like Wilson, Grace's stunting led him into acting, and his first leading role was in *The Flying Fool* (1925) for Sunset Productions. In this, Gaston Glass plays the villain who frames Grace for a burglary in the hopes of stealing his fiancée. He only had one more chance for a starring role, and that came in 1927 in *Wide Open*, again for Sunset.

Throughout the twenties, stunt pilots like Grace and Wilson were much in demand, but there were few films that revolved around aviation. Most had aviation scenes that were woven into the stories. However, the greatest aviation picture of the silent era was about to be made, and Grace played a significant role in its success.

Wings was conceived and written by former army training command flyer John Monk Saunders and was directed by William Wellman, who was a combat pilot during World War I. Another stunt pilot, Frank Tomick, was hired as the chief pilot for the picture, and Grace was hired for the two main crashes in the film, one in a Spad and one in a Fokker. Both of the World War I planes were in poor condition, and Grace oversaw something of a "renovation" before he would fly them.

The first crash—in the Spad—would take place in a trench-lined, barbed wire–covered battlefield. First, the ground was dug up and the dirt replaced to make it as soft as possible. Then, the wooden posts were replaced with those made from balsa, and the barbed wire was replaced with twine. Although the nosedive crash came off, with Grace unscathed, he missed the fake posts and barbed wire by 17 feet and hit the real thing. Upon surveying the crash, he realized there was the jagged edge of an airframe member jutting through the fabric just 17 inches from his head.

The second crash was to take place in a steel-framed Fokker, a more substantial plane, making the stunt exceptionally difficult. In each crash, Grace had to saw the frame at strategic points so the plane would crumple, as necessary. Although this occurred as planned, the half-sawed landing gear did not cause the greatest impact on the fuselage. Because of this, Grace's straps broke, and his head went through the instrument panel. When pulled from the wreckage, it appeared he was okay, except for some cuts. He was even photographed beside the plane following the crash. A short time later, it was discovered he had broken his neck and crushed four vertebrae.

Although Grace was told by doctors that he would be incapacitated for a year with a neck brace, he left the hospital six weeks later, shedding the brace. The following year he was coordinating the airplane stunts for Colleen Moore's *Lilac Time* (1928). Grace performed two crashes perfectly in which the plane hit the ground in a preplanned sequence that included the wheels, wing, and nose. One scene in the film has Moore fooling around in the cockpit of a plane and accidentally hitting the throttle. After scattering every military man at the airfield, the taxiing airplane eventually runs between two trees, shearing off both its wings. Grace, however, did not perform this stunt. He was out of town, and it was handled by Charles Stoffer, who came so close that the fuselage was within inches of one of the trees.

Although the silent film era was quickly drawing to a close, Grace's career as a stuntman continued for many years to come. During World War II, he joined the Army Air Corps and flew several missions with the 8th Air Force as a B-17 co-pilot. It is said that, during his movie career, he performed 45-50 crashes and broke over 80 bones in his body. Unlike many of his contemporaries, it was not a stunt that brought an end to his life. Emphysema took him in his sleep in 1965, when he was 67.

Other Aerial Stunt Work

Quite often, there was no explanation for a tragic outcome. Stuntman Dick Kerwood was asked to perform the switch from a moving airplane to a moving automobile, a stunt he had executed many times, this time for a film starring Franklyn Farnum. He made his way over the fuselage and down the rope ladder, but no one saw what happened after that. He was found at the bottom if Pico Cañon, where he had fallen 500 feet to his death.

Still others had no one to blame but themselves. During the filming of *The Great Circus Mystery* in 1925, a scene called for a race between an airplane and an automobile along a mountain road. Cameramen were told to keep cranking as the car was to skid and turn over. It did, however, but at the wrong point. Former circus acrobat Frank Tully was killed, and his companion, Tony Brack, seriously injured.

There was one incident involving an aerial stunt that, for all its sadness, is humorous in its own way. A stunt flyer was asked to crash a plane for one of the larger studios. He knew he would get hurt, so he told the studio he would have to have $3,000 for the job to take care of his wife while he was in the hospital. The studio agreed, he got the $3,000, gave it to his wife, and did the stunt. Just as he predicted, it required a stay in the hospital, six months to be exact. However, when he came out, he found that his wife had run off with another stuntman and the $3,000!

Why Did They Do It?

So, why *did* the stuntmen risk their lives to perform stunts for other actors? There was no glory involved. For the thrill, perhaps? What about the chance to become stars themselves? Cameraman J. B. Scott probably had the most incisive answer to these questions. Immediately after filming "Speed" Osbourne's ill-fated motorcycle stunt, he was asked why his daredevil friend had attempted a stunt that not only failed but resulted in compound fractures of both legs. Scott simply replied, "For twenty-five dollars."

SOURCES

PERIODICALS

The Air Patrol review, *Variety*, January 18, 1928.

Billboard. October 10, 1919.

Carter, Charles. "Without Benefit of Thrills." *Picture Play Magazine* (January 1922).

Grace, Dick. "Stunt Men, The Boys Who Risk Their Lives for a Thrill." *Photoplay* (August 1925).

Gray, George Arthur. "Stunts!" *Photoplay* (September 1919).

Sky High Saunders review, *Variety*, December 14, 1927.

Three Miles Up review, *Variety*, October 5, 1927.

BOOKS

Baxter, John. *Stunt: The Story of the Great Movie Stuntmen*. London: Macdonald & Co., 1973.

Brownlow, Kevin, and John Kobal. *Hollywood: The Pioneers*. New York: Alfred A. Knopf, 1979.

Brownlow, Kevin. *The Parade's Gone By*. New York: Bonanza Books, 1968.

Golden, Eve. *Golden Images: 41 Essays on Silent Film Stars*. Jefferson, NC: McFarland, 2001.

Grace, Dick. *Squadron of Death*. London: Constable & Co. Ltd., 1930.

Sennett, Mack. *King of Comedy*. Garden City, NY: Doubleday & Company, 1954.

Wynne, H. Hugh. *The Motion Picture Stunt Pilots*. Missoula, MT: Pictorial Histories Publishing Company. 1987.

CHAPTER 18
Vitagraph: Three Men and Their Baby

ॐ

Our initial plunge was $936, spent in building of the first machines and purchase of films . . . In less than a decade, two youths and a kindly, blustery gentleman who they had invited into their partnership were earning a figure close on the heels of a million dollars.

—Albert E. Smith

Three Men

The Vitagraph Company could be said to have had its genesis as the International Novelty Company, which is what three Englishmen—Albert E. Smith, J. Stuart Blackton, and Ronald A. Reader—called their vaudeville act, which made its first public appearances in 1894. The act included magic, cartooning, magic lantern slides, and more. All three had migrated to New York from their homeland in search of their fortunes.

When the vaudeville act failed, the three men went on to other jobs. Blackton was serving as a cartoonist for the *New York Evening World* when he was sent to interview Thomas Edison. He and Edison hit it off when Blackton did some sketches of him, so much so, in fact, that Edison asked Blackton to do some of his drawings for the motion picture camera. He did, which led Blackton and Smith to purchase a projection machine and 10 films from Edison for $800.

Albert E. Smith gave a different story in his 1952 autobiography. He claimed that he and Blackton were intrigued by Edison's peep show Kinetoscope but realized that being able to project the images on a screen, the same way they had done magic lantern slides in their vaudeville show, would be much more profitable. So, Smith invented a projector. They secured some of the Kinetoscope films, and Vitagraph made its debut at Tony Pastor's New Fourteenth Street Theatre on March 23, 1896.

Smith and Blackton, with Reader as projectionist, continued their vaudeville acts, but with the addition of motion pictures that were typical of the day—a train coming into the station, Niagara Falls, a man shoveling snow, a boy romping with his dog—anything that showed movement. As Smith noted, audiences were intrigued by "clouds that floated, branches that waved, and smoke that puffed."

Their first story picture was shot May 16, 1897, on the roof of their office building and was entitled *The Burglar on the Roof*. The film was only supposed to involve a burglar (played by Blackton) and a policeman; however, when the "policeman" began struggling with the "burglar," Mrs. Olsen, the wife of the building's janitor, came on the scene. Thinking she had happened upon the real thing, she began beating the "burglar" with her broom.

At first worried that their film was ruined, they were pleased to see the favorable reaction from the audience at Pastor's the following evening.

Filming History

The reputation of the American Vitagraph Company was bolstered greatly by the filming of some major historical events around the turn of the 20th century. One of these was the Spanish-American War. When the dead from the Maine explosion were brought back to Arlington Cemetery in Washington, D.C., Vitagraph was there to film it—with emotional results. Smith and Blackton then managed to gain passage to Cuba on the same ship occupied by Teddy Roosevelt and his Rough Riders. Eventually, they accompanied Roosevelt on his famous charge up San Juan Hill.

When Smith and Blackton returned to New York, everyone was hungry for news from the battlefront, so, of course, their films were a tremendous success. They also foolishly claimed to have taken film of the Battle of Santiago Bay, although they had not! So, to accommodate this demand to see their films of the battle, they staged the confrontation in what was probably the first use of miniatures in a film. It was filmed in an improvised bathtub with the "smoke of battle" provided by Blackton's cigar and Mrs. Blackton blowing smoke from a cigarette. Crude as it was, it still proved believable to the moviegoers of the day and was a popular attraction.

Another major event that helped establish Vitagraph's reputation was their actual footage of the Boer War in South Africa. In late 1899, Smith sailed to the site of the conflict and spent quite a while there in the midst of some of the worst fighting. Smith mentioned in his book, *Two Reels and a Crank*, that England's jubilation over their victory in the war couldn't have matched his and Blackton's jubilation over the fact that the Boer War pictures netted them Koster and Bial's Music Hall as a regular venue.

Some of the other notable historical events filmed by Vitagraph during these early years were the Galveston flood of 1900, the 1901 assassination of President McKinley, the 1904 inauguration of President Theodore Roosevelt, and the aftermath of the 1906 San Francisco earthquake. They were present at the first successful flight by the Wright Brothers, on December 14, 1903, at Kitty Hawk, North Carolina, but failed to get pictures because of their skepticism once they saw the brothers' "fool contraption." Vitagraph was also the first to film one of Mark Twain's stories (*A Curious Dream*, 1904) with the author's blessings, no less.

William T. "Pop" Rock (left) was brought on board after founders Stuart Blackton (center) and Albert E. Smith had Vitagraph up and running for a few years. Approximately 20 years his partners' senior, Rock provided the company with the business acumen the others lacked.

Enter "Pop"

The most notable event for Vitagraph prior to the turn of the century was the addition of a third partner to the company— William "Pop" Rock, a fellow Englishman. It is unclear why Blackton and Smith invited Rock, a local film distributor, to join their ranks, especially with Rock being named as president, Smith as treasurer, and Blackton as secretary. Smith said in his autobiography that Rock, who was some 20 years senior to his youthful partners, had "mature business judgment," while Blackton was the creative force in the team, and he (Smith) was "a sort of trouble shooter." Smith is being modest about himself, though, because it was his acute business sense that carried Vitagraph through some of its hardest times.

Smith reported that Vitagraph's profits in 1899 were $7,975 and fell to $6,742 in 1900, but he attributed the decrease to the expenses he incurred on his Boer War excursion. However, the first years of the new century were successful indeed for the blossoming company as they moved to newer and larger offices, began to add employees to their roster, and, in 1905, built their first studio in the Flatbush area of Brooklyn.

In 1904, despite the construction of the new studio and opening a film office in Chicago, the company was able to claim profits of $25,750. The profits rose to $38,860 in 1905, which Smith said was attributable to increased foreign operations. By 1906, they had leapt to $120,749. So successful were the foreign operations that Vitagraph opened offices in London, Paris, and Berlin in 1908.

During those first 10 years of the century, Vitagraph claimed such luminaries on their acting roster as Broncho Billy Anderson, Annette Kellerman, Paul Panzer, Florence Lawrence, Florence Turner, Maurice Costello, Gladys Hulette, Julia Swayne Gordon, and many others. One of their most successful series of films was the "Happy Hooligan" comedies about a tramp, featuring J. Stuart Blackton in the role.

During these early years, Vitagraph and other film companies were constantly under threat of lawsuits from Edison, who claimed, according to Smith, that he owned the very concept of making pictures move. However, the situation was clouded somewhat by the fact that many patents were floating around, controlling various aspects of the motion picture camera, and not all of them belonged to Edison. Vitagraph and several other companies got together in 1908 to discuss pooling their patents so that all could benefit from them. However, they realized the endeavor was futile unless the major patent holder, Edison, was in on the deal.

Amazingly, Edison liked the idea, and, in 1908, Edison, Kleine, Méliès, Pathé, Vitagraph, Selig, Essanay, Lubin, Kalem, and Biograph formed the Motion Picture Patents Company (MPPC), in which any producer could make use of the patents by paying the patent holder a license fee. The arrangement proved to be very lucrative for Edison but virtually locked

When 48-year-old John Bunny signed with Vitagraph in 1910, he quickly became one of the most popular comedians in the world, predating Charlie Chaplin's film debut by four years.

out any company from the motion picture production field unless they were members.

The MPPC went a step further. They formed a distributing company called General Film, which became known as "The Trust." No theatre could obtain a film produced by one of the "Big Ten" except through them. The "Trust" would be challenged by some highly innovative and strong-willed independents.

By 1909, "[F]ilm had come of age, thanks, to a large extent, to the Vitagraph Company," writes historian Anthony Slide. In February of that year, the company began to release three reels of film a week and had 30 actors and actresses and seven directors under contract, in addition to technical and business staff.

Smith said that, by 1908, the Vitagraph directors were producing eight films a week, "mostly one- and two-reelers cast from the studio's stock company of four hundred players."

One of the Most Popular Comedians in the World

The second decade of the twentieth century saw the first of the John Bunny films released by Vitagraph, with *Doctor Cupid* gracing screens in January 1911. Bunny, who had come to Vitagraph from a successful career on the stage and was 48 years old at the time, became one of the most popular comedians in the world during the next few years, predating Charlie Chaplin and Roscoe Arbuckle. Bunny, a butterball of a man, reached his peak when teamed with tall, thin Flora Finch in a series of marital situation comedies. When he died on April 26, 1915, the world mourned, and Vitagraph lost its most famous comedian.

The year 1910 proved to be a pivotal one in Vitagraph's history, not only because it was the year John Bunny came to the company, but due to several other significant events, as well.

- On July 2, 1910, a fire destroyed virtually all the negatives of every film the company had made since 1896. In his diary, Smith simply commented, "All [were] heartbroken over the loss."

- In 1910, the company initiated a monthly newsreel, *The Vitagraph Monthly News of Current Events*. (Smith quotes 1910 in his book while Slide says the newsreels were first released in 1911). This soon became the *Hearst-Vitagraph Weekly News Feature*, with semi-weekly releases.

- In 1910, Vitagraph sent their first permanent company to California. At this time, the company had 20 (or more) directors making films at Flatbush and one in California. Ten years later, virtually all filming was done in California, and activity at Flatbush was confined almost entirely to laboratory work.

- In 1910, profits had risen to $695,372, more than doubling the previous year's take. Films were being turned out in greater numbers, requiring the construction of a new laboratory building for processing film.

- In 1910, Vitagraph's reputation grew rapidly, due to the quality of their films. *The Life of Moses*, the first of a series of Biblical pictures, was released in five parts between December 1909 and February 1910. The following year, Vitagraph continued to test the public's reaction to longer films and released a pair of three-reelers based on classic literature: *A Tale of Two Cities* and *Vanity Fair. A Tale of Two Cities* was released in three parts; however, *Vanity Fair* was released at one time as a three-reel feature. "In doing so," Slide writes, "Vitagraph moved one important step ahead of its competitors by accepting that audiences were willing to sit through a film more than one reel in length."

Smith said the company made two "super productions" in late 1913 and early 1914—*A Million Bid* at five reels, and *The Christian* at eight reels. Unaccepting of exhibitors' claims that the public would not sit through a film lasting more than an hour, Smith said, "We sent them reams of material telling them how to put a feature picture over, how to bring patrons into their houses in greater numbers than ever before," but, he noted, the exhibitors were still unconvinced.

Smith said he and Blackton decided to "test our faith in big pictures" and did something no other producing company had done at that point—*they* became exhibitors. They leased the Criterion Theatre on Broadway in New York, renamed it the Vitagraph Theatre, and opened it on February 7, 1914, with a sketch, a short, and the feature *A Million Bid*, which starred Anita Stewart and Julia Swayne Gordon. The opening was an unqualified success.

In May, they leased the Harris Theatre on 42nd Street and opened with *The Christian*, starring Earle Williams and Edith Storey. This, too, was a success. Exhibitors became concerned about this new venture and confronted

Vitagraph's 20-acre studio in Hollywood as it appeared in 1923. When the company was sold in 1925, it also included a studio in Brooklyn, 50 exchanges around the country, and an elaborate system of exchanges in several foreign markets.

the Vitagraph officials. After a meeting with a committee of exhibitors, Vitagraph announced it would acquire no more theatres, although this was to become a common practice of film producers in the ensuing years. Vitagraph, however, was the first to do it.

Growing by Leaps and Bounds

Vitagraph was expanding, and they soon began to release their features through their own exchanges, while the General Film Company continued to handle their shorts. By 1915, the Motion Picture Patents Company came to an end. There were several mitigating factors, but the final, undeniable blow was a federal court decision that the company represented an illegal restraint of trade under the Sherman Antitrust Act.

It became necessary to form a new releasing organization, and Vitagraph, Lubin, Selig, and Essanay joined forces to form the VLSE. The partnership proved to be a lucrative one but was dissolved when Vitagraph purchased the stock and interest of Lubin, Selig, and Essanay in September 1916.

Other actors were added to Vitagraph's roster who would go on to be among the most famous names of the silent era. Norma Talmadge and Anita Stewart came to Vitagraph straight from Erasmus High School in Flatbush. Norma joined the company in 1910, and Anita followed soon afterwards at the suggestion of her brother-in-law, Ralph Ince. Wallace Reid joined in 1911 after a brief stint with Selig. One of the most famous cowboy stars of the 1920s, Fred Thomson, started his career with Vitagraph. Jane Novak came to the studio in 1913 because her aunt, Anne Schaefer, was already a star with Vitagraph. Clara Kimball Young made her first Vitagraph film in 1912. Both Bebe Daniels and Mabel Normand spent a short time with the company. Antonio Moreno entered films with the Vitagraph Company in 1914. Alice Joyce's name was added to the roster in 1916 when Vitagraph purchased the Kalem studio, for whom she was already a star. Another of the company's biggest drawing cards was Jean, the Vitagraph dog.

Probably the most popular series of comedies to come out of the Vitagraph studio, next to the films of John Bunny, were those of Mr. and Mrs. Sidney Drew. During the teens, Sidney Drew and his second wife, Lucille McVey, introduced a type of humor that was antithetical to the knockabout slapstick being seen in comedy shorts of the day. The humorous, polite, domestic stories so adroitly performed by the Drews were more akin to the situation comedies of the early television era.

Smith asserts in his book that there were three great Vitagraph comedians. Already mentioned are John Bunny and Sidney Drew. The third, he said, was Larry Semon, who joined the company in 1917. Semon worked well in the Vitagraph family for the first couple of years, but, as his popularity grew, so did his ego. He began spending extravagantly on his films, which resulted in many conflicts with Smith, even to the point of his filing a lawsuit against Semon at one time. Semon finally left Vitagraph in 1924, his career rapidly declining; he died in 1928, aged 39.

Vitagraph was also a leader in serials. They released their first one in 1915, a tongue-in-cheek affair entitled *The Fates of Flora Fourflush or The Massive Ten Billion Dollar Vitagraph Mystery Sequel*. It starred Clara Kimball Young in an uncharacteristic comedy role. The company's first serious serial was *The Goddess*, released in 1915 and starring the romantic team of Earle Williams and Anita Stewart. They only released one serial in 1916, although there were three in 1917, and several more in the ensuing years. Their last was *Breaking Through*, starring Carmel Myers and Wallace MacDonald, which appeared in theaters in 1921.

A Crumbling Partnership and a Sale

"Pop" Rock died in 1916, leaving Smith and Blackton to run the company without their elder mentor. And then, Blackton resigned in 1917. He went into independent production for a while, but it proved to be an unsuccessful venture. He also unsuccessfully took a turn at producing films in England, but he returned to Vitagraph as 1923 as an equal partner once again with Smith.

Some of Vitagraph's most difficult days were in the late teens and early twenties. Due to the war, the foreign market for films was gone, and in 1919, the General Film Company folded. In the early twenties, the company was feeling the effects of the bigger film companies who were then emerging, buying up theatres across the country and releasing more, and bigger, pictures than Vitagraph. In September 1922, the company estimated its losses to be nearly a million dollars.

Though most of the company's features in the 1920s were programmers, two top-quality productions enjoyed both critical and financial success: *Black Beauty* in 1921, and *Captain Blood* in 1924—both starring Smith's wife, Jean Paige. Smith's acute business sense kept Vitagraph alive and solvent. In 1925, though, he decided to sell the company. Its financial standing varies somewhat depending on the source. In his autobiography, Smith said the estimated value of Vitagraph in 1925 was $4.2 million, with no indebtedness, and he reached an agreement with the Warner Brothers to purchase Vitagraph for $735,000, which was split equally between Smith, Blackton, and "Pop" Rock's son.

In their 1998 history of Warner Bros., authors Cass Warner Sperling and Cork Millner state that Vitagraph was in debt for $980,000, and that Harry Warner agreed to pay that debt plus an additional $800,000 for the company. The authors went on to note, however, that in 1925, Vitagraph had a studio in Brooklyn, a 20-acre studio in Hollywood, the largest motion picture library in the world, over 50 distributing exchanges in 30 principal cities around the country, plus an elaborate system of foreign exchanges: four in Canada, 10 in England, and 10 in continental Europe. Although no purchase price was mentioned, the Vitagraph holdings were confirmed in a 1925 *Motion Picture News* article about the sale.

In light of these holdings, Smith's estimation of the company's value may have been correct. Also, the two versions of the sale price aren't that far off; Smith just didn't mention the indebtedness in his autobiography. After the sale, though, Smith would continue as chairman of the board.

Smith poignantly recalled the day the company changed hands: "I remember that day in February 1925. I shook hands with Harry Warner. He walked out

This 1920 ad clearly shows that some of the most popular stars of the day were among Vitagraph's stable of players.

and there was a terrible silence in the room, as if every living hope had gone with him, and I was left in a vast empty amphitheater swept clean of memories near and dear."

SOURCES

PERIODICALS

"Vitagraph Company Purchased by Warner Brothers." *Motion Picture News* (May 2, 1925).

BOOKS

Hampton, Benjamin B. *History of the American Film Industry from Its Beginnings to 1931*. New York: Dover Publications, 1970.

Slide, Anthony. *The Big V: The History of the Vitagraph Company*. Metuchen, NJ, and London: Scarecrow Press, 1976.

———. *The New Historical Dictionary of the American Film Industry*. Metuchen, NJ, and London: Scarecrow Press, 1998.

Smith, Albert E. *Two Reels and a Crank*. Garden City, NY: Doubleday & Company, 1952.

Sperling, Cass Warner, and Cork Millner. *Hollywood Be Thy Name: The Warner Brothers Story*. Lexington, KY: The University of Kentucky Press, 1998.

INTERNET

The Internet Movie Database. IMDb.com

CHAPTER 19
Reginald Hitchcock and Alice Taaffe:
The Most Ideal Union
⁊

He saw her face for the first time on the screen—she had a small part in a forgettable picture. But that face—for some unknown reason, like a photograph in an album of memories—remained with him.

Then, a year later, there she was. He was directing a picture at Universal—and there was that face, watching him work—the face of the one with whom he fell in love and would spend the rest of his life.

Half a World Away

Reginald Ingram Montgomery Hitchcock was born in Dublin, Ireland, in 1893. Seven years later and half a world away, Alice Frances Taaffe was born in Vincennes, Indiana. How Fate leads two soulmates together is a mystery, but without a doubt these two lives were meant to come together and be shared—and that they did for 29 years of marriage, without a hint of discord or the threat of parting.

Hitchcock migrated to the United States to seek his fortune, enrolled at Yale, and, through his roommate was introduced to Thomas Edison's son. Soon, young Hitchcock found himself employed by the Edison Motion Picture Company as a jack-of-all-trades, including actor. By the time he had served apprenticeships with Edison and Vitagraph, he joined Fox Films and changed his named to Rex Ingram. It was with his next employer, Universal, however, that he first took on the role for which he would be remembered—that of director.

Alice Taaffe's family moved from Indiana to Los Angeles when she was 15. Enid Markey (Jane, in the original 1918 version of *Tarzan of the Apes*), who was already somewhat of a star, lived in the same building and convinced her to try for a job at Inceville, producer Thomas Ince's studio. Bits and pieces of work that included acting and film editing led to nothing, and her confidence in herself as an actress was nil . . . that is, until she met Rex Ingram. And, under his mentorship and with a name change to Alice Terry, she became one of the most respected actresses of the silent era.

The Fateful Meeting

A 1921 *Picture Play Magazine* article says the meeting mentioned above took place in the summer of 1916. Terry told Ingram biographer Liam O'Leary that the couple's first meeting was in 1917 when the director was making a picture with Henry B. Walthall, probably *Humdrum Brown* for Paralta Plays, in 1917. (Ingram had married actress Doris Pawn that same year; they would divorce in 1920.) Terry said she "worked extra" for two or three days, and Ingram left for Canada to join the Royal Flying Corps and do his part in the war.

Ingram was only in the Corps for the last three months of 1918. One report said that, as a flying instructor, he was involved in a serious crash in which the metal of a propeller entered his lung. Although the army has no record of such a crash, it is a fact that he came back from service, ill, and without a job.

But he had not forgotten Terry. "Alice used to come to the studio I shared with another amateur sculptor and talk to me and pose for me," he recalled. "I did two heads of her." Ingram had attended art school in Ireland and was an accomplished sculptor.

Then, for some unknown reason, they did not see each other for a matter of months. In the meantime, Ingram had gotten work with Metro, and again he thought of Terry. Whether Ingram requested her or not is unknown, but Terry received a call to do extra work in a picture he was directing (*Shore Acres*, 1920). According to Terry, "He spoke very harshly to me, and I started to cry—and I walked off the set and refused to go back. The next morning, Rex called for me himself and apologized and said to come back and that soon he was going to change studios and he would have a part for me." O'Leary pointed out, "It was clear that Rex was deeply attracted to Alice at this stage," and, it turns out, the feeling was mutual.

Why is one person attracted to another, and what special chemistry takes place to make that attraction mutual . . . and passionate? Maybe it's the little things. Terry remembers being on location for a film, and she and Ingram had adjoining rooms. The connecting door would lock on Ingram's side but not hers. Apprehensive about Ingram's intentions, she sat up all night only to find he had had a good night's sleep.

In another instance, a slight hint of jealousy reared its head. After a streetcar ride to the end of the line, Terry still had a significant distance to walk to the studio. A taxi driver would pick her up and take her the rest of the way each day, free of charge. One day, Ingram heard the driver say, "Goodbye, Alice. I'll see you tomorrow morning." When he realized the driver was on a first-name basis with Terry, he arranged transportation for her himself.

ALICE TERRY and REX INGRAM.

Rex Ingram and Alice Terry are pictured in Paris, in 1925. Ingram realized his dream of leaving Hollywood and purchasing a studio in Nice, France. Unfortunately, he was only able to shoot three films there before losing the studio two years later.

And Terry was enamored by the "older man" and his good looks, equal to any leading man of the day. Terry said the Prince of Wales was considered one of the handsomest men in the world at the time, but she thought Ingram was even more so.

Respect

Of course, no relationship will survive without respect—and these two held a deep respect for each other. She, from the very beginning, knew he was an exceptional director. He held a high regard for her acting abilities, even though she, herself, had little confidence, at least in the beginning. According to Ingram, when he offered Terry the lead in *Hearts Are Trumps*, "To my amazement, though her eyes brightened, she shook her head. 'No, Mr. Ingram,' she said, 'I can't. I haven't had enough experience in the playing of important roles like that.' 'Just give it a try,' I urged. 'You're the right type, and you can leave the acting instructions to me.' She refused, shy and frightened at the idea for a long time, but, finally, she consented to try.'" Ingram told *Moving Picture World*, "The part of Dora Woodberry fits Miss Terry like a beautifully tailored suit."

And it was not only her acting he respected—he was open to her suggestions regarding both direction and business. Ingram commented, "If Alice had been married to someone else when I met her, I think I would promptly have engaged her as my business manager."

In a 1921 article on their engagement, Ingram referred several times to the fact that he and Terry were "pals" in the beginning. They would meet at a Pasadena tearoom and talk about their lives and their ambitions. Terry would occasionally cook for him. Unknown to them, this sharing of the little things in their lives was building the foundation for a rock-solid relationship that would last until Ingram's death.

Success Together

The two also experienced success during this period, the greatest of which was *The Four Horsemen of the Apocalypse*, released in 1921. It proved mutually beneficial, solidifying his reputation as one of the greatest directors of his day, and establishing Terry as a major star.

All these pieces came together to cement a relationship that, at the time, did not seem destined for anything so formal as marriage. It took a separation to make Ingram realize just how miserable he was without Terry by his side. According to an interview he gave in 1921, he was in New York after the release of *The Four Horsemen of the Apocalypse*, when he asked himself, "What the deuce is the matter with me?" He immediately called her on the telephone and, from 3,000 miles away, he asked her to marry him.

The same 1921 article noted that, during their engagement, the couple would

> take motor trips together to Pasadena or the beach, dine, and usually ride home early, sometimes hardly exchanging a word when Ingram happens to be weary or engrossed in thinking out a story. At other times, they talk over his work.

> "I don't know how she puts up with me," said Ingram with affectionate gallantry. "I never take her to the theater, nor do I care much for dancing. I'm absorbed in my work much of the time when other girls would, I'm sure, think I should be with my fiancée. But she's always the same serene companion, genial, sympathetic and helpful."

The couple finally married on Saturday, November 5, 1921. They spent most of the day at the movies on Sunday, and Monday morning they were at the studio, filming *The Prisoner of Zenda*. Terry later told an interviewer, "My first day back at the studio, there was my new husband directing a scene with Lewis Stone and ordering him to kiss me, not once, but over and over, until the effect was just right. Everybody was amused and took no trouble to hide it. That added to my embarrassment and distress. Of course, my nervousness didn't help the scene a bit. But it did seem too dreadful to have a husband of only two days, who professed to love his wife, shouting instructions how to kiss another man."

Marriage: Detriment or Advantage?

Terry admitted that she felt marriage was a detriment rather than an advantage when an actress is married to the director. Nevertheless, it was obvious that she was totally devoted to her husband and his career, which was far more important to Ingram than Terry's career was to her. It is possible she may not have even pursued her career had it not been for Ingram. O'Leary described Terry as "a most capable housewife," adding that she "did not allow her career to interfere with her domestic chores . . . she was not consumed with a burning ambition to get to the top and stay there at all costs," he said.

In a 1924 article, Terry said, "Real love, the kind that lasts and brings companionship and happiness to one's old age, must be founded on mutual respect and trust—a sort of glorified friendship . . . Some of the finest love matches which I have seen among my married friends have begun as friendships and ripened into a truly beautiful love."

In a 1925 *Photoplay* article, writer Herbert Howe commented, "The marriage of Alice and Rex is the most ideal union of individuals I've known, because each maintains the right of individuality. There is mutual understanding and confidence. Rex has never lapsed into the state of a complacent husband. He's always the adoring suitor, marveling at his good fortune."

Working Side by Side

And the two were not only lovers; they were, indeed, best friends. Terry was Ingram's favorite actress, and he exhibited an unfailing confidence in her abilities. Ingram was Terry's favorite director, and she was at her best under his guidance. The two also worked side by side, with Terry offering advice and assistance on his movies, being more than just an actress to him.

Although Ingram's usual style of directing was brash and driving, he adopted a different style for his wife. A 1923 article noted, "With Alice Terry, Ingram's method is different. He will rehearse her just as many times, but he doesn't storm. For the most part he simply suggests. Abrupt criticism only invites calamity with Alice. She is hypersensitive. Upon one occasion, when he had been a little more vigorous than usual, the tears welled into her eyes—and tears were not in demand just then. The rest of the scenes were carefully punctuated with, 'That's fine, Alice dear.'"

Ingram's longtime dream of leaving Hollywood behind and making films in Europe was realized in 1925 when he acquired the Victorine Studios in Nice, France. Being from Ireland, Ingram was more at home in Europe, but, without question, the shy little girl from Indiana was right at her husband's side, far away from the land she had known as home for the past 26 years.

As if to validate her contentment to be wherever her husband was, Ingram's first film at the studio was Terry's favorite, and, most likely, her best performance. As Freya Talberg, a beautiful spy working for the Germans during World War I in *Mare Nostrum* (1926), she was at her best and most captivating. The two couldn't have been happier with their lives or each other.

Ingram's behavior was not always predictable, yet Terry remained the devoted, and most understanding, wife. For instance, Ingram and Terry had lengthy separations while he was busy with a project or whatever was interesting him. As a matter of fact, while he was preparing for his 1927 movie *The Garden of Allah*, Terry returned to Hollywood to make *Lovers*, with Ramon Novarro. But, as soon as this was completed, she was back in Europe with her husband, playing the lead in *The Garden of Allah*.

Rex Ingram directed Mare Nostrum, *co-starring Alice Terry and Antonio Moreno, in 1926 at his studio in Nice. This was Terry's favorite of the films she and Ingram made together.*

Ingram became enamored with North Africa and the Arabic culture in general when he filmed parts of *The Arab* (1924) on location in Tunisia. This "strange affinity," as O'Leary called it, that he felt for the Arab people, was, no doubt, why he chose to make such films as *The Garden of Allah* and *Baroud* (1932), as well as adopting a young Arab boy, Abd-el-Kader.

A Mutual Understanding

Terry allowed her husband the freedom to fulfill his dreams and desires, even to the point of stepping out of the way when necessary. O'Leary noted that during the period of *The Magician* in the early days at the studio in Nice, "Alice lived her own life more or less independently."

The couple's lifestyle led to some assumptions in a British magazine that Ingram was leaving filmmaking because of his "revulsion" for Hollywood, that he and Terry were having marital difficulties, and that he had converted to Islam, none of which was true. He sued the magazine's publishers and won.

Although these years at the Nice studio were heady days for Ingram, Terry is the one who apparently "kept her head" and steered her husband toward wise investments — an area in which Ingram was not especially adept.

It wasn't all smooth sailing for the Ingrams, either. After a few years in Nice, he lost his beloved studio. He was able to make only three films there: *The Magician* (1926), *Mare Nostrum* (1926), and *The Garden of Allah* (1927). MGM stopped financing any further Ingram movies when they realized it was costing far more to film in France than in Hollywood.

Sound in films suited neither Ingram nor Terry. Terry retired, and Ingram made only one more film, *Baroud* (1932), which he starred in and directed. Terry co-directed the film, a task she had assumed many times before when Ingram was not inclined to take on the day's duties.

By 1934, the Ingrams had left Nice and were living in Cairo. However, Terry soon moved to California to be with her dying mother. She would not see her husband again for the two years he was wandering in North Africa and writing his first novel.

Back to the U. S.

Ingram and Terry reunited and settled in the San Fernando Valley of California, where they maintained two adjacent homes, one as a main residence, and one where Ingram could take refuge when he shunned visitors or wanted to indulge in his sculpting.

World War II came, and his precious collection of art that he had left with the Cairo Museum could not be retrieved until after the war. He took an extended trip in 1947 and 1948, during which time he regained his treasures and visited his father and brother one last time. He had been suffering from ill health, and, when he returned to Terry and their California home, he was obviously declining.

In July 1950, he entered the hospital to have some tests and X-rays made. The day before he was to be released, Terry visited him there. He instructed her to pick him up the following morning for a visit to a clinic in the Valley and to pick out something for her birthday, which was coming up shortly. However, by the time she arrived home, the hospital called and said he was unconscious. Terry rushed back and was at his side when he passed away, a short time later.

Although Alice Terry was only 51 years old when she lost her husband, she never remarried. She remained in her home, and for most of the rest of her life she shared it with her elder sister, Edna. Alice Terry passed away on December 22, 1987, some 37 years after she lost her beloved husband.

Wouldn't Have Been the Same

Looking back over their lives, it is obvious Rex Ingram and Alice Terry had few regrets, and this is due in no small part to the fact that they were able to share 29 years of their lives together. Ingram's films would not have been the same without Alice Terry. Nor is it likely that he could have pursued his dreams or indulged his passions the way he did with anyone but her. It is also safe to assume that Terry, the reluctant performer, would not have become the person or actress she was without Ingram by her side, guiding her career. And, because of his love for her, his confidence in her abilities, his respect for her as an actress, and through the masterpieces he has left, fans can still see that face . . . yes, that face just as Ingram saw it and fell in love with her all those years ago.

SOURCES

PERIODICALS

Benthall, Dwinelle. "Some Women Have All the Luck." *Motion Picture Magazine* (January 1927).

Bodeen, DeWitt. "Rex Ingram and Alice Terry." *Films in Review* (February–March 1975).

Cheatham, Maude. "The Darkest Hour." *Motion Picture Classic* (November 1922).

Evans, Delight. "She Wants to Be Wicked." *Photoplay* (December 1922).

Johaneson, Bland. "Alice & Miss Terry." *Photoplay* (January 1924).

Moving Picture World (June 12, 1920).

Robinson, Selma. "A Rex-Ray View of Alice Terry." *Motion Picture Magazine* (November 1924).

Sebastian, Dorothy. "The Alice Terry I Know." *Motion Picture Magazine* (February 1926).

Thayer, Mamie. "Alice of Old Vincennes." *Picture Play Magazine* (May 1921).

BOOKS

O'Leary, Liam. *Rex Ingram: Master of the Silent Cinema*. Dublin: Academy Press, 1980.

Slide, Anthony. *The Idols of Silence*. New York: A.S. Barnes and Co., 1976.

CHAPTER 20
Three Crusty Characters
✂

Ernest Torrence, Theodore Roberts, George Fawcett... these three fine actors did not achieve the ranks of stardom accorded to, say, John Gilbert or Rudolph Valentino. But their contributions to the silent screen remain invaluable.

Ernest Torrence

This lumbering 6′4″ giant of a man could portray the epitome of evil as he did in *Tol'able David* (1921), or a big "softie" as he did in *Mantrap* (1926). He was never the star of a film himself, but he contributed immensely to the stardom of others, including Richard Barthelmess, Clara Bow, Betty Bronson, Lon Chaney, and Buster Keaton with his supporting roles.

Torrence came to America from Scotland. He was a veteran of the stage, and it was one of his stage performances that led to his film debut as the brutal Luke Hatburn in *Tol'able David*. The film's director, Henry King, saw Torrence perform on Broadway in 1920 and selected him for the role. He was an immediate hit as the title character's thoroughly despicable nemesis.

Just as intensely as they had hated him in *Tol'able David*, audiences fell in love with him as the crusty veteran of the plains, Bill Jackson, in *The Covered Wagon* (1923). Although boasting such stars as J. Warren Kerrigan, Lois Wilson, Alan Hale, and Tully Marshall, it is Torrence who consistently gets the acting honors in this film. As the tobacco-chewing best friend to Kerrigan's character, Will Banion, Torrence gets to play a tough guy when he urges Will to go ahead and gouge Sam Woodhull's (Alan Hale) eyes out in a "free" fight—and a comedian when he begs Will to let him throw Woodhull back in the quicksand from which he was just rescued.

Another memorable Torrence performance was as Captain Hook in the silent adaptation of J. M. Barrie's *Peter Pan* (1924), starring Betty Bronson. In reviewing that film, James Card, founder of the George Eastman film archive, said, "And Ernest Torrence as the 'not altogether unheroic' Captain Hook, after his triumph as the dust-encrusted scout of *The Covered Wagon*, was brilliant casting."

Born in Scotland, Ernest Torrence landed his first movie role in the U.S. in Tol'able David *(1921) in which he was the personification of evil. He was just as adept at comedy, as can be seen in his role as Buster Keaton's father in* Steamboat Bill, Jr. *(1928).*

In *Mantrap* (1926), he plays a lovable backwoodsman in need of a wife. The most unlikely coupling imaginable comes about when Torrence's character marries city girl Clara Bow, the quintessential carefree "flapper." Even in a loveable role such as this, Torrence switches convincingly to a menacing hulk at a moment's notice when he goes looking for his errant wife and the man with whom she has run off. In the end, she realizes she really loves him and comes back to him, and, somehow, Torrence makes us believe this is possible.

His performance as Buster Keaton's embarrassed father in *Steamboat Bill, Jr.* (1928) is a gem! Some of his other films include Lon Chaney's *The Hunchback of Notre Dame* (1923), in which he portrayed Clopin, the king of the criminals and outcasts; *The King of Kings* (1927), as Peter, one of the disciples; the comedy *The Ruggles of Red Gap* (1923), as Cousin Egbert Floud, who wins British valet Ruggles in a poker game; *Twelve Miles Out* (1927), in which he is John Gilbert's rival for women, gunrunning, and diamond smuggling; and his final film, *I Cover the Waterfront* (1933), starring Claudette Colbert, in which he is Eli Kirk, a fisherman who smuggles Chinese migrants into the country.

Because of his ability to play a variety of roles, Torrence was in high demand during his short 15-year career. Between 1918 and 1933, he made 51 films, each one enriched by this "giant" of a man—not only in size, but in his presence on the screen.

Torrence died May 15, 1933, at age 55.

Theodore Roberts

Cigar-chewing Theodore Roberts was also a veteran of the stage, which is where he and Wallace Reid became good friends. Roberts worked in support of Reid in many of his pictures, including *Nan of Music Mountain* (1917), *The Source* (1918), *The Roaring Road* (1919), *Hawthorne of the U.S.A.* (1919), *Double Speed* (1920), *Excuse My Dust* (1920), and *Too Much Speed* (1921).

Roberts gives one of his trademark performances in *The Roaring Road* as J. D. "The Bear" Ward. He provides the perfect antagonist for Reid, constantly snarling and impatiently chewing on a cigar, with smoke billowing about his head. A reviewer for the *Motion Picture Magazine* opines that given "the number of close-ups of Theodore Roberts smoking a cigar, I should say it was starring a new brand of tobacco." *Photoplay* said, "Theodore Roberts is excellent as the blustering J. D."

Around this same time, Roberts was being used by Cecil B. DeMille in some of his most popular films, such as *Don't Change Your Husband* (1919), *Male and Female* (1919), and *The Affairs of Anatol* (1921). In *Male and Female*, he still has the cigar but, in contrast to his aggressive character in *The Roaring*

Theodore Roberts almost always played gruff but likable characters. In the teens, he could be seen in several Wallace Reid movies, but he was also a favorite of Cecil B. DeMille, appearing in at least 11 of the director's films.

Road, he plays the passive Lord Loam, who lets his daughters (played by Gloria Swanson and Mildred Reardon) rule the roost. When they are all stranded on a desert island, he willingly accedes to the rule of his butler (played by Thomas Meighan). He does add a comical touch to the film, though, such as the scene where the shipwrecked party panics when they see something rustling in the undergrowth. While the women recoil in fright and the men brandish their firearms, out comes Roberts, presumed dead in the shipwreck, on his hands and knees, still in his bathrobe, glasses down on his nose, and, of course, the ubiquitous cigar clenched tightly in his teeth.

It is a tribute to this old veteran's talent that, just four years after playing the clueless patriarch in *Male and Female*, he would turn in a first-rate performance as Moses in Cecil B. DeMille's Biblical epic *The Ten Commandments* (1923). A review in *The New York Times* mentioned, "Theodore Roberts, who recently was seen in the character of a businessman with a cigar in his mouth, gave an excellent portrayal of Moses, the Lawgiver. His make-up was faultless, and the sincerity with which he acted this part made the whole affair doubly effective."

Roberts's health began to go downhill in the mid-twenties, and his film work was reduced accordingly. He didn't appear in a single picture in 1924, he made only one each in 1925 and 1926, and two more in 1928. He died on December 14, 1928, at the age of 67, depriving the coming sound era of a great character actor.

George Fawcett

George Fawcett is one of those actors who seems to pop up in film after film. This is understandable when one realizes he made 129 pictures between 1915 and 1931, an amazing record for a 16-year period!

D.W. Griffith was very fond of Fawcett, and he can be seen in several of the great director's films of the late teens. In the World War I drama *Hearts of the World* (1918), he is the good-natured and lovable village carpenter who takes money from M. Cuckoo's purse to give to the Little Disturber. He hugs and kisses "The Boy" when he meets his fellow villager in the trenches and laughs while having dinner as the little boys stick items from the table in his ears and mouth.

In contrast to this performance, he effectively plays Bobby Harron's stern, pious father in another Griffith film, *A Romance of Happy Valley* (1918). John Logan Jr. (Harron) wants to go to the city to try and make his fortune. Because his father's objections are so emphatic, he decides to steal away one night to fulfill his dream. His father discovers this deception, and a tense, emotional confrontation ensues. Fawcett, Harron, and Kate Bruce, who plays Harron's mother, handle the dramatics to perfection. The end of the movie is less effective,

*George Fawcett was used regularly by D.W. Griffith in his Biograph films; he later
distinguished himself in character parts requiring maturity. Between 1915 and 1931, he
appeared in an amazing 129 movies.*

though, with an episode of misunderstandings in which Fawcett thinks he has mistakenly killed his son. Fawcett's performance, nevertheless, rises above the melodrama.

Before deciding on the casting for his 1919 masterpiece, *Broken Blossoms* (1919), Griffith had begun rehearsing Fawcett in the role of the Yellow Man, which Richard Barthelmess would make famous. Barthelmess commented later, "I can state that after having watched Fawcett rehearse . . . I merely went into rehearsal myself and copied every mannerism that he had given the part. I couldn't have done better, as Fawcett was a fine actor."

In 1919, Fawcett appeared in four Griffith productions: *The Girl Who Stayed at Home*, in which he portrays Harron's father once again; in *True Heart Susie*, as a stranger; in *Scarlet Days*, as a sheriff; and in *The Greatest Question*, playing, for the third time, Harron's father. His final film for Griffith was *Lady of the Pavements* (1929), as Baron Hausemann. Of that performance, Griffith historian Edward Wagenknecht writes, "Indeed, the only player who suggests anything that had appeared in earlier Griffith films is George Fawcett, who performs valiantly in what he has to do, which is not enough notably to affect one's final impression."

Fawcett proceeded through the 1920s being called on by a variety of stars and a variety of companies. He is an eccentric tramp in one of the Johnny Hines comedies, *Burn 'em Up Barnes* (1921). Cecil B. DeMille called on him to play a judge in *Manslaughter* (1922), starring Leatrice Joy. And he was Blanche Sweet's father in her 1924 version of *Tess of the D'Ubervilles*.

A typical role for Fawcett can be seen in *The Mad Whirl* (1924). His rugged face, large nose, piercing eyes, and intimidating scowl make him the perfect, old-fashioned, Victorian parent, somewhat reminiscent of his role in *A Romance of Happy Valley*, but without the religious bent. He is a simple country store owner who is trying to raise his daughter (played by May McAvoy) properly among the Jazz Age partygoers. To the frustration of Fawcett, his daughter is attracted to a young partygoer named Jack Herrington (Jack Mulhall), whose wealthy parents not only condone the all-night parties—they participate in them. In the end, the old-fashioned values of Fawcett's character win out, but not before he gives the Herringtons a severe tongue-lashing about their lifestyle.

One delightful scene has young Jack entering Fawcett's store, looking for the daughter without admitting the real reason he's there. He bides his time, ordering ice cream he doesn't want and dawdles around while Fawcett squints, frowns, snarls, and generally intimidates the young man.

MGM used Fawcett effectively in some of their biggest pictures of the late twenties. In *Flesh and the Devil* (1926), with Greta Garbo and John Gilbert, he is Pastor Voss, who christened Leo (Gilbert) and Ulrich (Lars Hanson) and has watched the two young men's friendship grow over the years. However, Felicitas (Garbo) comes along and creates the first division in this friendship. After a lengthy trip away, Leo returns to find Felicitas married to Ulrich. In a palpably intense scene, Pastor Voss surprises Leo by telling him he must end the friendship with Ulrich—because he is still in love with Felicitas. Leo surely realizes this but hearing it from the Pastor is disconcerting at best. Gilbert's character looks expressionless, and somewhat still in shock over the surprise marriage. Fawcett's downturned mouth, cold, steely eyes, and chiseled face seem to say, "You will do as I say!"—without either man uttering a word.

Fawcett appeared the year before with Gilbert in Erich von Stroheim's *The Merry Widow* (1925), as King Nikita, and once more with Gilbert and Garbo in *Love* (1927), as the Grand Duke. He played a final time for von Stroheim in the 1928 disaster *The Wedding March*.

By the time Fawcett made his last film in 1931, he had been acting for 43 years, having started out on the stage in 1888 as a young man of 28. He passed away on June 6, 1939, at the age of 79.

A 1928 *Motion Picture Magazine* article commemorating Fawcett's 40 years as an actor stated, "Fawcett has on the screen today few rivals"—an understatement, most certainly.

As silent film buffs gaze in awe at the performances of Barthelmess, Gish, Garbo, Gilbert, Reid, Keaton, Chaney, and others, it's easy to overlook the character actors who portrayed The Judge, The King, The Tramp, The Pastor, The Carpenter, The Father, or The Businessman in their films. But try to imagine the loss if superb actors such as Ernest Torrence, Theodore Roberts, or George Fawcett hadn't been there to lend their great talents to these cinematic gems.

SOURCES
PERIODICALS
Calhoun, Dorothy. "From Females to Flappers." *Motion Picture Magazine* (December 1928).

The Roaring Road review. *Motion Picture Magazine* (July 1919).

The Roaring Road review. *Photoplay* (June 1919).

The Ten Commandments review. *The New York* (NY) *Times*, December 22, 1923.

BOOKS
Card, James. *Seductive Cinema: The Art of Silent Film*. New York: Alfred A. Knopf, 1994.

Schickel, Richard. *D.W. Griffith: An American Life*. New York: Simon and Schuster, 1984.

Wagenknecht, Edward, and Anthony Slide. *The Films of D.W. Griffith*. New York: Crown Publishers, 1975.

CHAPTER 21
The Fair Virginia Brown Faire
❦

She was born Virginia La Buna in Brooklyn, New York, on June 26, 1904. Her mother had some stage experience, which may have led Virginia to appear in various film productions in New York and Fort Lee before being named one of four winners in *Motion Picture Classic's* "Fame and Fortune" contest in 1919, when she was just 15.

"How did I feel when I learnt I was one of the contest winners?" she said in a 1920 interview. "Why, very happy. At first it seemed too good to be true, and when Universal offered me the five years' contract and the generous salary—well, I just didn't know anyone could be so happy."

Reportedly, there were as many as 50,000 entries for the contest, which was judged by Mary Pickford, Cecil B. DeMille, Maurice Tourneur, J. Stuart Blackton, artists Howard Chandler Christy and James Montgomery Flagg, photographer Samuel Lumiere, and *Motion Picture Classic* magazine publisher Eugene V. Brewster. This illustrious panel concurred that Faire "is of an extraordinary beauty, sculptural, classic. Artists pronounce her close to perfection. She has the exquisiteness of youth. She has a super-delicate sensitiveness, easily—and rarely—lent to dramatic art. She is finely different, because of her sense of innocence and touch of the young Madonna in poise and feature."

Her mother told a reporter that Virginia was just beginning her first year of high school, but that she quit due to her good fortune in winning the contest. "Virginia will not give up her studies, however," she said. "She is fond of them, in the first place, and we realize that the wider her knowledge, the more conversant she is in different subjects, the better her work will be. She is particularly fond of French and literature, but there will be other subjects as well. One of the first things we'll attend to when we reach California is securing a good tutor."

A year later, the 17-year-old actress was asked what her goals were. She answered: "To work until I become a big, big star—not what I call a floating one, here today and gone tomorrow. I want to make each picture a real feature, something that will stand out because of special merit."

Virginia La Buna entered movies after winning Motion Picture Classic's "Fame and Fortune" contest in 1919 at age 15. Universal decided a name change was in order, and Virginia Brown Faire was decided upon.

"And then?" the interviewer asked.

"To go right on just as long as the public will let me, for I love motion pictures and cannot think what my life would be without them."

Her Biggest Break to Date

At the time of this interview, she had made only a handful of shorts and one feature. Universal had sought a name change for her, so she took "Brown" from her stepfather, but fearing that too common, she was named Virginia Faire. That, too, presented a problem: Elinor Fair was already a known actress in Hollywood. Thus, Virginia Brown Faire became her stage name.

Faire was apparently overjoyed at her selection for the lead female role in the Robert Brunton production *Without Benefit of Clergy* (1921), Rudyard Kipling's tale of a British engineer in India who defies social structure and takes a native girl as his bride. "They tried out thirty-two girls," Faire said in an interview. "It didn't seem possible that I could win, and after a week of hopes and fears, I nearly died of joy when I was given the part." The article went on to note that when production supervisor Randolph Lewis spoke to Rudyard Kipling in England about the upcoming production, Kipling "repeatedly declared that everything depended upon the girl who would play Ameera, saying she was the very life, the heart of the story, and he urged that much care be given to the matter of her selection." It went on to say, "Mr. Lewis feels that Virginia Faire absolutely fulfills every qualification emphasized by Mr. Kipling." In typical *New York Times* fashion, their review of the film praised Faire's performance, but in a "back-handed" fashion: "Virginia Brown Faire, as Ameera, the little Indian girl whom Holden, the British engineer, marries 'without benefit of clergy,' gives, perhaps, the most appealing performance, although she does not surprise in effectiveness."

Variety also gave mixed praise: "The acting was satisfactory. Virginia Brown Faire wasn't pretty in our sense of the term, but certainly she made Ameera wistful, pathetic . . ." As a side note, the picture's producer and owner of Brunton Studios, Robert Brunton, became her personal manager at this time.

Next was a smaller role in the Will Rogers comedy *Doubling for Romeo* (1921), followed by a western, a genre she would frequent in her later career. William Desmond was a popular early western star and *Fightin' Mad* (1921) was typical fare of the time. But this was not her first rodeo. Some of those first two-reelers for Universal that she made upon arriving in California were cowboy pictures. As she remembered, "I came out, and the first thing they did was stick me into western two-reelers. I had learned to ride, English saddle, of course, in Central Park, so they immediately put me in a western in a western saddle. The horse took off. I managed to get in the saddle, and the cowboys applauded. I didn't know it, but I had made a flying mount."

A more important role followed for the then-18-year-old Faire, one of two female leads in John Gilbert's *Monte Cristo* (1922), a major production of the famous Alexander Dumas story for the Fox Film Corporation. *Variety* said, "Virginia Brown Faire, as the Arabian princess, scored the beauty hit and acquitted herself exceptionally well."

A newspaper brief from April 14, 1922, reported that Faire had been involved in an automobile accident. Although it claims she was "severely injured," the article went on to say that she "is in bed suffering from nervous shock and minor bruises." The accident was caused by another motorist, who "collided with her car, smashing and jamming it to the curb."

An Artistic Triumph

Omar the Tentmaker (1922) was a major production that received ample notice. Writer Richard Walton Tully selected Faire for the lead female role of Shireen, Omar Khayam's beloved, after seeing her in *Without Benefit of Clergy*. The picture was well received. *Variety* said, "It may not be unwise to predict that *Omar* will shoot the gross ahead of the usual release, for this is a spectacle of a film production." However, the reviewer was not impressed by the ingénue. "Virginia Brown Faire 'registered' well enough as Shireen, but it seemed more registration than playing."

According to Faire, this film "started me in good parts. It was called an artistic triumph. Those artistic triumphs don't usually make money, but at least it did give me the recognition for better parts." Director James Young was impressed enough with her that he asked her to star in his next picture, *Trilby* (1923), but she opted instead to make *Vengeance of the Deep* (1923) for the minor studio, American Releasing Company, because it was being filmed in Hawaii. A passenger list shows Faire sailing from San Francisco for Honolulu on October 4, 1922, aboard the SS *Matsonia*. However, after making this movie, Faire realized the foolishness of her choice, noting that *Vengeance of the Deep* was "a very bad picture."

Another role she accepted with a minor company, Film Booking Offices (F.B.O.), was as the female lead in a feature pairing brothers Wallace and Noah Beery. This was followed by another attention-getting role, that of Dot Marley in *The Cricket on the Hearth* (1923) for Selznick. It did not live up to expectations. *Variety* called it "pleasantly mild," and simply said, "Three pretty women—Virginia Browne (*sic*) Faire, Fritzi Ridgeway and Margaret Landis—provide an unusual assortment of feminine pulchritude for one picture."

WAMPAS

Pan dancing at Bacchanale with a dryad in a Billy Sunday tabernacle under the eye of a policeman. A swirling sea of white faces against a backwash of kaleidoscopic colors. An atmosphere heavy with the reek of Turkish cigarettes and exotic perfumes, defying the vari-colored beams of half a hundred limelights and shot with the sensuous throbbing of tireless orchestras with heavy burdens of evening wraps. Beautiful women in gorgeous gowns dancing with men in somber evening clothes. Visions of loveliness paraded before 10,000 eyes by a raucous-voiced master of ceremonies competing unequally with the incessant prattle of thousands of tongues.

No, the above is not describing a scene from a movie. It is an evocative look at the WAMPAS (Western Association of Motion Picture Advertisers) Baby Stars event, held at Warner Bros. studio on Sunset Boulevard on April 21, 1923. One of Hollywood's biggest events of the year, the naming of the year's WAMPAS Baby Stars meant national recognition for a group of fortunate young starlets and the affirmation that their work up to this point showed talent and potential.

Virginia Brown Faire was one of the 13 being feted at this event, along with Eleanor Boardman, Evelyn Brent, Dorothy Devore, Betty Francisco, Pauline Garon, Laura La Plante, Margaret Leahy, Helen Lynch, Derelys Perdue, Jobyna Ralston, Kathleen Key, and Ethel Shannon. As can be seen from the list, some WAMPAS Baby Stars passed into obscurity while others went on to become major stars of the silent era. Obviously, being selected brought attention to the rising star, attention that had the potential to give a much-needed boost to her career. Nevertheless, the burden of talent and charisma still rested with the individual. As author and WAMPAS historian Roy Liebman stated, "Whether their designation as Wampas Baby Stars speeded the initial groups of actresses toward fame or their subsequent fame gave cachet to their designation, to be named a Baby Star soon became an extremely prestigious honor. It was to prove a major plum for the studios as well as for the young women."

Although being selected a WAMPAS Baby Star was certainly a high point for Faire, the year was not without its problems, including a Hollywood scandal. In April 1923, screenwriter H. H. Van Loan was sued for divorce by his wife on the grounds of desertion. His story credits included two of Faire's films up to that time, *Fightin' Mad* in 1921, and *Stormswept* in 1923. Publications in those days were not above passing on gossip, and an April 1923 article stated, "Somewhat more than a fortnight ago the names of Van Loan and Virginia Brown

Faire, young leading woman, were mentioned in one and the same breath, and those who had followed studio gossip were not backward in asserting that Van Loan and Miss Faire were engaged and would wed as soon as Van Loan had his divorce." Van Loan said he and his wife had been separated for two years, and, while denying the rumor, admitted that he and Faire "have been going about quite a bit." Faire said somewhat flippantly, "The rumor is absurd. Becoming engaged to a married man is not being done this season."

Later that same year, her photo was plastered on the newspaper page, garnering more column inches than the negative article to which it was attached. Apparently, her stepfather, Dr. Spencer Brown, was being sought for questioning in the supposed "accidental" shooting death of Lewis J. Hauschild, attorney for some beer runners. Pinkerton detectives were questioning Faire as to the whereabouts of her stepfather. Nothing more was mentioned regarding her, and, apparently, neither incident had an impact on her burgeoning popularity.

Faire remained busy throughout 1923 and 1924, with a couple of westerns with William Desmond and Harry Carey, a drama for First National with Owen Moore, a little-known film with John Gilbert entitled *Romance Ranch* for Fox, one for poverty row studio Producers Distributing Corporation with Florence Vidor and Noah Beery, and one of Al Wilson's typical air adventures.

The film with Owen Moore was entitled *Thundergate* (1923), in which Faire plays Jen Jue, a white girl raised in China who becomes the slave-bride of a Chinese lord. There is an intriguing human-interest story attached to this film, which may, or may not, stem from the imagination of a publicity department. As the story goes, Faire won the affection of the Orientals on the set who rechristened her Suey Sin, which means Water Lily. At one point, an elderly Oriental named Chan Ing was moved to tears in a scene that did not call for them. Director Joseph de Grasse asked Chan Ing why he was crying. He responded that his small fortune was used up in his search for his lost daughter, also named Suey Sin. Now, his only means of support was as an extra in movies. He went on to explain that tears came as he watched Faire in her Oriental dress, feeling that he has found the counterpart to his lost child in the actress.

"Do you believe in fairies?"

If she's mentioned at all today, Virginia Brown Faire is best known as Tinker Bell in *Peter Pan* (1924). Admittedly, this may be the best-known film in which she appeared, but when shown as something other than a light darting about, she is shown from a distance to emphasize her miniature size. Faire was disappointed in *Peter Pan* because much of the screen time originally planned for Tinker Bell was cut. She said, "That was a very exciting thing because I worked alone most of the time. You know, five inches high. Also, Jimmy [James Wong] Howe, a wonderful photographer, had figured out how he could have close-ups of me, but [*Peter Pan* creator] James Barrie said, 'No close-ups of Tinker Bell, because it would spoil the illusion.'" Because of this, it is difficult to find mention of her in reviews, although *Photoplay* had this to say: "The beautiful bits done by Virginia Brown Faire as Tinker Bell lent an enchantment that was needed to make the picture perfect."

Interestingly, a newspaper article announced at this time that Faire was being signed to play the feminine lead opposite Al Wilson in "The Phantom Flyer." More than likely, this is the film mentioned earlier that she made with Wilson in 1924 entitled *Air Hawk*, released by Universal in December. Many times (more often in westerns, it seems) a title was something generic and not descriptive of anything in the film. This is likely the case here since Wilson did make a film entitled *The Phantom Flyer*, but it was four years later, in 1928, and it co-starred Lillian Gilmore, not Faire.

Faire appeared in a bit part as a half-caste girl in The Lost World *(1925), Arthur Conan Doyle's story of the Prehistoric era.*

Another "big picture" appearance for Faire that has nothing to recommend it for her fans is the famous *Lost World* (1925). Faire plays a half-caste girl in an uncredited role. The part is so small, it is likely she may not even be seen in currently circulating prints.

Much more appealing for anyone wishing to see how Virginia Brown Faire brought so much to the screen are the surviving features made over the next few years. There are no major productions—Faire was not too proud to take whatever parts were offered, nor was she a temperamental actress. Instead, she was one who took direction and gave each film her best, regardless of the studio or the production's budget. While working on *Thundergate*, a reporter noted, "She puts her whole heart and soul into her work. The day was hot and the many lights on the set added to that heat, but there was not so much as a murmur of complaint from her. Always she was cheerful, stopping now and then to speak to an electrician or a fellow player, and with a smile and a cheery word for everyone." Co-star Owen Moore added, "Miss Faire is one of the finest little ladies in the picture business. She is always striving to do her best, and I have never seen her angry or heard her complain."

Fashionable Poverty Row

Even though there were offers (and acceptances) of studio contracts, Virginia preferred to freelance. As she explained: "We all used to do quickies in between [assignments] because it was good money, twice as much as you got for a big studio production. And nobody looked down on it because everybody did it. We worked fast in those days."

Whether just for publicity or not, Faire claimed in the summer of 1923 that she was required to maintain her 110-pound weight lest she violate her new contract with First National. Faire went on to describe her exercise routine that centered around swimming: "I wish I could impress upon every non-aquatic girl in the country the joy, satisfaction, health and beauty that come from swimming and diving."

As noted, Faire appeared in several westerns, and two of the best that are still available to view are *The Calgary Stampede* (1925) and *Chip of the Flying U* (1926), both with the amiable Hoot Gibson. Also, both films are Universal-Jewel productions, which means Universal lavished more money, effort, and talent on them than the run-of-the-mill fare. That's not to say they feature enormous sets or crowds of extras, but the extra attention can be seen in the strong storylines—for example, western scenarios that are devoid of the typical good guy-bad guy, shoot-em-up clichés. The two Hoot Gibson features

Faire supported Hoot Gibson in three of his silent westerns; this is from Chip of the Flying U *(1926).*

she made, for instance, are good drama-comedy-love stories, acted out in a western setting.

The Calgary Stampede has Gibson traveling to big rodeos, the biggest of which is the Calgary Stampede. In this, he falls in love with a French-Canadian girl (Faire), whose father is killed, an accident for which Gibson is blamed. In *Chip of the Flying U*, he's a bashful cowhand, and when the boss's sister comes to visit, he immediately falls in love. Since she's a doctor, he fakes an accident to get her attention. She is enamored of Chip, too, but is angered and insulted when she finds that he has faked his injury. He must find a way to win her back.

The chemistry between Faire and Gibson works, and she provides the winsomeness and charm to make a perfect love interest for Gibson's shy characterizations.

Wedged in between these two westerns is a drama of Jewish life in New York City's lower East Side entitled *His People* (1925). The film starred Rudolph Schildkraut as the father of two sons who are straying from family traditions. Faire said, "I remember Rudolph Schildkraut. He was so wonderful...I became so enthralled just watching him, and the tears started rolling down my face." Another Universal-Jewel, *Harrison's Reports* said, "No truer picture of the

Ghetto, and more human, has ever been produced. None of the details of Orthodox Jewish life has been overlooked." The film also benefited from the direction of the talented Edward Slocum, whose films are all too scarce today.

With Garbo

Faire's next four films (all made in 1926) are apparently lost. They were made for such low-budget studios as Rayart, Ben Wilson Productions, and Ell-bee Pictures. Her co-stars were second-echelon actors such as Robert McKim (who typically played heavies, often for Douglas Fairbanks), Reed Howes, and Cullen Landis. The highlight of the year, though, was a coveted role in Greta Garbo's second feature, *The Temptress,* which does survive. Obviously, the movie was a success and got good reviews. The reviews focused on Garbo, of course, Antonio Moreno in the male lead, Fred Niblo as director, and Vicente Blasco Ibáñez as the author. Faire is billed last in the opening credits, so it's no wonder it's difficult to find a mention of her. Nevertheless, her dark features were perfect for this tale of the Argentine, and her performance as Moreno's hometown love, although small, adds to the appeal of the film.

The Temptress *(1926) was Greta Garbo's second film in the U.S.; her co-star was Antonio Moreno. In this scene, Moreno returns to his Argentine home and is welcomed by his former sweetheart, Celinda, played beautifully by Virginia Brown Faire.*

The production, though, was not without its problems. Faire said Garbo was still trying to master English in this, only her second film in the United States. "Mauritz Stiller was a big director in Sweden, but he, by this time, I guess was a pretty sick man, although nobody seemed to know it," she said. "And every scene he'd make her do over twenty times at least . . . And all they were getting in the front office, in the rushes, were close-ups of Garbo. The poor girl was in tears most of the time. Finally, they took him off after two weeks. They put Fred Niblo on the picture, and he finished it." She continued, "Garbo was difficult and remote. We all tried—Lionel Barrymore, Tony Moreno, everybody tried to make her feel at home, but she, I guess, was upset that Stiller was taken off, and she was in a foreign country. It was impossible to get close to her."

Faire only made three brief appearances in the film. When Robledo (Moreno) returns from Paris to the Argentine, along with virtually the entire village, Celinda (Faire) is there to greet him. She stands there, looking longingly at Robledo in her sharp gaucho outfit. Later, she comes into Robledo's work cabin—he is busily poring over papers—and sits on the desk near him. In a few lines she notes that she is not happy, nor has he been since the arrival of Elena (Garbo). She then adds that Elena is not happy, an observation that appears to be a revelation for Robledo. The scene fades. Faire doesn't appear again until the end of the film when a crowd in Paris is waiting outside to see the famous Argentine architect, Robledo. He comes out of the building with his wife, Celinda, on his arm. All told, Faire has less than five minutes of screen time, a true shame since her dark beauty was so well-suited for the setting of this film.

Three more films, all minor, rounded out 1926 for Faire—a drama with Thunder the Dog and Reed Howes for Fox, a William Fairbanks feature for a minor studio, and a western with Buck Jones.

Her first film in 1927 paired her with Louise Dresser and Jason Robards, Sr.; Pat O'Malley was her co-star in the second. Neither picture has survived the passage of time. The third film in 1927, *Tracked by the Police*, with Rin Tin Tin, is extant and was available on video at one time. (It was pulled from distribution because Warner Bros. asserted the film remains under copyright until it falls in the public domain in 2022.) *Harrison's Reports* said the film was "just ordinary melodrama," but added that "it is fairly exciting, though it lacks originality." The film once again paired Faire with Robards, and the review did say she filled the role of the heroine "capably."

True, the story is nothing out of the ordinary. Virginia's father is in charge of building a dam in Arizona. Robards is his foreman. The ever-capable Tom

Faire supported several western stars, including Hoot Gibson, John Wayne, Tom Tyler, Jack Perrin, and Harry Carey. This publicity photo is for Gun Gospel *(1927), starring Ken Maynard.*

Santschi makes a superb villain who tries to sabotage things for another company that wants the contract. Rin Tin Tin does his usual amazing acting, stunts, and rescues. The rescue at the climax has Faire clinging to a rope on a beam hanging over a river with rushing rapids. The film was shot on location at the Laguna Dam on the Colorado River in Yuma, Arizona, and the rushing water is real and intimidating. In the long shots, it is assumed that Faire is replaced by a double, although the stunt is made believable by some adroit editing. The close-ups of the rushing water effectively convey the danger, resulting in a truly gripping sequence.

A curiosity for 1927 is a film entitled *The Devil's Masterpiece*, which had a New York opening of April 29, 1927, yet it reportedly premiered in England in October 1926. The movie was produced by Stanford F. Arnold and "handled" by Goodwill Pictures, a minor company. *Variety* had virtually nothing good to say about it, stating, "a short bank roll, an unknown cast and a star (Faire) of little name or note do not produce pictures that mean much. This one is a state rights proposition designed for a limited market and for that market good enough to suffice and even satisfy. There have been a lot worse 'quickies' than *The Devil's Masterpiece*." It's a melodrama about the Royal Mounties ferreting out dope smugglers. There is no mention of Faire's acting in the review, and no other review could be found in major publications.

Her penultimate film for 1927 was *Hazardous Valley* with Vincent Brownell. It's a standard story of Brownell helping his father fight against a rival lumber company owner and falling in love with the rival's daughter.

Her last 1927 release was another western, *Gun Gospel*, starring Ken Maynard. She, of course, is the love interest for Maynard, whose character must avenge the death of his friend, Dad Walker, and put a stop the rustlers.

Marriage and Marital Vacations

Biographical briefs on Faire indicate that her first marriage was to a Dick Durham. No record of this marriage can be found, but it is not unusual for the stars to "hide" knowledge of a marriage that took place when they were very young and/or before coming to Hollywood. The union with Durham would have taken place in the early 1920s since Faire was only 15 when she was on the "Fame and Fortune" contest in 1919.

A marriage that was covered in the press, though, took place in 1927. It can be assumed that Faire and Jack Dougherty, mainly a cowboy star but with some other roles to his credit, met through her association with westerns. They had not appeared in any films together up to this time and would co-star in only one after they were married. At any rate, there seems to be no media coverage of a love affair between the two until after they were married on February 6, 1927.

After the wedding, the couple received no publicity until trouble started brewing later that year. The only mention of Faire in the newspapers at that time is an announcement that she, along with MGM actress Dorothy Phillips, would be making some personal appearances. A May 5, 1927, newspaper ad announced her appearance at the Hotel Oakland (CA) on Saturday, May 7, at the T&D Theater on Sunday, May 8, and as hostess in Capwell's Millinery Department, on Monday, May 9.

Then, the media wags began. A little over six months into the marriage, Faire and Dougherty announced they would be taking a "marital vacation." An article with the headline, "Actress on Stage Tour to Get Perspective View on Problems of Marriage," reads, "She will, in the first phase, make her appearances on the stages of several cities. In the second, she will leave her husband, Jack Dougherty, for a few days or weeks in the hopes that certain petty difficulties may be straightened out." Neither wished to specify what those difficulties were, but Faire was quoted as saying, "There is a slang phrase to the effect that the first year is the worst. Perhaps it is true, for Mr. Dougherty and myself have found, even though we are very happy, that a few days of vacation might aid us in making some of the adjustments necessary in married life."

It's not clear what personal appearances she may have been referencing (she had spent time in San Diego) because only four days later, the newspapers announced that she had returned, and that she and her husband had left on a second honeymoon. "I am sure it may be worked out," she said. "We are leaving today on a trip, and I am sure this will be the last story written about us—unless it is about some anniversary."

It wasn't the last story. In April 1928, it was announced in the press for the second time that Faire and Dougherty "are trying a marital vacation." Dougherty explained, "We are trying this experimental separation to see whether or not we want to get a divorce or stay married." He claimed this came about over "petty matters" that "caused difficulty," specifically noting his disapproval of one of her hats and her disapproval of his choice of ties. Faire, who was reportedly living with her mother, estimated the separation would last "a month or so."

"Jack and I departed the very best of friends," she said. "It is solely because we were not able to get along happily—an accumulation of minor troubles rather than one big thing." Dougherty, confirmed, too, that they remained the best of friends, and neither would admit to an impending divorce. That was short-lived, however, as Faire admitted the next day they would "probably" file for one.

That they did. They divorced in July 1928, with Virginia claiming he was "cruel, morose and sullen." The divorce was finalized one year later.

Interestingly, their only film together was released in July 1929: *The Body Punch*, a western (of course) for Universal.

However, back in December, between the first and second marital vacations, Faire was a guest at a Christmas party hosted by Mr. and Mrs. Al Rogell. Rogell was a director who specialized in westerns, but he stayed active in the movie industry until the early 1950s, when he moved his talents over to television. Guests for the dinner included Marian Nixon, Jeanette Loff, Carlotta King, Priscilla Bonner, Dorothy Manners, and Billy Sullivan. Interestingly, there is no mention of Dougherty being present at this party.

Another article notes that Dougherty was present at a Christmas party hosted by Lottie Pickford in her home. Reportedly, the police were called once to "warn the party to be more quiet and a second time to halt the fight." The fight apparently took place between Dougherty and Daniel Jaeger, only identified as "retired." Dougherty fled the home after biting and beating Jaeger, the article noting that Dougherty "almost amputated" Jaeger's finger with his teeth. Jaeger refused to press charges. The article said the two were fighting over the "affections" of Pickford.

Going to the Dogs

Faire opened 1928 with another Rin Tin Tin film, *A Race for Life*, the story of a boy (Bobby Gordon) who runs away from home to become a jockey. Her second film of 1928, *Queen of the Chorus*, although a relatively basic chorus girl love story for a minor company (Morris R. Schlank Productions); it is thoroughly enjoyable and a good showcase for Faire's beauty and talent. Lloyd Whitlock, with his small, rakish mustache, was most often cast as the villain, albeit a sophisticated one, and a part he played extremely well. Such is the case here. The married Gordon Trent (Whitlock) is in love with chorus girl Queenie (Faire). Queenie considers him a good friend, and that's all. While Trent is away in Europe with his wife, his secretary, Billy (Rex Lease), is given access to the home, servants, car—everything. Billy meets Queenie, and they fall in love, but he leads her to believe he's rich. Billy also uses Trent's charge account to buy things for Queenie, which he assumes is permissible and with plans to repay whatever debts he incurs. He freely tells this to Trent when he returns, and, when he confides his plans to get married, Trent offers to pay the debts as a wedding present—that is, until he learns the identity of the bride-to-be. Trent immediately goes to Queenie with an offer of marriage—after he secures a divorce. When Queenie rebuffs his offer, he threatens to have Billy arrested for

Although she made several films for small, poverty row studios, Faire is still a delight to watch in films such low-budget offerings as The Queen of the Chorus *(1928).*

his use of the charge account unless she allows the two of them to be caught in a compromising position, thus giving him grounds to divorce his wife.

Variety gave it a brief-but-positive review, saying it "should prove generally satisfactory." The critic felt that Whitlock "over-acts heavy role," but said Lease and Faire "entertain in a light way." *Photoplay* was less kind: "If you don't pay more than the price of a malted milk to see this picture, you'll get your money's worth."

Faire continued to work regularly, albeit for minor studios most of the time. The next four films were for Rayart, Gotham, Sterling Pictures, and one for First National. She also got away from westerns somewhat as three of the films were contemporary dramas, and only one a western.

One of the dramas, *Danger Patrol* (1928), with William Russell and Wheeler Oakman, was important, not because of its stars, but because of its director/ producer, Duke Worne. More on him later.

She made another film in 1928, this one entitled *House of Shame* for the Poverty Row studio, Chesterfield Pictures. Once again, Lloyd Whitlock was in the cast, as was Creighton Hale. This is an enjoyable drama with excellent performances by all three leads. Harvey (Hale) and Druid (Faire) are husband and wife. Harvey has been stealing from his employer, Kimball (Whitlock). When discovered, he convinces Druid to go and plead his case. Kimball agrees to look the other way in return for Druid's company. Since the relationship is not to be sexual (at least in the beginning), Druid agrees. In the meantime, Harvey is having an affair with the gold-digging Doris, played admirably by Florence Dudley. As noted earlier, Whitlock was generally typecast as bad guys, and his character in this fits that description, at first anyway. In a unique twist, Whitlock falls in love with Druid, and she begins to have feelings for him, but is determined to keep her marriage honorable. She is unaware of her husband's infidelity, but Kimball is determined that she will see Harvey for the cad he is. In the end, Harvey gets his just desserts, and Kimball and Druid can act on their love.

Variety opined that the production "may be considered meritorious since it brings a finer product into the states-rights field than has been available previously." And although the publication felt the film would do well "in the minor stands, split weeks and daily changes," the reviewer did find faults. For example, "Miss Faire, who photographs well and looks snappy in certain poses, has been subjected to more and longer close-ups than suitable. Girl looks good but can't stand a close camera for long, difficult facial contortions" — an assessment that belies Faire's lovely performance. And although the reviewer acknowledges its "[f]airly smooth continuity resulting in a picture which moves along at a good speed," the overall direction was "not any too good."

The year was rounded out with her third Hoot Gibson western, *Burning the Wind.*

Duke Worne and Her First Talkie

A March 1929 article announced the dissolution of Faire and Dougherty's marriage and noted that the divorce would be finalized that July. The article also conjectured that Faire would then marry director Howard Duke Worne, Jr., a statement that Faire refused to confirm or deny. Obviously, keeping in mind the fact that her divorce was not yet final, she stated that she had "no announcement to make at present, maybe later. You must realize that it is impossible for me, under the present circumstances, to say anything."

In addition to *Danger Patrol* the year before, Worne directed her in two films in 1929, *The Devil's Chaplain* with Cornelius Keefe, and *Handcuffed* with Wheeler Oakman. Unfortunately, it appears all three films are lost.

Her most notable film for 1929 is *The Donovan Affair*, Frank Capra's first talkie. The film also features Jack Holt, Dorothy Revier (who had the feminine lead), William Collier, and Agnes Ayres. *Variety* praised the film, noting,

"Columbia has a strong dialog feature here that can stand the deluxe test anywhere. In addition to a well-conceived and neatly developed cock robin yarn, there are laughs liberally sprinkled along the way, obtained through by-play and with a minimum of mugging." *Variety* did not single out Faire for comment. *The New York Times*, which also failed to mention Faire, chimed in with praise: "It is a yarn that sustains the interest, and because of its farcical quality, it affords good entertainment."

In addition to the aforementioned titles from 1929, Faire made one more picture that year, an action-adventure-crime story entitled *Untamed Justice*, with Gaston Glass for Biltmore Productions.

Then, in January 1930, Faire and Worne were married in Big Bear Valley, a resort area about 100 miles east of Los Angeles. An announcement reads:

> Miss Faire and Worne, both dressed in mountain togs, appeared at County Clerk Harry L. Allison's office at noon yesterday [January 29, 1930] and obtained their license to wed. They had filed their intention last Saturday, Miss Faire signing her legal name as Virginia Cecelia Labuna. She said she is 25 years old. Worne gave his age as 41.

The marriage did not last long. Worne passed away on October 13, 1933, at age 43. Reportedly, his death was attributed to a tooth infection that spread throughout his body because he refused to see a dentist. He had quit the movie business shortly after the wedding and went into real estate. Faire continued in films, starring in four films in 1930, one mystery and three westerns, all for minor studios.

Soldiering On

Of the films credited to her for 1931, two of them—a western and a crime-drama—appear to be lost. However, two others have survived: a serial, and another Ken Maynard western. The serial, bearing the title *The Sign of the Wolf*, has Rex Lease as the hero. The plot concerns a discovery by Faire's father: an East Indian method of turning sand into jewels. While others attempt to obtain the secret, a mysterious man from India is there to both protect her father and return the method to its country of origin. This represents the worst of what a serial could be, with bad acting, a silly storyline, and interminable repetitiveness in each chapter. As lovely as she is, Faire isn't given a chance to act.

On the other hand, the western *Alias the Bad Man*, is quite enjoyable. Maynard is a Texas Ranger infiltrating a gang to learn who killed his father. An

Faire's last appearance on film was in Tom Tyler's 1935 western Tracy Rides. *Unlike most B-westerns, wherein the heroine is basically a part of the scenery, Faire has a significant role that is essential to the better-than-average storyline.*

aspect of the story that adds to its enjoyment is the fact that Faire dislikes Maynard because his father and hers were supposedly enemies.

The next year, her film work began to taper off. Only two films, both westerns, were made in 1932, two in 1934, and then a final one in 1935. Fortunately, her last three films, all westerns, survive. *West of the Divide* (1934) stars John Wayne. With a storyline similar to *Alias the Bad Man*, Wayne impersonates a bandit to join up with the local gang. Once again, Faire co-stars with Lloyd Whitlock, and, once again, he takes on the role as the heavy. As a testament to how quickly these films were made, Faire is identified in the credits as "Virginia Faire Brown."

Rainbow Riders (1934) is a short with Jack Perrin; the final feature, *Tracy Rides* (1935), has Tom Tyler attempting to clear Faire's brother of a murder charge.

Leaving Hollywood Behind

Sources state that Faire left Hollywood in the late 1930s and worked in radio in Chicago; she also appeared in industrial films before retiring to the West Coast.

Newspaper articles from December 1937 state that Faire and her then-husband William Bernstein, a Chicago furniture manufacturer, returned from a lengthy trip to Europe. The world was in a state of unrest at the time: this was less than two years before the outbreak of World War II. According to Faire, England was "friendly," France was "terrified," and the dictatorship in Italy was making "reasoned progress." She said they avoided Germany, but they did visit Austria, where she observed fear among both Aryan and Jewish fugitives.

No record can be found of Faire's marriage to Bernstein. However, there *is* record of a September 1939 wedding to Chicago businessman William Bayer, a union that was to last the rest of her life. A 1940 census shows Bayer and Faire living in the Evanston Township of Chicago, Illinois. His age is given as 42; hers as 35.

When Faire left pictures, she left the limelight, and little information can be found on her over the next several decades. Supposedly, she volunteered for the Red Cross and enjoyed oil painting. Bayer served as a major in the U. S. Air Force during World War II.

In 1977, Anthony Slide wrote an article for *Films in Review*, noting that Virginia Brown Faire was seeking some of her films to view, but the vast majority were not available to collectors.

Faire spent her last years at Leisure World, still visited by fellow silent movie stars and close friends Priscilla Bonner and Mary Brian. Slide said the last time he saw her was in late 1979, and he observed that "her face evidenced" the cancer which was to take her life. She passed away on June 30, 1980. Bayer passed away at age 88, in 1986.

With such a large percentage of silent films categorized as lost, it is fortunate for fans today that at least 14 of her films have been or are available on home video. These include *Tracy Rides* (1935), *West of the Divide* (1934), *Alias the Bad Man* (1931), *The Sign of the Wolf* (serial, 1931), *The House of Shame* (1928), *Queen of the Chorus* (1928), *Tracked by the Police* (1927), *The Temptress* (1926), *Chip of the Flying U* (1926), *His People* (1925), *The Calgary Stampede* (1925), *The Lost World* (uncredited, 1925), *Peter Pan* (1924), and *Monte Cristo* (1922). There are others, such as *Doubling for Romeo*, *Without Benefit of Clergy*, *Cricket on the Hearth*, and *The Donovan Affair* (albeit without its sound discs) that reside in archives. Hopefully, more will become available. Only then can future generations truly experience the charisma, charm, winsomeness, and beauty that Virginia Brown Faire brought to the movies.

SOURCES

NEWSPAPERS

"Actress Expected to Marry Director," *The Los Angeles* (CA) *Times*, March 14, 1929.

"Film Star on Vacation from Hubby," *The Des Moines* (IA) *Register*, April 7, 1928.

"H. H. Van Loan Sued by Wife: Screen Writer Charged With Desertion; Engagement Rumor Denied by Virginia Brown Faire." *The Los Angeles* (CA) *Times*, April 11, 1923.

"Learn to Dive and Keep Your Weight Down," *Arizona Republic* (Phoenix, AZ), June 17, 1923.

"Miss Faire Takes Rest from Home: Actress on Stage Tour to Get Perspective View on Problems of Marriage," *The Los Angeles* (CA) *Times*, September 20, 1927.

"Murder Meshes Beauty in Booze Plot, Say Police: Virginia Fair (*sic*) is Questioned in Amazing Chicago Liquor Case." *Oakland* (CA) *Tribune*, November 21, 1923.

"Roles Varied as Did Her Costars," *The Los Angeles* (CA) *Times*, July 7, 1980.

"Screen Pair Decides on Separation: Jack Dougherty and Wife, Virginia Brown Faire, Say They're Still Friends." *The Los Angeles* (CA) *Times*, April 6, 1928.

"Screen Star Hurt in Yule Party Battle," *Arizona Republic* (Phoenix, AZ), December 26, 1928.

"Society of Cinemaland: Christmas Party." *The Los Angeles* (CA) *Times*, December 30, 1928.

"The Screen." *The News-Palladium* (Benton Harbor, MI), December 29, 1923.

Untitled article. *Oakland* (CA) *Tribune*, July 29, 1923.

"Virginia Brown Faire Back," *The Los Angeles* (CA) *Times*. December 17, 1933.

"Virginia Brown Faire Planning Divorce Suit," *The Los Angeles* (CA) *Times*, April 7, 1928.

"Virginia Faire Cuts Marital Recess Short," *The Los Angeles* (CA) *Times*. September 24, 1927.

"Virginia Faire Hurt," *Oakland* (CA) *Tribune*, April 2, 1922.

"Virginia Faire Won Contest and Found Stardom in It." *Evening Public Ledger* (Philadelphia, PA), May 19, 1921.

"What Becomes of 'em? Here's One Prize Beauty That Has Really Made Good." *The Wichita* (KS) *Beacon*, July 16, 1922.

"Without Benefit of Clergy" review, *The New York* (NY) *Times*, June 20, 1921.

OTHER PERIODICALS

Allen, Barbara. "A Rose in the Bud." *Motion Picture Classic* (June 1920).

Cheatham, Maude. "Fulfillment." *Motion Picture Magazine* (July 1921).

His People review. *Harrison's Reports* (November 14, 1925).

The Cricket on the Hearth review. *Harrison's Reports* (February 23, 1924).

The Cricket on the Hearth review. *Variety* (March 12, 1924).

House of Shame review. *Variety* (August 29, 1928).

Monte Cristo review. *Variety* (August 25, 1922).

Omar the Tentmaker review. *Variety* (January 25, 1923).

Peter Pan review. *Photoplay* (March 1925).

Slide, Anthony. "Films on 8 & 16." *Films in Review* (November 1977).

Queen of the Chorus review. *Photoplay* (August 1928).

Queen of the Chorus review. *Variety* (June 6, 1928).

Tracked by the Police review. *Harrison's Reports* (May 7, 1927).

Without Benefit of Clergy review. *Variety* (June 24, 1921).

BOOKS

Liebman, Roy. *The Wampas Baby Stars: A Biographical Dictionary, 1922–1934*. Jefferson, NC: McFarland, 2000.

Slide, Anthony. *Silent Players: A Biographical and Autobiographical Study of 100 Silent Film Actors and Actresses*. Lexington, KY: University Press of Kentucky, 2002.

INTERNET

"Virginia Brown Faire." Internet Movie Database.

"William Bayer." Ancestry.com

OTHER

United States Census, 1940.

CHAPTER 22
The Novak Sisters
Part I: Jane

~

It is a disservice to Jane Novak's memory that her reputation seems to be limited to having been William S. Hart's leading lady and one-time fiancée. The truth of the matter is that Jane made 58 silent features and several shorts, only five of which were as Hart's co-star. A look at her career will show she deserves to be remembered for so much more.

Information on how Jane came to Hollywood can differ depending on the source—and even reminisces in both she and sister Eva's later years may be a bit suspect.

Jane (Johana) was born at home, 2401 South Twelfth Street, in St. Louis, Missouri on January 12, 1896. She and Eva had six siblings—two girls and four boys. Their parents were Joseph and Barbara (née Medek) Novak. Joseph was a native of Prague, and a newspaper writer; he passed away from tuberculosis in December 1901. Jane was not yet six, and Eva was two months shy of turning four. Jane, as well as Eva, was educated at Notre Dame High Convent in St. Louis.

"Yes, I went from Notre Dame Convent in St. Louis right straight into vaudeville," Jane told a fan magazine reporter in 1922. "Another girl and myself made up a team, and the manager booked us. But he was a naughty rascal, and our act went broke. We almost had to walk home. Then I did some work in my uncle's stock company until the stage virus had thoroughly got in its deadly work with an inoculation of motion picturitis."

In Movies, It's Who You Know

It is a fact that the Novak sisters' aunt, Anne Schaefer, a well-known actress who was starring in Vitagraph shorts in 1913, was Jane's ticket into the movies. One day while having breakfast with Schaefer, Jane was spotted by Ruth Roland, who was then working for Kalem. Roland suggested the 17-year-old appear in a party scene in her current picture.

An autographed fan photo of a young Jane Novak taken in the teens, likely during her tenure with Vitagraph.

The film also included an actor named Frank Newburg, 10 years older than Jane. Newburg would soon become Jane's one and only husband in her life-time, albeit for only a short time. There appear to be only three Kalem films at this time in which Newburg and Roland were starred – *The Raiders from the Double L Ranch* released July 1, 1913; *The Tenderfoot's Luck* released July

23, 1913; and *Hoodooed on His Wedding Day* released August 1, 1913. The timing flows well with the date of Jane's first release for Vitagraph, which was in October. So, in which of these three did Jane appear? Since she was an extra, her name, of course, is not associated with any of them. Also, being lost films, their descriptions do not help to determine which may have included a "party scene" as the story goes.

The first two films Jane made for Vitagraph were *Anne of the Trails*, a two-reel western drama released October 6, 1913, and *At the Sign of the Lost Angel*, released October 27. By early 1914, she had become one of Vitagraph's four main leading ladies, along with her aunt, Myrtle Gonzalez, and Patricia Palmer.

In *The Return of Jack Bellew* (January 26, 1914), Jane has two suiters, Jack Mower and Robert Thornby. It's the story of two sailors, who, while out to sea, come to blows while fighting over Jane's hand in marriage. In the midst of this altercation, one pushes the other overboard. Of course, the "dead man" returns, scaring his competitor so badly that he falls into the sea, never to return.

Jane's growing popularity can be ascertained by looking at newspaper advertisements of the Vitagraph shorts. In some of them, although she may not have been the star, the billing would read: "Jane Novak in . . ."—with no mention of other cast members. For one of her films, *An Innocent Delilah*, the newspaper identified her as "Jane Novak, the famous Russian actress." Jane's 23 shorts for Vitagraph over the next year and a half proved to be a good training ground for her.

In late 1914, Jane went to the Bradbury Mansion on the corner of Hill and Court Streets, in downtown Los Angeles. The 35-room home, in the Bunker Hill section, was built in 1886; in 1914, it provided shared studio space for the fledgling Universal and Hal Roach. Jane was there to try out for a part in a Universal picture. Although she lost out to another actress, she was offered a job by Roach, appearing opposite Harold Lloyd in four one-reelers for the Rolin Company. The first of these was *Willie Runs the Park* (released January 2, 1915), in which the neophyte comedian assumes the character Willie Work.

Before her next Lloyd film was released, more than three months later, three of her Vitagraph shorts hit the screens: *The Worthier Man* (in February) co-starring Jack Mower and George Stanley; *The Other Man's Wife* (released in March) co-starring the same two leading men; and *Her Gethsemane* (in early April) in support of her aunt Anne Schaefer.

April 19, 1915, saw the release of the Hal Roach–produced *Just Nuts*, with Lloyd once again in his Willie Work character. This is the only one of the four films she made with Lloyd that survives today. Harold Lloyd biographer Annette D'Agostino Lloyd said of Jane:

> Her work with Lloyd, as a result, can only be fully assessed from that one surviving film. While it can be said that character development was not high on the list of priorities at that point (even for the starring character of Willie Work), Novak makes an impression, not because of her work with her co-stars, but because of her face, which was bright, vivacious, perennially smiling and quite attractive. In that one reel, she can be seen as a promising young actress who, given the right vehicle with better material, could really shine.

Roy Stewart appeared in both films. Although not a comedian, he was only in his second year as an actor and was, thus, finding his way. Roach wisely saw that there was more to the tall, rugged Stewart than to be wasted as a foil for a slapstick comedian. Stewart was the star of the next two films in which Jane appeared for Roach—with Lloyd in minor supporting roles.

From Italy's Shores, released May 19, 1915, was a two-reel drama about an Italian couple (Stewart and Novak) who have just arrived in New York and are taken advantage of by thugs. This was followed by *Into the Light*, a.k.a. *The Hungry Actors* (released June 17). Stewart is a burglar who surprises Jane one night when he breaks into her home. Later, repentant, he becomes a parson who takes pity on a bandit, played by Lloyd.

These were certainly better roles for Jane than simply serving as the "pretty girl" in Willie Work comedies; they did also prove to be the precursor of a better career for Stewart. He signed with Triangle the following year, became a star, and soon found his niche as a western hero.

On March 15, 1915, Roach, Lloyd, and Jane went to the official opening of Universal City, a huge movie-making complex on the 230-acre Taylor Ranch property in what is now the North Hollywood area. It was a gala affair with state-of-the-art film stages on display, daredevil stunt pilots, personal appearances of Universal's idols, and more. Roach, who was a friend of Universal head Carl Laemmle, introduced Lloyd and Jane to the great man and Pat Powers, at that time, Universal's treasurer.

Powers had formed his own movie company but merged with Laemmle in 1912. Jane would remain close friends with both men for the rest of their lives. However, when she met Laemmle, he asked her if she would like to work for *him*. At first, she said she could not as she was working for Roach. Assuming that the arrangement would be on a temporary basis, Roach gave his permission for Jane to appear for Universal while he was in New York. But Jane did not return. She stayed at Universal through five features, one serial, and 22 shorts.

After making a two-reeler for Universal, Jane was finally cast in her first feature film, *The Scarlet Sin*, with Hobart Bosworth as her leading man. Bosworth, born in 1867, had been a sailor (starting at a young age), a semi-professional boxer, a wrestler, a rancher, and a painter before deciding on a theatrical career. He worked on the stage for a few years, but life soon found him working in a mine in Utah and then touring as a magician's assistant. Back on the stage in his early twenties, he gained a reputation and soon became a lead actor. A bout with tuberculosis robbed him of his stage voice, a loss that would go unnoticed in silent films. He began with the Selig Company in 1908, and by 1913 he had formed his own company. By the time he worked with Jane in 1915, his reputation on the silent screen had been firmly established.

The onscreen partnership of Jane Novak and Hobart Bosworth was, within the Universal fold, a boon to Jane's career. *The Scarlet Sin*, a four-reeler, has Bosworth as a small-town pastor who confronts the story's villain over the safety of the local mine. In the midst of the pastor's troubles, his wife (Jane) leaves him. In the end, she returns to ask forgiveness but loses her life while saving their baby from a fire. *Variety*'s review heaped praise on Bosworth, the film, and Jane. "She looked well, acted convincingly, and did all that was expected of her admirably." *Film Daily* agreed, saying that she played her part "exceedingly well."

Jane's beauty rarely went unnoticed in reviews. The sole two-reeler she did for Universal, released two months prior to *The Scarlet Sin*, was *The Mysterious Escort*. An unidentified columnist for *The Chronicle-Telegram* in Elyria, Ohio, gushed:

> Now it would be an utter impossibility for me to continue with my
> story this week if I did not take this opportunity of voicing my opinion
> of this charming little actress. I will admit that I had never heard of
> Jane Novak, although I understand that the youthful leading lady has
> been a star in comic opera and very successful in pictures. However,
> I dropped into the beautiful projection room at the Universal New
> York offices the other day to see one or two new pictures, and I was
> indeed startled, for on the screen I beheld one of the most bewitch-
> ing faces I have ever seen. I was fascinated and determined to find
> out all I could about her. And I did. She is a new Universalite and is at
> Universal City playing in Rex Films. I know you will be charmed with

her. What impressed me perhaps more forcibly than her extraordinary beauty was her evident desire to please her audiences. . . her remarkable beauty and real ability to act will win Jane Novak worldwide fame. At least, such is the opinion of a mere fashion writer. I shall send for her photograph and hope to have her on my page very soon.

The release of Jane's first feature-length film—with good reviews—was not the only significant event for her in 1915. Two months prior to the film's release, in May, Jane had married Frank Newburg, an actor she had met at Kalem back in the summer of 1913. Jane was 19 years old, and Newburg was 29. It was not destined to be a happy union. Her screen partnership with Bosworth would be much more successful.

By the time Jane co-starred with Hobart Bosworth in The Scarlet Sin *(1915)*, he was an established star. Jane and Bosworth would make a total of five films together—just as many as she made with William S. Hart.

A Little Brother of the Rich (released in September), based on a successful novel and stage play, tells the story of a small-town boy who leaves his fiancée for a city woman. The jilted girl (Jane) joins a stock company and reforms an alcoholic actor (Bosworth), who falls in love with her. Disillusioned by the city girl's insincerity, the boy returns to his paramour. Seeing the two together, the actor goes back to drinking. Of course, the girl rebuffs the boy, and the actor and the girl eventually marry. *Photoplay* magazine's description of her performance is just what one would expect: "Jane Novak gives sweetly sympathetic support as Sylvia Castle."

Jane's tenure at Universal was essentially what made her a star. She was being given first-rate stories, good production values, and the ongoing assist of the redoubtable Hobart Bosworth. *The White Scar*, which hit theaters in December 1915, is set in the Northwest. This time, Bosworth is a fur trapper; Jane is the girl he loves, a romance that is complicated by the fact that the girl is already engaged to someone else. An interesting side note is that Frank Newberg was once again in a film with Jane—this time as her brother, who is framed by her intended for stealing skins.

Filming began in September in the Bear Lake Mountains near San Bernardino. The hotel in which the company was staying caught fire, and it was reported that the cast and crew served as "firemen." The only one without a bucket of water was the cameraman, who gained some authentic footage for future use.

Continued Next Week . . .

Graft, a lost serial, consisted of 20 chapters, released weekly from December 1915 through April 1916. The premise involved a young lawyer, Bruce Larnigan, whose district attorney father was killed for going after a powerful graft trust. Larnigan is elected the next district attorney and vows to bring to justice the group of unidentified men known as "The Fifteen." A different Hobart—Hobart Henley—was the original star of the film. However, due to an automobile accident that crushed his ankles, he had to withdraw from the role. He later returned, wheelchair ridden, to appear in some later chapters. Henley can be seen in chapters 1, 2, 3, 7, 11, and 12. Harry Carey, in the role of Larnigan's brother, Tom, stepped in the lead for chapters 4, 5, 6, 8, 9, and 10. Actual filming was done at Henley's room in the hospital—Carey, as Tom Larnigan, receives instructions at his brother's bedside. The final eight chapters had Richard Stanton, the director of the serial, along with George Lessey, a late addition, leading the fight for justice. Jane, as Dorothy Maxwell—the love interest for Bruce Larnigan—was in all 20 chapters.

Political corruption is the subject of *The Iron Hand* (working titles: "Tainted Money" and "The Man Who Made Good"). It was directed by Ulysses Davis for Universal and released May 29, 1916, at least five months after its completion. Hobart Bosworth plays an unscrupulous political boss, and Jane is the daughter of Bosworth's reforming adversary.

Although Bosworth received top billing, he and Jane were being advertised as a team, indicating the growing value of Jane's name at the box office. She was also attracting more attention in the fan magazines. One interesting tidbit reveals her aptitude for baseball. In December 1915, an all-female baseball club was made up of actresses from the Universal lot. About 20 girls tried out for positions, and, although a final first-string line-up had not been chosen, Jane and Dixie Carr were closely tied for the first-base position.

Jane was nearing the end of her brief tenure with Universal, but it had been a productive association. She was paired yet again with Hobart Bosworth, this time in a five-reel western entitled *The Target*, which was released in March 1916.

The reasons for Jane leaving Universal are unknown. Nor is it clear why she was absent from the screen for the last seven months of 1916; it is also perplexing that her next two films were for minor studios, Continental and Clune.

Entrepreneur Robert Goldstein announced in June 1916 that his Continental Producing Company would make a nine-reel historical spectacle entitled *The Spirit of '76*. The epic film, which was said to be inspired by D.W. Griffith's *The Birth of a Nation*, was released at the same time as the United States' entry into World War I. Goldstein, a German Jew, wrote and produced the film. The story is based on a supposed love affair between King George III of England and a Quaker girl, Catherine, who wanted to be Queen of America. (Interestingly, that is not the part played by Jane; she, instead, was the third feminine lead.) The film depicted many factual events from the Revolutionary War, such as Paul Revere's ride, Lexington, Valley Forge, and the signing of the Declaration of Independence. However, his depictions of the British bayonetting babies, raping unarmed women, as well as the Wyoming and Cherry Valley massacres, landed producer Goldstein in trouble with the federal government. When the film premiered in Chicago, the local police censorship board confiscated the print because of its apparent anti-British sentiment. Goldstein had to make judicious cuts if he wished to continue its exhibition. *The Chicago Daily Tribune*'s regular movie reviewer Mae Tinee (a fake name intended to sound like "matinee") defended the film by asking and answering: "Is it unpatriotic? It is not." When it was shown in Los Angeles later, the offending scenes had been restored. Goldstein was later charged with aiding and abetting the German enemy, and the film was seized again. He was charged with violating the Espionage Act and sentenced to 10 years in prison, later commuted to three years by President Woodrow Wilson. Goldstein's career was over in the U.S., so he later tried to establish himself as a filmmaker in Europe, without success.

Based on a best-selling novel by Harold Bell Wright, *The Eyes of the World* (1917) is the story of a young man (Jack Livingstone), who is convicted for a crime he did not commit. The novelist himself cast Jane in the leading female role of Sybil Andres. According to a trade magazine: "Mr. Wright, who assisted in the filming of his book, said this young woman was precisely the kind of girl he imagined when he wrote the tale of California love and adventure." The same article described Jane as "one of the most beautiful women in the realm of film." Although the producers had a solid story with a proven track record, director Donald Crisp failed to do an effective job of bringing it to the screen. One reviewer described the seven-reeler as "a bit long drawn out, entirely unconcentrated. Much scenery—not much else!"

Jane had one more film released in 1917: *The Innocent Sinner*. Produced for the Fox Film Corporation, it was directed by Raoul Walsh, and starred Miriam Cooper. The story concerns a woman from the country (Cooper) who falls in love with a man from the city (Jack Standing); she goes back with him and becomes enmeshed in the underworld. Jane plays a Good Samaritan who befriends Cooper when her life is at its lowest point. *The Innocent Sinner* wrapped in June of that year—which means Jane worked late into her pregnancy. On August 24, 1917, she gave birth to Virginia Rita Newburg. Jane would have a close, loving relationship with her daughter for the rest of her life.

The Stoic Cowboy

The year 1918 was a significant one for Jane's career as it marked the debut of the first of five features in which she co-starred with William S. Hart. *The Tiger Man*, which was shot on location in New Mexico and released in April 1918, is one of Hart's trademark good-bad man roles as a leader of a gang of outlaws who falls in love with a minister's wife (Jane). When Indians attack a wagon train, he prevents them from sending a distress signal until he can leave with the minister's wife. He does, but later repents and turns himself in.

In a 1921 interview with *The Los Angeles Times* movie editor and columnist Grace Kingsley, Jane recalled the first time she met Hart. It was her friend, actress Vola Vale, who wanted Jane to meet him. Jane, who had recently seen the rugged western star in a film in which he played a loathsome character, told Vale, "No I'm scared of him. I don't want to go. If he was the only actor in the world, I wouldn't go to meet him."

Hart had previously told Vale he was looking for a "little blonde girl" for his next picture and asked her if she knew anyone. Vale told him she did: her friend Jane. "Well," Hart said, "I don't know who Jane is, but whoever she is, bring her over." Finally convinced to go, when she met Hart, he asked if she would do a screen test. She said she was so afraid she could barely speak, but Hart patiently asked her to sit down, and she eventually calmed down enough to do the test. She passed with flying colors.

"The very first day I worked with Hart, he spanked me," Jane recalled. "No, I don't remember why, but I think it was because I had put my hair up high on my head. Anyway, it was a regular cowboy initiation. Imagine sitting there frightened to death of Bill Hart—and then, all of a sudden, he's catching me up and, holding me by the arm as though I were a naughty child, giving me a couple of good spanks. Then somebody nailed me in a packing box and kept me there all the afternoon. They put signs on the box, 'Don't feed the monkey,' sprinkled me with water and exclaimed, 'You'd better get out of there; it's rain-

Jane, with sister Eva, in a photograph from the early 1920s. The sisters were often photographed together and remained close throughout their entire lives.

ing.'" She was even handcuffed, and subjected to such unflattering adjectives as "slow," "awkward," and "lazy." Members of the crew repeatedly told her they couldn't wait until the picture was over so they could get "a *real* leading lady." Jane remained stoic and smiling throughout the entire initiation.

Having lost her fear of Hart, she decided to get back at him the following day. At one point he had to give a serious speech, which would be translated into a lengthy intertitle. She and another girl kidded him from the sidelines. As she laughingly recalled: "I broke him up so badly it took him two hours before he could straighten out his face enough to appear serious in the scene."

Jane admitted that she found it difficult to cry when she was called upon to do so in a scene with Hart: "[T]he idea of play tears, of merely pretending to be sad when one has gone through some of life's realest and deepest experiences, suddenly made me laugh when Mr. Hart told me I must cry. Everybody looked at me. I couldn't cry; that was all. It took me the rest of the day to turn on the tears. But once I had wept, the made-to-order grief came easily for me."

Jane said she was very frustrated once when her efforts failed to impress the company. She explained, "In that picture I had to play 'Nearer My God to Thee' on a quaint little organ in a church scene. I can't play, but I just made up my mind to learn that piece. I took lessons on it, worked awful hard, and kept thinking about the surprise I'd have for the company when I played the organ. The time came. I walked up the church aisle, sat down at the organ, and started to play. Do you know, after all that work and anxiety, that organ wouldn't play one note! Not a single key sounded. It was just an old dummy!"

As did virtually all of Hart's films, *The Tiger Man* received good reviews. One reads: "Incidentally, his new leading lady, Jane Novak, is not only a very charming girl but [is] also well cast in this picture. I liked the unaffected way in which she played the part of the minister's wife who realized that there were things more important than life."

Another Hart film, *Selfish Yates*, followed a month later. In it, Hart is a hardened individual who runs a disreputable saloon in the Arizona desert, but Jane's character ends up reforming him. Thelma Salter, a 10-year-old child star at that time, played Jane's younger sister.

Jane was announced to be Charles Ray's leading woman in three films, the first being *The Claws of the Hun*. As the title implies, this was a departure from Ray's typical homespun, bucolic setting. He is the son of a munitions manufacturer who becomes entangled with enemy agents. With the nation embroiled in World War I, it was obviously made to cash in on the patriotic fervor sweeping the country. However, the other two Ray films centered around his country

Charles Ray set aside his country boy character to cash in on the World War I fervor with The Claws of the Hun *(1918). The story concerns the son of a munitions manufacturer who becomes embroiled with enemy agents. This was the first of three films in which Jane appeared with Ray.*

boy character. Jane was cast in both films as the sweet and innocent girl who loves him with undying faith.

There was one more film for Jane in 1918, wedged in between two of the Ray pictures—*The Temple of the Dusk*, starring Sessue Hayakawa. Japanese-born Hayakawa was unique in that he was the first Asian-American star of the movies. His reputation was made by playing the male lead to Fannie Ward in the immensely successful 1915 Cecil B. DeMille picture *The Cheat*. Hayakawa's popularity had grown to such a degree that he formed his own production company (along with his director, William Worthington), Haworth Pictures Corporation, the previous March. *The Temple of the Dusk* was only his second film as an independent. Jane's contribution is limited to the beginning of the film. Her character lives in Tokyo, where her deceased parents were missionaries. Hayakawa is a poet who loves her, but she marries an unfaithful American. After giving birth to a daughter, Jane's character becomes ill and dies—and the poet vows always to protect the child. Later, the father marries his mistress, kills her lover, and the poet accepts the blame to protect the little girl (Mary

Jane made two films with Sessue Hayakawa for his company, Haworth Pictures: The Temple of Dusk *(1918), and* His Debt *(1919, pictured).*

Jane Irving) from humiliation. He escapes from prison to see her one last time, dying in the attempt.

A newspaper blurb in that year of war noted that tanks were on display at Central Park in Los Angeles as several groups raised money for the Fourth Liberty Loan. The notice read: "'Bill Hart Night' took place at this location on the evening of October 4, 1918. Jane Novak, Dora Dale, and other William S. Hart studio stars were on hand to "add their loveliness to the occasion."

Jane kicked off 1919 with back-to-back westerns, one with Hart, the other with Tom Mix, whose popularity was then growing by leaps and bounds. Mix served his apprenticeship in one- and two-reelers, and his westerns were popular in their time and remain entertaining today. Mix had a certain charisma and devil-may-care attitude in his films that was new for a western star. Also, Mix's westerns provided action and stunts not previously seen in cowboy pictures of the teens. The rising cowboy hero was a breath of fresh air after the heavy acting of the screen's first cowboy star, Broncho Billy, and the dour William S. Hart—and, unlike those stalwart men, Mix was strikingly handsome and possessed of a good physique.

Treat 'em Rough, filmed on location in Arizona, opened five days into the new year, 1919. A rancher calls Mix in to hunt down some cattle rustlers. The romance—as far as it typically goes in a Mix western—begins when Jane nurses him back to health from a rattlesnake bite.

Back with Hart for her next picture, *The Money Corral* has the star as a cowhand who wins a shooting contest. As a result, he is hired by a railroad magnate to go to Chicago and guard his vaults. Jane is the magnate's niece and the reason the cowhand, who is reluctant to go to the city, finally agrees to do so.

Continuing the year with one film on the heels of another, her next release was *The Fire Flingers*, directed by and starring Rupert Julian. He plays dual roles, one as a mean, alcoholic husband and a poor printer with a shady past.

The husband owns the printing company, and when he learns that the printer is an ex-con, he discharges him without pay. The printer goes to the husband's home to ask for his salary, resulting in fisticuffs between the two men. During the altercation, the husband is accidentally killed. Due to their striking resemblance, the printer seizes the opportunity to pose as the deceased. The story would be particularly interesting to see because the wife (Jane) prefers the fake husband to the real one! Jane received one of her most glowing reviews for her performance. *Variety* said: "Jane Novak plays the role of the wife and scores decidedly. Miss Novak shows in this production that she is destined to eventually climb to the top in pictures. She is a striking blonde that screens well, and she certainly knows how to use her eyes, and is every inch a trouper."

His Debt, with Sessue Hayakawa in a story of miscegenation, came out in May. Both stars received excellent notices. A newspaper critic had this to say: "Jane Novak . . . is a striking blonde beauty and one of the most talented emotional actresses in the silent drama . . . Miss Novak creates an appealing and human character and registers emotionally with convincing effect."

Lewis Stone (best remembered as Andy Hardy's father in that MGM series during the 1930s and 1940s) was a popular leading man in the silent era. In the late teens, he had his own production company. *Man's Desire*, released in July 1919, was one of his productions, based on a story he wrote. Set in a Northwest lumber camp, Stone valiantly attempts to rescue his wife when the camp bully kidnaps her. During filming in March, Jane was on location as exteriors were shot in Eureka and Truckee, California. The troupe was snowed in during what was called "the worst blizzard in 23 years." With snow piled 15 feet high, the company had to dig themselves out of their two cabins and set to work. "A fierce gale" came up, and Jane suddenly disappeared. Everyone rushed to the spot where she had been, and with shovels, branches, and anything else they could find, they began digging. Finally, a very wet and frightened Jane was rescued from a hole that had been masked by the snow. According to Stone, "If instant help had not been at hand, she would now be taking her long sleep there, with several feet of snow for a shroud."

The company was low on provisions, with no prospect of getting more, and the road leading to the resort was completely covered, making it impossible for any vehicles to traverse the mountain. They voted to make the trek on foot, which took them four hours of walking in the snow. It was noted that Jane "was game" to make the trip.

Man's Desire required a set that included a western gambling hall. Apparently, the company enjoyed playing the various games of chance, and Jane

Wagon Tracks (1919) was Jane's fourth film with William S. Hart, the star with whom she would forever be associated.

won $55,000 on the first day in "tentative" money. She lost 73 cents in real money the following day.

Back with Hart for the second time in 1919, Jane co-starred in *Wagon Tracks* (released in July). In this tightly knit story, Buckskin Hamilton (Hart) tries to determine who killed his brother, Billy—supposedly in self-defense—during an altercation on a riverboat with two gamblers, one of whom is Jane's brother. Later, they are all crossing the country on a wagon train. Jane admires Buckskin for his kindness to everyone and confesses that the shooting was not done in self-defense—although she is uncertain as to which of the two men fired the shot. Buckskin takes a long walk in the desert with the two suspects to extract a confession.

During the filming of *Wagon Tracks* in the Mojave Desert, Hart and company set up their own township, Cactus Center. Hart, of course, was mayor, and Jane was appointed sheriff. Anyone who misbehaved was punished by being "chapped" (which is basically being "spanked" with a pair of chaps). One wonders if Jane administered the "chapping."

Jane stepped out with something totally different for her next film. A Vitagraph production, *The Wolf* hit screens in August and starred Earle Williams, who was 16 years Jane's senior and had been in films since 1908. Also in the cast were George Nichols, who had acted in many of the Biograph films for D. W. Griffith, and the perennial villain Robert McKim. This is a heavy drama laid in the Canadian Northwest and featuring a girl who is seduced and impregnated. She is left to wander into the forest, where she is ultimately devoured by wolves—hardly light entertainment. But that's not the part Jane plays. McKim tries to take her away later, but the boy who loves Jane—and is the brother of the girl devoured by wolves—ends up killing McKim.

The film reviewer for *The Los Angeles Times* was more than a bit smitten by Jane: "Any time that lovely and expressive bit of skirt, Jane Novak, appears in a picture, I'm going to see it! Who wants to wager she won't be a star within a year? Certainly, nobody has won the luminous niche by more consistently good work or greater personal charm than this young woman. Jane Novak, to me, was the best part of *The Wolf*."

In 1919 alone, Jane worked for Vitagraph, Paramount-Artcraft, Robertson-Cole, Haworth Pictures, Universal, and Fox. She wasn't under contract, but she was in demand, with seven films in 1919, and one more to go—the only film she made in which she dies, and in a most unpleasant way. Little known by silent movie fans until its home video release in 2017, *Behind the Door*, a Thomas H. Ince production, has gained a certain degree of popularity due to its intense and gruesome story by Gouverneur Morris.

Hobart Bosworth stars as an American of German ancestry in a small Maine town during the war. Knowing he would be ostracized by the township if they learned his Germanic last name, Krug, he secretly marries a local girl, Alice (Jane), enlists, and on the strength of his seafaring background is given command of an American ship. Alice, who has been turned out by her father because of the marriage, stows away on the ship. The ship is sunk, and Alice and Krug are picked up by a German U-boat. Krug is set adrift—swearing vengeance on the captain as the U-boat sinks into the water. Alice is gang raped, killed, and her body is released into the ocean. A year later, Krug is in command of another ship and captures the U-boat captain, who does not recognize him. Playing on their mutual German heritage, the U-boat commander's tongue becomes loosened the more he drinks. This is when Krug learns the terrible fate of his wife. He takes the commander behind closed doors and makes good on his earlier threat—he skins him alive.

Wallace Beery—who never disappoints in a role—is excellent as the evil U-boat commander. However, it's difficult to watch Jane being brutalized. Although hardly a typical silent film, it received enthusiastic reviews. *The New*

York Times called it "grim and gruesome," but also said it is "compelling by its force and precision," praising the acting of Bosworth, Jane, and Beery, as well as Irvin V. Willat's direction. The ending has Krug's spirit rising to meet Alice's, but as the *Times* astutely pointed out, the ending "would be beautiful in another story, but nothing can be convincingly beautiful arising out of such a substance of horror and hate as *Behind the Door* is made of." *Motion Picture News* called it "an opus in brutality—an intermezzo in gory revenge."

Marriage Woes

In the almost five years since they were married, little was said of Jane's marriage to Frank Newburg outside of the announcement of the birth of Virginia in August 1917. In the summer of 1920, however, the couple found themselves all over the newspapers.

Jane and Newburg had separated in April, and in May she sued for divorce. The couple, who resided at 6629 Hollywood Boulevard, found themselves in the courtroom of Judge Crail, where testimony began on June 18.

Jane claimed that, because of her husband's jealous nature, he struck her on two occasions. In one instance, she explained, "He came home under the influence of liquor and, walking up to me, struck me with his fist with such force that I fell into the bathtub." Several times, she asserted, he pretended to take poison. He succeeded in terrifying her, and, she claimed, "It tended, in a measure, to frighten [our] four-year-old daughter, Virginia."

She said that he was frequently intoxicated and that he followed her from their home to the studio and spied on her often. In addition, she said, he called her "a rat," and told her he would "see her in the gutter," adding, "You will crawl to me yet." In addition to cursing her, he once threatened her with the revolver they kept in the house. "Then he said I was a chuck-headed fool," she testified.

A charge was not specified, although she said she did have him arrested once. Newburg denied all accusations and countered that Jane's reason for divorce was her sudden prosperity and "rise in filmland." In response to the charge that he knocked her in the bathtub, he said he threw up his arm to ward off what looked like a blow and accidentally struck her on the cheek. He also claimed that he was responsible for getting her more money as an actress and he categorically denied having called her "opprobrious names."

"She told me we were too close together all the time," he continued, "and that one of us ought to take a trip somewhere. I could not afford to go to New York at that time. I admit, in a business argument, I told her she did not look at things like I did and that she did not have any sense." Newburg claimed that while his wife was acting, he often washed the dishes and took care of the baby to help her out. "Now that she is up and I am down, she wants to get rid of me. I sacrificed my whole future in order to push her forward. I have been a good manager and a good husband. I have saved that woman commissions and expenses on her wardrobe; now she wants to throw me off."

Judge Crail said, "The husband seems to want to take her back." He addressed Jane. "What do you say?" Jane simply shook her head.

Newburg testified that he had met Jane's aunt years before and saw a photo of Jane on the bureau. He asked who the girl was, and the aunt replied, "She is my niece." Newburg said he told her, "She would make a dandy motion picture star." From that encounter with the aunt, he began corresponding with Jane.

It was brought out in the trial that Jane was earning $600 a week. She said she had earned $34,000 during their married life and had a wardrobe worth about $12,000. The judge asked her if she had saved any money. She replied that she had saved all she could after paying the bills.

Jane was granted a divorce on June 19 on the grounds of mental and physical cruelty. The final judgment on the division of property, however, was delayed for another week.

Coincidentally, just as Jane was in the throes of the divorce proceedings, a one-page article about Jane and daughter Virginia appeared in the April issue of *Picture Play Magazine*. It reads:

> Her name is Virginia Rita Newburg. She is the manager of Jane Novak, the picture star, whom Virginia calls "Muzzer." At home, "Muzzer" Jane is Mrs. Frank Newburg . . . "Daddy was an actor," Virginia said. "Now he's just Daddy." And the timing of the following comment must have taken Jane aback while pleading her case against Newburg in court: "It really was Frank's confidence in me that made everything possible. I am not a star, but I have what many stars have not—good parts in good stories."

Details of property settlement and visitation (twice a week) of Virginia were ironed out, but in October, Newburg had Jane back in court, charging that she was intending to violate the court order by taking their child from the jurisdiction of the court to New York. However, Jane did obtain a court order, allowing her to take Virginia with her on location in Oregon until December 15.

In October of the previous year, it was announced that Jane was chosen for the first picture in Marshall "Mickey" Neilan's new production company (with releases through First National). His first picture would be *The River's*

End (1920), a drama by James Oliver Curwood. Jane starred once again with the dependable Lewis Stone.

Set in the gold fields of the Canadian Northwest (although filmed in Bear Valley, California), the story has Stone in the dual roles as a man falsely accused of a murder and the Canadian mounted policeman pursuing him. The movie received excellent reviews, most praising Neilan for his direction and cinematography (including superb double exposures of Stone in his dual roles). Stone, of course, received his share of credit, and Jane was being noticed as well. *The New York Times* paid a nice compliment by saying that she "plays up to her own high standard." And, as usual, her beauty did not go unnoticed. *Variety* said she was "sweetly pretty and prettily sweet."

Her next picture was in theaters in June. Goldwyn Pictures' *The Great Accident* starred Jane and Tom Moore. It is the story of a former alcoholic who accidentally becomes mayor, cleans up his act, and cleans up the town. As were so many movies in this era, *The Great Accident* was taken from a serialized story in *The Saturday Evening Post*.

In September 1919, Jane was in San Francisco, meeting with the American Lifeograph Company, a short-lived studio based in Portland, Oregon. It was later announced that she would appear in their production of *The Golden Trail*, with Jack Livingstone and Jean Hersholt, which was to be filmed in the Portland area. This tale of murder has Jane playing two parts—the innocent Jane Sunderlin, who accompanies her brother to Alaska, and "Faro" Kate, who works in the Golden Trail Saloon. It's interesting that the *Variety* review of the film identifies Jane as Juanita Hansen, who was a star of modest popularity and bore no resemblance to Jane. *Motion Picture News* opined that she had "never appeared to greater advantage than in this picture."

Her last release for 1920 was *Isobel; or The Trail's End*, which came out in December, another James Oliver Curwood story set in the Northwest. House Peters is a mounted policeman out to get Jane's husband for murder, and he falls in love with her.

Engagement Denials

In March 1921, Hart was busy answering questions about an engagement and denying the claim. His statement of denial appeared in newspapers across the country. "The fact that Miss Jane Novak is now working with me [Jane was then co-starring in her fifth film with Hart, *Three Word Brand*], and the fact that I have a great admiration for her, as well as a high opinion of her ability as an actress, has probably given rise to the present rumors which, unfortunately for me, are positively not true." Although Jane was not quoted directly, Eva, speaking on her sister's behalf, also denied the rumor.

The headline blared, "Movie Star to Wed Jane Novak," and, in typical florid style of the day, the accompanying article reads:

> The screen beauty has played the leading role opposite Hart in several of his pictures of the great outdoors. In order to make the pictures end, as someone seems to have ruled that all pictures must end, it became necessary many times for bighearted "Bill" Hart to pose before the camera with the star in his arms. In so doing, it is told, Miss Novak awakened the love in the actor's heart. The play scenes gradually became transformed into settings of reality.

For essentially all of 1921, fan magazines and newspapers carried stories claiming that Jane Novak and William S. Hart were engaged to be married. Both stars vigorously denied the rumor whenever questioned about it.

Reporters, it stated, were unable to interview Jane or Hart, but "an intimate friend" of the two was found and vouched for the truthfulness of the engagement.

The stories continued, and later in March, one headline proclaimed that not only was Hart to wed Jane—he would also retire from the screen. In its defense, the writer states that such rumors have been "without confirmation." Of course, this very "dependable" news report also mistakenly said Jane and Hart co-starred in *The River's End*. This was not a Hart picture, but, as stated earlier, it co-starred Lewis Stone.

Then in May, it was said she was wearing a diamond ring, the diamonds numbering 33 and that "[s]he said she is to be married in August." However, in September, when asked about the engagement reports, Hart said, "There was nothing to that." He continued, "Miss Novak appeared as my leading woman in five pictures, and her sister, Eva, in two, so that the name of Novak runs through seven of my films. Usually, I change my leading woman for every picture, so the fact that Miss Novak stayed so long in my support probably started that report. She is a sweet, lovely girl, but there's no such good luck in the cards as my marrying her. In fact, there's no one I'm going to marry." Hart also denied the rumors of his retirement. Yet vigilant reporters did question why Hart was making enlargements to his home in Beverly Hills and that he had been seen away from the set, socializing with Jane.

The August issue of *Picture Play Magazine* devoted an entire article to the marriage as a foregone conclusion. It began: "So Bill Hart is going to marry Jane Novak! Anyway, that's what folks say." Author Helen Ogden noted that she had been on the set with Hart and Jane in the past and observed, "Somehow you're not a bit surprised to see Bill pick Jane up, as happens every once in a while, and kiss her." It's difficult to believe Hart typically did this with his leading ladies—other than onscreen, of course. As noted, Ogden wrote of the impending marriage not as a rumor, but fact. Her next observation would confirm it was more than a platonic relationship: "They don't go out to cafés or big parties, these two, but they often keep Sister Mamie Hart happy, of evenings, at Bill's big house in Beverly Hills. They go to the theater together a good deal, too, and enjoy long motor trips to seaside and mountains in Bill's big car." The presence of Mamie Hart should be noted as she would become very prominent in court proceedings about 20 years hence.

However, December brought an end to the rumors. "Is it true that you are engaged to Jane Novak?" the reporter asked bluntly. "Boy," he said, "she's the finest little woman in the world—one of God's own creatures—but there's no engagement. And I guess there won't be one." The "I guess there won't be one" is a little suspicious—was Hart turned down by Jane? Jane would not publicly admit there had ever been an engagement until nearly 60 years later. In articles published long after the silent era, it would be stated that she was once engaged to Hart, a fact Jane neither confirmed nor denied. However, in a 1976 interview, the reporter said she was engaged to Hart for nearly five years—and that during that time, they came close to tying the knot twice. Jane said in this interview that she was the one who "backed off," but added that she could not remember exactly why.

On December 8, 1921, an announcement hit the newspapers that Hart had married Winifred Westover, a "minor player" in some of his films. Westover had appeared in a secondary role in only one Hart film, *John Petticoats* (1919). Her career was a respectable one, if a bit short. She had done a couple of westerns with Buck Jones and one with Harry Carey. She was also the female lead to such popular leading men as William Russell, Charles Ray, Eugene O'Brien, and Conway Tearle. She even had the title role in *Anne of Little Smokey*, released in 1921 by a minor company, Wisteria Productions. However, by the following September (1922), she and Hart were in divorce court. They had separated in May, and divorce proceedings had begun while she was still pregnant. After the divorce, Westover disappeared from the screen.

A January 1922 article in *Photoplay* magazine predated the December 1921 wedding announcement since periodicals are typically on the magazine stands a full month before the cover date. It reads,

> Aside from her screen reputation, Miss Novak's chief claim to fame
> has been the frequency with which her engagement to William S. Hart
> has been announced. When the papers are shy a picture for Monday
> morning, they publish a pretty one of Jane Novak above the rumor
> that she and Bill are going to be married soon.

Apparently, this issue of *Photoplay* was also "shy a picture" because they filled a full page with a portrait of the lovely Jane with just such a caption below.

Despite the profuse amount of publicity regarding the engagement, Jane was one busy actress. First up in 1921 was *The Other Woman*, an April release for J. L. Frothingham Productions, a company that seems to have lasted about two years. She did have some recognizable names with her in the cast—Helen Jerome Eddy, William Conklin, and Kate Price. Her leading man, though, was Jerome Patrick, a forgotten name. (This may be because he died at 41 years old

Three Word Brand *(1921) was the last of the five films Jane made with William S. Hart.*

in 1923 and only had 10 film credits.) *The Other Woman* was of the soap opera variety, with an amnesiac forgetting his wife and children, marrying another, and, in the end, his first wife nobly concedes that the second wife should have his name. Jane was the second wife. *Motion Picture News* said it "has been called the strangest story ever screened."

Jane's final William S. Hart movie—*Three Word Brand*—came out in October and was greeted by the press and the public with much hoopla.

Some of the publicity surrounded Hart playing not one, not two, but *three* separate roles in the film—a man and his twin sons. The movie didn't exactly "wow" the critics. *Harrison's Reports* said "[I]t is not the kind that one would rave about." *Variety* scathingly said the movie was overshadowed by the single reel cartoon that was shown before it. Interestingly, the reviewer mentioned the love story part of the film, adding, "[F]rom the manner in which the star shares his close-ups with her, it is quite evident that she means more than just a leading lady to him and that there may be more than a rumor in the stories that they are to wed."

Last up for 1921 was *Kazan*, yet another James Oliver Curwood Northwest story, this one dealing with a dog who protects the female lead. Jane is the star of this picture, and the forgotten Ben Deely is the love interest who helps her succeed in bringing to justice the murderer of her father and brother—with the canine Kazan's help, of course.

A star's popularity could be measured by the appearance in newspapers or fan magazines of the time like *Photoplay, Picture Play, Motion Picture Classic*, etc.—as well as newspapers that were hungry for feature material on the stars. Jane was beginning to see her name and photo appear more and more in these publications.

Grace Kingsley was the first motion picture editor and columnist for *The Los Angeles Times*, so being interviewed by her was a boost to any actor's career. Jane's interview, in the September 18, 1921, issue of that publication, was at the height of the Hart-Novak fervor. However, Kingsley made only one reference to the engagement rumor, saying that some people have said that the relationship "has ripened into romance."

Kingsley said she met Jane at her bungalow, which she shared with Eva. Expecting to see a pretense of being the perfect homemaker, she said she quickly learned there was no pretense. Jane was, indeed, a devoted homemaker, cook, and mother. As a matter of fact, the dinner Kingsley had that evening was prepared entirely by Jane.

Motion Picture Magazine writer Gordon Gassaway said, "She loves to be at home; she loves to cook things like roast beef and baked potatoes—not goulash or chop-suey or whatever it is Bohemians eat."

"I'm not a bit Bohemian in tendency if Bohemianism means being flighty and queer and bobbed-hairish," Jane explained.

In 1924, *Motion Picture Classic* writer Dorothy Donnell continued to emphasize Jane's reputation as a homebody:

> You don't see her pale golden head among the jazzing dancers at the
> Cocoanut Grove, she does not care for the noisy gaiety of film night
> at the Montmartre, and bootleggers do not have her address. In short,
> Jane Novak is an old-fashioned girl—the kind women would pick out
> as daughters-in-law, the sort men think their mothers must have been,
> a girl such as girls used to be before they became vamps, cuties, flap-
> pers, Shebas and baby dolls. She is almost the only star in Hollywood
> who still has a use for hairpins and hasn't any use for a match-box in
> her vanity case.

In the previously mentioned Kingsley interview, the reporter continued to describe Jane's personality, saying she is "absolutely fearless when it comes to doing any stunt in a picture. A fine emotional actress of the repressed school, she is yet quiet, gentle, serene as a May morning . . . She is quiet and shy but has positive opinions and reads Shaw and Mrs. Browning and H. G. Wells."

One of the reasons that "outdoor actors crave her services," Kingsley explained, is because she is "brave, a fearless horsewoman and swimmer, and a great lover of the open air. She takes long hikes by herself when on location . . . and loves talking to the birds and little creeping things whose shyness rivals her own."

For physical attributes, a fan magazine reported in 1921 that Jane was 5'7" and her weight was 135 lbs.

In the Clutches of Chester

Chester Bennett, the director-producer for whom Jane made seven films beginning in 1921. It was rumored that the two were involved in a romantic relationship.

Chester Bennett was born in San Francisco on February 12, 1892. Before entering movies as an actor in 1917, he had practiced law. His supposed service as an aviator in World War I is unconfirmed. He and actress Gladys Tennyson were married in December 1917 after appearing together in a Victor short entitled *In the Clutches of Milk*. That was Bennett's last appearance as an actor, next moving into the director's chair. When he formed his production company, and Jane went under contract with him, six of her nine films over the next two years would be for Bennett.

It was obvious that Jane and Bennett had a close relationship. She was recently divorced, and, although Bennett was still married, it is not clear if he and Tennyson had separated. It wasn't until August 1925 that Bennett's divorce from Tennyson was finalized. A month later, Tennyson married actor Earle Fox.

Final camera work was completed on Jane's first film for Bennett, *Belle of Alaska*, at the end of October 1921. In her most recent film (*The Rosary*, an undistinguished drama for Selig-Rork that she filmed after *Kazan*), Wallace

JANE NOVAK IN "COLLEEN OF THE PINES"

WHAT GHASTLY SIGHT FROZE THEIR EYES?

Jane and Edward Hearn starred in Colleen of the Pines *(1922), one of several films Jane made with a Northwest setting.*

Beery had played the heavy. This time, that designation was given to his brother, Noah Beery, who is Jane's husband in the film. He basically abandons her in Seattle on the way to the gold fields of Alaska. A dance hall owner falls in love with her and, in the end, the two men fight it out for the girl. *Exhibitors Herald* called it an excellent drama and said it had "one of the best fights in the final reel ever screened." Upon its release in March 1922, *Motion Picture News* said, "Jane Novak is deserving of no small credit for her work in this production, assuming the role of a Kansas housewife with ease and familiarity that is almost convincing, even to a native Jayhawker."

Jane's first collaboration with Bennett proved to be a success. But long before they knew what the reception would be, they were hard at work on Jane's second picture for the producer. Sometime toward the end of November, the company was at Big Bear Lake in the San Bernardino Mountains, about 100 miles east of Los Angeles. They were filming scenes for what was then called "The Starveling." The location filming was finished around the second week of December, which made it possible for Jane to spend Christmas at home with her daughter, who by this time was nicknamed "Mickey." Eva was on break, too, and the sisters were able to spend Christmas together.

Jane's métier seemed to be outdoor pictures, and *Colleen of the Pines* (the final title for "The Starveling," released July 9, 1922) was no exception. In the Northwest, Joan (Jane) claims an illegitimate baby as her own to protect her younger sister from their father's wrath. Joan also inherits a murder charge against her sister and is taken into custody by a dashing Northwest mounted policeman who doesn't realize Joan is the "colleen" he had met earlier. All is cleared up in the end when the younger sister is exonerated after the supposedly murdered man (the baby's father) shows up alive. She gets married and claims her baby. Of course, Joan and the mounted police officer end up together as well.

Jane and Chester Bennett once again had a successful picture on their hands. So, to continue the formula for success, their next picture, *The Snowshoe Trail* (released September 17, 1922) was again set in the Northwest. Virginia (Jane), her guardian (Herbert Prior), and their guide, Bill (her old friend Roy

The Snowshoe Trail (1922) pairs Jane with Roy Stewart, with whom she worked back in her Rolin days in 1915. Stewart helps her travel to the snow-covered Northwest in search of her errant husband, but, in the end, she and Stewart fall in love.

Stewart from her Rolin days) set out to locate her worthless fiancé. However, her affections are transferred to Bill when he twice saves her from danger.

Jane was sick with an unidentified illness for about three weeks in January and February 1922, just prior to beginning work on *The Snowshoe Trail*. However, within the next month, she would be in Truckee for the movie's snow scenes. She told reviewers around this time that she could seldom keep up with the seasons since her life was just "one darn snow or rainstorm after another." The company returned to the studio long enough to replenish supplies and equipment and then headed back out for filming at Keane's Camp, an area presently in the Death Valley National Park.

Thelma, based on the 1887 Marie Corelli novel of the same name, is the story of a Norwegian girl from a small village who marries an English nobleman. In the original treatment, Jane's character was to be shown as a child. Several children were tested for the part, but all were deemed unsatisfactory. Members of the company were in Jane's dressing room discussing their dilemma when four-year old Mickey (Virginia), who was playing with her dolls in the corner, piped up and said, "I look just like mamma, and I want to be a star now 'cause when I grow up, I have to go to school!" The result: Mickey talked herself into a contract.

Unfortunately, Mickey's part was cut from the final film. Jane remembered that after it was previewed, the director decided to cut out the whole episode, and so when the proud Mickey went to the theater to see herself, "the air was rent with her heart-broken wails."

"Wasn't I any good?" she demanded. "Didn't I act right? Why did they leave me out?"

"It's rather a tragedy not to appear at your first appearance!" Jane told a reporter, "but I don't want her to go into the films—at least until she has had all the good times a girl ought to have first."

When the film was released November 26, Jane's portrayal received excellent reviews. One reads: "In the first place, Jane Novak, with her delicate blonde beauty and spiritual loveliness, is perhaps the perfect embodiment of Marie Corelli's heroine. Jane Novak makes Thelma live upon the screen. Her fine traits are thrown into clear-cut relief. As the central figure of an exquisite romance with a British nobleman, she lends a note of poignant appeal to this striking love story." Many reviews, too, pointed out the array of "dazzling" gowns she wore in the film. As most moviegoers were used to seeing her in outdoor dramas, the novelty, as well as her beauty in the gowns, garnered much attention.

A Sweet, Old-Fashioned Girl

Referred to as "Filmland's Old-Time Girl" in the press, it was said Jane began working for a salary of $1,500 a week in March. One reviewer said she reminded one of the song lyric "Sweet old-fashioned girl with eyes so blue . . .," noting that, to her off-screen friends, she is "ever the sweet, old-fashioned girl." Indeed, there was nothing flashy about her acting or appearance. She never exhibited the exuberance and buoyancy of a Clara Bow or a Colleen Moore, and never projected herself as a "jazz baby." Her acting style may be more comparable to, say, a Claire Windsor or Alice Joyce. One reviewer wrote that there was a "charm of simplicity" about her; "somehow, when one meets this exquisite young star—hears the low, modulated voice, sees the soft, dainty blonde beauty of face and hair, and observes the demure charm in her mannerisms, which today are thought quaint—then it is that one realizes her simplicity."

In one fan magazine interview, the writer observes, "She is beautiful. With her natural pallor, her corn-silk hair, her large blue eyes and those emotional mouth corners, I think she is more beautiful off the screen than she is on, and that is saying a great deal."

One fan magazine interviewer in 1922 described Jane thusly: "With her natural pallor, her corn-silk hair, her large blue eyes and those emotional mouth corners . . . she is more beautiful off the screen than she is on, and that is saying a great deal."

To illustrate that beauty is in the eye of the beholder, a female writer for *Photoplay* had this to say about Jane's appearance. She wrote, "She is medium tall, with a slim, girlish figure that adapts itself well to the straight-cut, heavy tweeds she affects. Her eyes are rather light blue—Swedish blue—and not at all out of the ordinary, save perhaps for their expression, which is unusually sweet and placid. Her hair is a nondescript blonde. Her mouth is pretty and very expressive. But, altogether, she is the sort of a person you wouldn't notice in a crowd."

For the frugal Jane, a savvy person who was known for investing and doing a good job of growing her finances, it is somewhat surprising that the Artists Booking Exchange took out a suit against her for $198.20 in June 1922. According to the suit, booking agent John Lancaster had obtained work for her with Selig to appear in *The Rosary*. Jane disagreed over his commission, so the organization sued her and was awarded damages in full. Jane appealed to the Superior Court, but, as of June 8, the case had been stricken from the court calendar, indicating some sort of out-of-court settlement had been reached.

Robert Anderson co-starred with Jane in The Lullaby *(1924), a dismal story of a husband who is sentenced to hang for killing his friend who seduced his bride, and she is sentenced to 20 years as an accessory. Born in prison, her child is taken from her at the age of three.*

Jane's earliest appearance on radio took place on June 16, when she appeared on radio station KHJ just three days after the Los Angeles–based station went on the air. She was there to help promote the All Arts Ball at the Ambassador Hotel, an event to benefit the Art Center. The Art Center's mission was to develop young, artistic talent for those who do not have the funds to educate themselves. The event, being held that same night, included a variety of talent, with Tom Mix serving as the master of ceremonies.

Although Jane was still under contract to Chester Bennett, only one of her three films released in 1923 was directed by Bennett and produced by his company. This was *Divorce* (June 10, 1923), co-starring John Bowers. After that, she made *Jealous Husbands* with Earle Williams, which was directed by Maurice Tourneur and produced by his namesake company.

Then, later that year, Jane and Eva made their one and only joint appearance onscreen. The Metro Picture starring Percy Marmont was *The Man Life Passed By*. Jane and Eva are sisters who befriend Marmont who has fallen on hard times.

Filmed in late 1923, the Chester Bennett produced *The Lullaby* was a drama with Jane getting top billing. It was released in January 1924.

After working so steadily, Jane welcomed the opportunity to spend a few weeks with Mickey, who would turn six that year. On another occasion, a three-week break was necessitated by the onset of a severe cold. Not one to enjoy being idle, she could hardly wait to regain her health and get back to work.

On Location in The Big Apple

Jane traveled to New York for a film shoot in the summer of 1924. Apparently, the sticky hot July weather did not agree with her. As she wrote in a letter to the press:

> Here I have been in New York for the past month doing a picture for Whitman Bennett, and I won't be home for another month or so, as I am going to do a picture for Banner Productions. It is Democratic Convention week here, and you never saw such awful crowds. They simply take your breath away. The city is all decorated and is very inspiring with the national colors flying everywhere. But you should be glad not to be here. The heat and storms are terrible. I am becoming so thin you won't know me, and I am slowly smothering.

Despite the uncomfortable conditions, Jane reported to the former Fine Arts studio on Riverdale Avenue in Yonkers. Her co-stars were Kenneth Har-

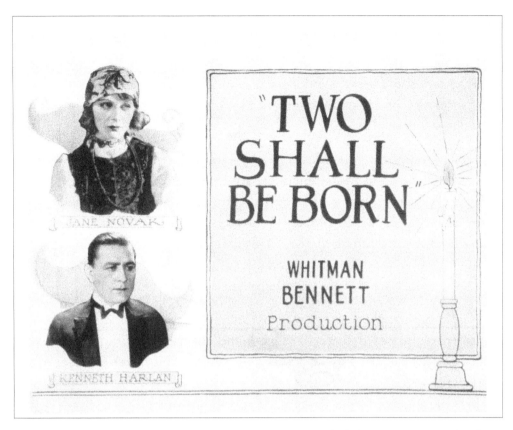

In Two Shall Be Born *(1924), Jane, as the daughter of a Polish count, is entrusted with delivering important documents to New York. She meets and marries Brian Kelly (Kenneth Harlan), a traffic cop who must rescue her when she is kidnapped by the evil Baron von Rittenheim.*

lan and the Swedish import Sigrid Holmquist. The picture, *Two Shall Be Born* (released in December), was produced by the obscure Twin Pictures Corporation and released through Vitagraph. In this opus, Jane is the daughter of a Polish Count who is entrusted to take some important documents to New York but is unable to establish contact. She meets and marries Brian Kelly (Harlan), a New York cop who was disinherited by his millionaire father. A Polish traitor kidnaps the princess and beats her severely to exact the whereabouts of the documents. Kelly, of course, rescues her, and the traitor is turned over to the police. A rather sensationalistic ad for this lost film is illustrated by a picture of Jane, hands tied to a post, her shoulders bared, as a grimacing man stands behind her with a whip.

Also filmed while she was in New York was *The Man Without a Heart* (released in September), a Banner Production, directed by Burton King. In one of the stranger scenarios, this one concerns a man (Harlan again) intent on saving his sister's marriage. To do so, he abducts the woman (Jane) he believes is guilty of infidelity with his brother-in-law. At one point, the abductee mistakes her captor for a vagabond and shoots him. She then proceeds to nurse him back to health.

That Jane's character is innocent of adultery in the picture should come as no surprise. The actress had resolved to retain her virtue onscreen. As one magazine writer explained:

> Jane Novak absolutely refuses to play a woman who goes wrong. She hates five reel and bath dramas, cabaret scenes, cigarets (*sic*) and society "dress up" parts. She adores pictures where little children in white nighties say their prayers in the moonlight at her knee, photo-plays where she can be the womanly influence that reforms rough men, parts with Bibles and gingham aprons and dish-pans in them. She is a real Harold Bell Wright heroine on the screen and off.

Harold Bell Wright was a former minister and a successful writer of fiction, whose characters epitomized hard work and concrete values. It was he who had personally cast Jane in the screen adaptation of his novel *The Eyes of the World*, in 1917.

In reviewing her career thus far, Jane said she was proud of the fact that she had never been called upon to enact a character who was "not open and above board—and a person to be admired." Regarding villains in movies, she said one never makes a hero out of a bad man or a bad woman.

Jane was respected by her peers and was always a hard worker, willing to do most anything for a part—a part she approved of, of course. "I don't believe in being late at the studio, and I don't believe in beating the clock when it comes to going home," she said.

The article stated:

> Some of the things Miss Novak would never do during her picture career are: Not to play with a woman star, not to be late at the studio, not to allow the casting director to put her in any part but one which would fit her type, and not to attend "movie" parties, whatever they are!

> For any girl who loves her family and loves her cute little home as does Jane, I'm here to say that she is certainly a bear for location stuff. She has established a reputation for herself as an 'out-door' (*sic*) girl, and so outdoors she has been!

And Then To Germany

After completing her film work in New York, Jane sailed to Bremen, Germany, in October 1924 to star in a British/German production entitled *The Blackguard*. The original title for its German release was *Die Prinzessin und der Geiger*, which translates to "The Princess and the Violinist." Her co-star was the respected German actor Walter Rilla, who had served as a drama critic before going on the stage and then into films. He worked in both German and French films, and, because of his bearing, he was usually cast as aristocrats. He and his Jewish wife were forced to flee Germany in 1933 as a result of the rising Nazi threat, and he continued his career in England. Although not the typically handsome Hollywood leading man, Rilla was, nevertheless, effective as the emotionally tortured violinist—if less so as a lover.

The Blackguard was filmed at Studio Babelsberg, Potsdam, Brandenburg, Germany, but was made in collaboration with Gainsborough Films, of London, England. It had its UK premiere April 20, 1925, and a German premiere September 4. The film was making the rounds in the U.S. by November.

The Blackguard presents Jane at her loveliest. Although directed by Englishman Graham Cutts, the film has all the hallmarks of German Expressionism,

Jane traveled to Germany to appear in a British/German production entitled The Blackguard *(1925). Jane plays a princess who is saved from the Russian Revolution by a French violinist (Walter Rilla).*

due in great part to cinematographer Theodor Sparkhul. He had photographed a dozen of Ernst Lubitsch's films before that director with the "velvet touch" immigrated to Hollywood in 1922. Shortly after *The Blackguard*, Sparkhul worked from 1928 to 1930 in England, and then in France for a couple of years before making his home in Hollywood. He is credited with being one of the main influences behind the "noir" style of low-key lighting. Through his lighting techniques, Sparkhul deserves much credit for enhancing Jane's beauty in this film. *The Blackguard* also holds a special place in cinematic history because Alfred Hitchcock wrote the screenplay from the Raymond Paton novel and served as both art director and assistant director.

In her *Los Angeles Times* column in January 1925, Grace Kingsley said she had received a letter from Jane while she was on location in Germany. Jane said Rilla was "a fine actor who ought to do well" in the U.S. She added, "I've been wined and dined, toasted, etc., and naturally love it. The voyage over was perfect, but our arrival at Bremen was very dismal. It was gloomy and fright-fully cold, but I had to be photographed, accept loads of flowers and all that. I made a personal appearance at one of the theatres in Bremen, and the box was draped in a huge American flag. When I entered, they played 'The Star-Spangled Banner.' I could have cried out—I was so homesick yet thrilled at the same time."

By mid-February 1925, reports had come in that Jane was ill with influenza at the Savoy Hotel in London. In a letter penned in March, she said she had recovered "a few weeks ago" and was at work on another British production.

One report said she was "lingering" in London due to an unnamed English nobleman who had become enamored with her. One account has their initial encounter occurring while each was out horseback riding. The gentleman did not know who this fragile beauty was, but being smitten, he introduced himself. As expected, when she was questioned about such a romance upon her return to Los Angeles in April 1925, she denied it.

Whether that story was true or not, it is a fact that Jane was at work in March in various European locations on *The Prude's Fall* (English release 1924), whose title was changed to *Dangerous Virtue* when it was released in the States in 1925. She was with the same director she had for *The Black-guard*, Graham Cutts, who had co-founded Gainsborough Pictures. Her co-stars included the English leading man Warwick Ward and the lovely American actress Julanne Johnston, who is likely best remembered as the Princess in Douglas Fairbanks's *The Thief of Bagdad* (1924).

She continued in her letter, "I am at Lake Como, a perfectly gorgeous place, doing *The Prude's Fall* . . . We go to Venice from here, then to St. Moritz, Switzerland, and to London for interiors. Julanne Johnston will meet us in Venice . . . We are the only 'foreigners' in it."

Jane always retained fond memories of the time she spent overseas making movies. Late in life, she told an interviewer, "It was heady stuff," adding that, in Berlin, she had lavish living quarters, a household staff, private dressing room at the studio, dressers, limousines, drivers, and deference on the set never accorded her in Hollywood.

In other words, no one put her in a box and nailed it shut, or sprinkled water on her and told her it was raining.

Back in Hollywood

Jane returned to Los Angeles April 7, 1925, where she was met at the train station by Chester Bennett and Eva. Jane was not scheduled to make another film for Bennett, nor did she for the rest of her career. His frequent presence in her life could lead one to question the depth of their relationship, but, then again, no confirmation of an affair could be found.

With little down time after returning from Europe, Jane reported to work at Columbia for *The Danger Signal* (released in August). For the first time, Jane was cast as the mother of two grown boys (played by Gaston Glass and Robert Gordon), one trustworthy, the other a "bad egg"—and both working for the railroad. A near collision of a passenger train and a freight train was the highlight. *Moving Picture World* said Jane gave "a smoothly-balanced, appealing portrayal of the mother."

Once filming was completed on *The Danger Signal* in late May, the Frank Borzage company left Los Angeles for Kernville, 150 miles west, to begin filming *Lazybones* for Fox, which was to star Buck Jones in a departure from his signature cowboy roles. Established in 1858 as a gold camp, at one time in the 1800s Kernville was better known as Whiskey Flats. When work began on the Lake Isabella reservoir in 1948, the town relocated to higher ground. The Kernville of *Lazybones* has been submerged under the waters of the reservoir since 1954. Over the years, prior to the construction of the reservoir, Kernville was a favored location for westerns.

Jones is Steve Tuttle, the town's recognized "lazybones," who takes on the raising of a fatherless girl, causing a scandal in the town. His sweetheart, Agnes (Jane), leaves him when he refuses to give up the child. Years later, when he returns from the war, he discovers that he loves the now-grownup girl (Madge

Bellamy). However, she weds another—and the film leaves the question open as to whether Steve and Agnes may reunite.

Jane had finished her work on *Lazybones*, so she left Hollywood June 19 on the Santa Fe Limited to begin filming *The Substitute Wife* (released in October) for the low-budget Arrow Film Corp. in New York. Wilfred Noy was imported from England to direct this story of two women who are so much alike that the blind husband of one cannot tell them apart. *Film Daily* liked the film and referred to the "fine acting" of both Jane and Niles Welch, who played the blind husband.

Jane made her third cross-country trip that year on the Santa Fe Limited and, ever the homebody, she admitted she was weary of travel. Keep in mind that she had just returned from Europe in April, Jane said she would be returning home the moment filming was finished in New York in early November.

Lifestyles of the Silent Rich and Famous

Although single and helping to support her mother, Jane was working steadily, earning a good salary and living very comfortably. An indication came with one of those tidbits that studios were so fond of sending out to newspapers—bits and pieces of the star's personal life that fans were so eager to devour. It was reported that Jane had purchased a Chandler automobile, a moderately priced vehicle in those days and an indication of her thriftiness. When she glimpsed the new Chandler Coach Imperial in the showroom window in the fall of 1925, she simply had to have it. The price? $1,595.

Regarding her driving, one interviewer wrote, "She has not become afflicted with chauffeur-itis, which means that she still drives her own coupe. She drove us from the Chet Bennett stage up into the busy parts of Hollywood with her own capable hands, and I'm here to say that she wields a mean throttle!"

Jane arrived back in Los Angeles November 4 looking forward to spending a Christmas season at home with her daughter. And, once again, it was reported that she had signed for four more pictures for Bennett and would be returning to New York in late December. However, Jane made it clear she did not want to continue working in New York. She preferred working in California so that she could spend more time with her daughter, mother, and Eva. Also, upon her return in November, she complained, "The weather back East has been wretched—cold and disagreeable."

Mickey was eight years old and very much the center of Jane's life. "When I'm not in the studio, I go to bed and rest," she said. "There isn't anything else to do. Of course, I help Mickey with her lessons."

One close observer said, "People who tell you, 'Oh Jane is a darling, but so shy—you'll have to do all the talking,' evidently never tried talking about Mickey."

Good News and Bad

Jane received some unexpected publicity in February 1926 when she was headed north to Sonora on Southern Pacific Train No. 64 with director Tom Forman's company. A fellow passenger, Mrs. Bessie Baldwin, was heavily pregnant and was riding in the chair car. Suddenly at 3 a.m., it became evident that she was about to give birth. When Jane learned of this, she immediately turned her drawing room over to Mrs. Baldwin. Fortunately, a registered nurse from Long Beach was on the train and took charge of the birth. When other passengers learned of the event, they passed the hat and raised $102 for the baby. The grateful Mrs. Baldwin named her newborn daughter after Jane.

Whispering Canyon, another western, was filmed at a large logging company outside Sonora, the Standard Lumber Company, located in a valley. Promotional material mentioned that the movie's "big scenes" that had been shot there included the dynamiting of the dam that provided power to the hero's sawmill, a fight between two gangs of lumberjacks, and the kidnapping of the heroine (Jane). Released May 10, 1926, *Whispering Canyon* pleased audiences and undiscerning critics. *Film Daily* said it had "a good plot full of action and intrigue." As for Jane: "Miss Novak charms the audience with creations of every conceivable description. In all of these habiliments, Miss Novak's slender figure appears to advantage, and her blonde loveliness and simple grace are a constant delight to the beholder."

Also around this time, an unwelcome bit of publicity for Jane hit the newspapers: she was one of 83 individuals against whom the Internal Revenue Service had filed suit for delinquent payments. According to the item, Jane owed $209.69 from her 1921 tax return. Wheeler Oakman was the only other actor named, yet his delinquent amount was far beyond Jane's—$7,014.50.

The Natural Look

In the early years of filmmaking, moviegoers were accustomed to seeing actors who were heavily made up for the camera. It is not uncommon to see eye shadow or lipstick— even on the male performers—and a discerning eye may sometimes see that an actor's neck and hands are darker than his face, particularly in the films from the teens. Heavy pancake make-up was required because the orthochromatic film stock of the day rendered pink skies as perpetually overcast, blond hair as washed-out, blue eyes nearly white, and red lips nearly black. The make-up was used, along with lens filters, to make everyone and everything appear as natural as possible. Panchromatic film, which reproduced a scene as it appears to the human eye, had been around since 1913, yet the cost was prohibitive—seven cents per foot as opposed to three cents per foot for orthochromatic; it also required special ordering. Kodak introduced panchromatic film as regular stock in 1922, but the cost was still far more expensive than orthochromatic. By 1926, however, prices were equalized due to increased competition, and from that point on, panchromatic was essentially the industry standard.

It's not a coincidence that Jane was one of a large number of stars who said they were no longer using heavy cosmetics in 1926. Cecil B. DeMille said there would be no greasepaint for the actors and actresses in his next film. Director Allan Dwan had recently directed the Paramount feature *Sea Horses* (1926) with Florence Vidor, Jack Holt, William Powell, and George Bancroft, none of whom used make-up—and Dwan reported that it was a success. Joining Jane in swearing off greasepaint were Esther Ralston, Mary Brian, Betty Bronson, Theodore Roberts, Wallace Beery, Ernest Torrence, Raymond Hatton, Alice Terry, and sister Eva, among others.

"Jane Novak Says . . ."

Photos such as this one of Jane from the late twenties were typically sent out to fans who wrote requesting a picture of their favorite star.

From the earliest days of motion pictures, stars endorsed various products for compensation; virtually everyone with box-office clout would turn up in one advertisement or another. Jane was no exception. Mayo-Wright Properties was a company promoting the sale of apartment-homes in a five-story complex known as the Los Altos, which had just opened in 1926. The apartments would soon become home to such luminaries as Bette Davis, William Randolph Hearst, Douglas Fairbanks Jr., Marion Davies, Howard Hughes, and Clara Bow. A May 12, 1926, ad in *The Los Angeles Times* was all about Jane's purchase of an apartment there; a large portrait accompanied the ad, along with PR quotes supplied by a professional copywriter. Interestingly, one such quote reads that she and her manager, Chester Bennett, agreed the apartments "provided an ideal home for this young star." Jane supposedly added, "In my work, we must have our time free from unnecessary domestic work since we never know when the call will come to be at the studio. Yet the ordinary apartment, and certainly a hotel, does not afford the privacy you feel you should have. The Los Altos gives me just the privacy I like yet does not burden me with needless responsibility."

(The Los Altos went bankrupt during the Great Depression. The building went into disrepair until 1993 when a local housing group rescued it from demolition. Los Angeles-based architectural firm M2A was hired and rehabilitated the 75-unit structure, bringing back its original decor. The firm restored or recreated the building's original light fixtures, hardware, carpets, plasterwork, awnings, and ornamental ironwork. This resulted in several preservation-design awards and earned a listing in the National Register of Historic Places.)

Fading Stardom

In the first half of the 1920s, Jane had worked for some prominent studios and producers—Marshall Neilan at First National, Goldwyn Pictures, William S. Hart at Paramount, William Selig, Maurice Tourneur Productions, and Fox Pictures. And although she had also worked for a few minor companies—American Lifeograph, for example—her production companies from about 1924 forward were more often poverty row studios such as Banner, Tiffany, and Arrow. She made seven films for Chester Bennett, an independent producer—not exactly a major studio, but Bennett typically had the distribution of his films through a respectable firm like Film Booking Offices (FBO). Also, when an actor or actress went overseas to make movies, it was usually a sign their star had begun to fade.

In early 1927 the latest Jane Novak picture, *One Increasing Purpose*, starring Edmund Lowe, Lila Lee, Holmes Herbert, May Allison, and Huntley Gordon, made its debut in theaters. Although Jane was not the female lead (that distinction belonged to Lila Lee), it was at least a return to a major studio—Fox Film Corporation. Still, her name sat at the bottom of the credits. She had been making pictures now for about 14 years and would be entering the dark side of 30 that January. The highest-grossing female stars of 1927 were Clara Bow, Colleen Moore, and Bebe Daniels—a clear indication that the public was very much in tune with the Jazz Age and the flapper genre. Jane, apparently, didn't possess what Elinor Glyn called "It!" Nor did she have the capital to produce her own pictures in the manner of industry superstars Mary Pickford and Norma Talmadge. The fact was, Jane was identified with the style of dramas that had been popular in the late teens and early twenties. Keep in mind that as far back as 1922, she had been given the nickname of "Filmland's Old-Time Girl"—not a tag anyone would want to carry around in 1927. And this label would not be going away anytime soon. One writer described her as an actress "whose peculiar, old-fashioned type of beauty is all the more striking in these days of bobbed hair and skirts." While this had surely been meant as a compliment, such comments only served to label her as passé.

Her last release of 1927 was *What Price Love?* for Morris R. Schlank Productions. Jane starred, but her supporting players were strictly third tier: Mahlon Hamilton and Charles Clary. Even the plot sounds tired. A disappointed romantic (Hamilton) sets about retrieving some stolen jewels so that the woman he loves (Jane), who had elected to marry another, can be happy with her husband (Clary). The critic for *Film Daily* must have been stifling a yawn when he wrote: "The old Russian jewels do the disappearing act again . . ."

Burning Bridges

Back in 1925 when Jane was beginning to film *Share and Share Alike* for Chester Bennett, it was announced that she had signed to do four more pictures for the producer/director—but her professional association with him ended with that picture, with no reason given. Then, in March 1928, Jane brought suit against the Chester Bennett Film Laboratories to be repaid $1,500 of a $9,000 loan she made to the production company in 1923. News articles stated that "the defendant" admits to borrowing and repaying $7,500, but that no more is owed. The suit was settled out of court.

Free Lips, co-starring newcomer June Marlowe and Frank Hagney, was Jane's only film in 1928. Filmed for James Ormont Productions and distributed by First Division Pictures (both minor concerns), this was the story of an innocent Indiana girl who turns hostess in the Free Lips Nightclub and attracts the interest of the tough-guy owner. Supposedly, she commits a murder, he takes the rap for her, the real murderer is discovered, and the tough guy goes straight and marries the girl. Jane, in the second feminine lead, had finally agreed to play a character who had gone astray.

Just about the time *Free Lips* was appearing in theaters, Jane and Mickey boarded the SS *Malolo* for a vacation in Hawaii. They met Eva and husband William there. The couple had hurried back from Australia due to the impending birth of their second child. They made it to Honolulu just one day ahead of the child's birth on June 28. Jane, Mickey, Eva, William and the newborn Pamela Eve returned to the states on July 20.

"It's not a comeback—it's a return!"

When it was announced in September 1928 that Jane would be co-starring in a picture, it was touted in at least one column as her comeback. "Jane is one of those unfortunate girls who made a big hit, had work all the time, and then began to slip little by little," the columnist wrote, adding, "Jane is fortunate in getting her chance to return to popularity. She has been in Australia making pictures but was never called in the Hollywood studios." Being branded a "has-been" must have been galling enough for her, but the columnist also confused her with Eva. It was *she* who went to Australia, *not* Jane.

Jane plays a schoolteacher for Native American children in her last silent film, Redskin (1929), with Richard Dix. This also marked the first time Jane's fans would see her in color.

Nevertheless, Jane had a good, solid part in a beautiful film to bring a close to her silent movie career. *Redskin* is a high-quality production filmed on location in Canyon de Chelly in Arizona. It was released by a major studio (Paramount), it had a director of note (Victor Schertzinger), and a major star (Richard Dix). It was also shot in Technicolor and the final six minutes were filmed in Paramount's new widescreen process, Magnascope. But despite the bells and whistles, the silent era was over, sound was in, and Jane was out. The fact that she was cast as a schoolmarm in this western drama was the inevitable omen that ingénue parts were now a thing of the past for the 31-year-old actress.

The Crash

More financial bad news was on the horizon. Once again, an income tax lien had been placed against Jane, this time in the amount of $346.57 in delinquent taxes from 1924. Not only did the two-paragraph news release refer to her as "a former well-known actress," the headline called her an "Ex-Actress." Jane's home address is given as 1515 North Hayworth, Hollywood, which helps to verify that an ad placed in *The Los Angeles Times* August 30, 1929, is indeed hers. The ad reads:

> Will invest. Want an apt.-house with large income. Location and prices must be desirable. Submit data in writing if possible. Jane Novak. 1515 N. Hayworth, Hollywood.

Jane wisely invested her acting money, the income of which allowed her to live a comfortable, financially secure life. However, following the Wall Street stock market crash of October 29, 1929, virtually all of Jane's assets were wiped out.

As 1930 turned the corner, Jean Hersholt and his wife hosted a "Margin Party." Guests were required to come dressed in old clothes as a sign of what they had lost in the stock market. Some of the industry members attending the party were Al St. John, Robert Edeson, Sidney Olcott, Edmund Breese, Pat O'Malley, Donald Crisp, Raymond McKee, Marguerite Courtot, Al Rogell, Jane, and a couple of dozen others. Columnist Grace Kingsley said that Jane was "looking awfully pretty and not a day older than when she was Bill Hart's leading lady, although she says that her little daughter is almost as tall as she herself is. Jane was wearing a simple little gingham frock and looked awfully sweet in it."

Some of Jane's silents were still being shown in theaters: *Redskin*, *What Price Love?*, *Closed Gates*, and *Free Lips*. Wiring a picture house for sound was not inexpensive. Smaller houses in rural areas—or even some of the bigger cities—just couldn't afford it, at least not right away. Of course, they would be forced to eventually, but, for 1930, second-run silent films had to be shown to keep them in business.

An issue of *The Los Angeles Times* (September 28, 1930) contains a classified ad offering a four-story brick building with 22 flats and a large vacant corner adjoining at 901 Exposition Boulevard. It says the owner would sacrifice all for $185,000, adding that there is still $77,000 owed on the property. The ad closes with, "Would prefer a clear grove in exchange for my equity. Courtesy to agents. Miss Jane Novak. WY 8903. EX. 4981."

Apparently, Jane had purchased an apartment building right before the crash. One can only surmise that, due to her substantial losses, she could no longer afford to keep the building. The address indicates this was the Neft Apartments, a block from the University of Southern California, built by jeweler Max Neft and a partner for $550,000, although this is likely an inflated cost projection. *Engineering News-Record* (November 29, 1923) lists a proposed three-story, 126 x 272 ft. building at the corner of Exposition and Vermont by Murstein and Neft of Seattle, Washington, at a cost of $200,000. However, *The Los Angeles Times* (May 18, 1924) states that the building had a frontage of 383 feet on Exposition Blvd., 240 feet on Thirty-Seventh Place, and 120 feet on University Avenue.

The entire project was never completed, and it is not known what Jane paid for it or its condition when she took ownership about five years after it was built. The next reference that could be found regarding the apartments is a January 1931 ad saying apartments were available for rent for $40 and up. (The apartment building no longer exists, and the corner is a part of the University of Southern California campus.)

Jane and sister Eva made it clear they had chosen to retire, although Jane's ability to do so comfortably was likely doubtful. According to records of the time, she was still listed at the same address—1515 North Hayworth, West Los Angeles.

Legal troubles would continue to plague her. She was back in court twice in 1932. The first time was to testify in a case against a real estate agent who had illegally used her name. A Mildred Furst gave a real estate agent $500 to enable him to close a "big real estate deal," and he gave Furst a note from Jane Novak as security for the loan. Jane appeared in court to testify that she had given the man the note on another deal, and that he had no authority to use it in obtaining money from anyone else.

The second appearance in court does not speak well of her finances at the time. A complaint was filed against her, claiming she had purchased $81.20 worth of rugs, mirrors, tea tables, and other furnishings for $20 down and failed to pay the balance.

In what seems to be such a short time since the silents went away, newspapers regularly published maudlin stories about the former stars, referring to them as "old-timers" or some other such term. In writing about a recent movie, columnist Wood Soanes reminisced about the stars of the late twenties, like Robert Agnew, Douglas MacLean, Corinne Griffith, Pola Negri, Theda Bara, Mahlon Hamilton, Johnnie Walker, and Thomas Meighan, among others. The closing paragraph reads: "Others are dead, some often wish they were dead, and many are on the ragged edge of existence. I run across many of the big names of yesterday as extras, as doormen, as house to house solicitors."

Apparently, down-on-their-luck stars made appealing copy.

The Depression

Jane would essentially disappear from public view for the next five years. During that period, the sisters lost their mother, Barbara Novak, who passed away February 20, 1934. The funeral was held two days later at the St. Ferdinand Catholic Church in San Fernando, California. Survivors were listed as Jane, brother Joseph, and sister Mrs. J. T. Ballak of St. Louis. Oddly enough, Eva was not mentioned.

Jane had not been in a film since 1929. However, her lengthy absence from the screen would come to an end in 1936. For Jane, there would be two movies and a stage play. The first of these would be in the Harry Carey western *Ghost Town* as a fellow gang member of the three male crooks. (Once again, the strait-laced Jane had let her character slip for a part.) This marked a return

Jane had a good role in Harry Carey's 1936 western Ghost Town. *She played a member of a gang to crooks. This was a return to working with Carey (pictured to Jane's right) after 20 years. He had been one of two leading men with Jane in the 1916 serial* Graft.

to working with Carey after more than 20 years. Although she does appear older, Jane was still attractive as she inched toward 40.

Hollywood Boulevard, a Paramount comedy released later that year, stars John Halliday as a has-been actor who agrees to write his memoirs for a scandal and gossip magazine. His daughter (Marsha Hunt) convinces him to desist for the sake of his ex-wife. The challenge, then, is to get the publisher to break the contract. Of interest to silent film buffs are the cameo appearances by such former stars as Jane, Esther Ralston, Francis X. Bushman, Maurice Costello, Betty Compson, Charles Ray, Herbert Rawlinson, Bryant Washburn, Jack Mulhall, Creighton Hale, and Roy D'Arcy.

Jane continued to have an active social life. In August, she was one of several former female screen personalities attending a luncheon hosted by Gene Raymond's mother at the Dominos Club. It is likely that the next announcement arose out of that luncheon. Jane would become the head of a drama group that would be dedicated to "the cause of theater" and proposed to "regenerate and restore the playhouse through a return to original methods, namely experiment and innovation."

That same month, she was among "names that made news in days gone by" who were "banding together" for their first annual dinner-dance at the Biltmore Bowl. The event was being sponsored by the Associated Cinema Artists. The executive committee for the group included William Farnum, Agnes Ayres, Charley Chase, Bryant Washburn, Jack Mulhall, Florence Turner, Maurice Costello, Flora Finch, Charles Murray, Helen Holmes, Creighton Hale, Lois Wilson, and Victor Potel. Jane, who was identified as "William S. Hart's former leading lady," was listed among those assisting with preparations.

Then, in late 1936 she appeared as "the fluttery and palpitating lady of the play" in *The Incredible Eve*, which was produced by Raymond Lee and Gilbert Davis. It opened at the Radio Playhouse in Los Angeles November 17 for a week's run. The play received good reviews when it opened; one reads: "amusing, tongue-in-cheek affair, wittily concocted and adorned with sparkling repartee." Jane's part was described as that of a ditsy lady "whose gushing, twittering flight through life is apparently entirely devoid of rhyme or reason. In fact, she is regarded by her children as the delectable but prize nit-wit of the ages." The reviewer went on to say, "Miss Novak was quite ravishing as the ebullient Eve, playing her comedy with deftness and esprit."

Hitting Bottom

Jane didn't appear in a film in 1937, but it was an unfortunate year for her for more serious reasons. In spite of the apparent normalcy in both work

This is a publicity photo that was released of Jane in connection with Hollywood Boulevard (1936). Still lovely at 40, Jane was one of several former silent stars who make an appearance in this Paramount comedy.

and her social life in 1936, the years had not been kind, and Jane's resources had just simply declined to almost nothing while her obligations mounted. So, unable to even keep up with her bills, the only thing Jane could do in 1937 was to file for bankruptcy. The headline blared, "Jane Novak, Once Screen Favorite, Admits Poverty."

Jane was in Superior Court to explain why she was unable to pay a $6,958 judgment against her by the Guaranty Liquidating Corporation on a real estate transaction. She told the judge she had less than $5 in her purse at that time and that her only source of income was a small salary paid her by her sister, Mrs. W.R. Reed of 8127 West Fourth St., for whom she keeps house. Jane was advised by her attorney to file for bankruptcy, and when the judge asked her if she intended to follow her attorney's advice, she responded, "Maybe." In 1938, headlines read "Jane Novak Broke," "Silent Star Bankrupt," and other similar sad proclamations when she did finally file for bankruptcy citing liabilities of $15,263 and only $100 in assets.

Nevertheless, there was good news yet to come. In November 1938, about a month after she filed for bankruptcy, it was announced that her daughter Mickey had secretly married Walter Seltzer of the MGM publicity department six weeks earlier.

Seltzer worked with MGM throughout the 1930s and served in the Marines in World War II. Prior to service, he was doing publicity for Columbia Pictures, and once out of service, he was Director of Publicity for Hal B. Wallis Productions. Over the next three decades he would work as a director of publicity and advertising for producer Hal B. Wallis, Burt Lancaster's Hecht-Lancaster Productions and Marlon Brando's Pennebaker Productions. He began producing in 1959 often collaborating with close friends Charlton Heston and Brando on their films. Over the years Jane must have been very pleased that her only daughter had entered into a successful, lifelong marriage.

After all the negative publicity concerning Jane's bankruptcy, she disappeared from public view for a few years.

Working Again

In 1940, Alfred Hitchcock gave Jane an uncredited bit part in *Foreign Correspondent*, with Joel McCrea, Laraine Day and Herbert Marshall. Hitchcock had remembered Jane from her trip to England back in 1924–1925 when she filmed *The Blackguard* and *The Prude's Fall*. As noted, Hitchcock was both scenario writer and assistant director on those films.

By this time, Jane was living with Mickey and her husband in Sherman Oaks. Seltzer would be going into the service shortly, and Mickey had taken on the role of columnist for an Eastern newspaper. For the next 13 years, she would write a column entitled "Hollywood Woman" for the *Philadelphia Evening Bulletin*. Also, during the 1940s, Mickey worked for the Warner Bros. publicity department and for the Margaret Ettinger Agency, one of the top publicity agencies in Los Angeles.

In 1941, Mickey had just volunteered to do publicity for the Studio City Red Cross, which was conducting a sweater drive for servicemen. She and Jane were also listed as the buyers of an acre of land in Van Nuys at 4172 Stansbury Avenue. The Seltzers would build a home there in the next year or so, and Jane would spend the rest of her days living with them.

The Hart Case

William S. Hart as he appeared in his heyday. In 1950, his ranch and holdings became the property of Los Angeles County. This occurred despite the contesting of the will by Hart's wife of less than a year, former silent actress Winifred Westover.

In a bitter, drawn-out legal battle that began in 1950, William S. Hart's former wife, Winifred Westover, was contesting Hart's will, which bequeathed most of his $1,170,000 estate, including his beloved 200-acre Horseshoe Ranch in Newhall, to Los Angeles County. Hart was always grateful to his fans. "While I was making pictures, the people gave me their nickels, dimes and quarters," he said. "When I am gone, I want them to have my home."

Hart married Westover in 1921 at the end of a year that was filled with speculation in fan magazines and newspapers that he and Jane were to be married. By all appearances, it seemed Hart was marrying Westover on the rebound.

Westover was pregnant when she left Hart, their marriage lasting only a matter of months. At the time of their divorce, Hart left a trust fund of $100,000 for his yet-to-be-born son. "I have made no provision in this will for my son," he wrote, "for the reason that I have amply provided for him during my lifetime." He also reached a settlement with Westover, and their divorce was finalized in 1927. But in 1950, Westover claimed that Hart was failing in mind and was unduly influenced before his death. He had died in 1946 at age 81, the will having been written two years earlier. The son's attorney mentioned that oil had been discovered nearby, which could greatly add to the property's value.

Jury selection began January 4, 1950. Some of those who knew Hart who were scheduled to testify included Jane, actor Joel McCrea, actress Edith Sterling, and actor/technical advisor Al Jennings.

As the trial progressed, Westover and her son claimed that Hart was so dominated by his sister, Mary Ellen (referred to as "Mamie" in a previously quoted 1921 article), that, at her insistence, he turned out his pregnant bride of five months. The attorney added that Mary Ellen even accompanied the couple on their honeymoon. He also contended that Hart would have married Jane, but the sister vetoed it.

According to the attorney, Hart was forced to choose between his sister and Westover. He supposedly said, "I owe everything I have to Mary. I can't give Mary up." She was "relatively a hypochondriac," the attorney added, spending most of her time in bed with a nurse in attendance from 1929 until her death in 1943. Westover claimed that she had returned from a day of shopping for baby clothes, and Hart met her at the door telling her, "You know you're not wanted around here—and you'll have to get out right now." Westover said she fainted, and that was the end of her relationship with Hart.

Hart reportedly formed a lasting attachment for his son. More than 300 letters and poems were produced as evidence that Hart had written to his son over the years.

Over the next several weeks, a number of witnesses took the stand—neighbors saying they didn't think Hart was of sound mind, others who had visited the ranch confirming Mary's dominance over Hart, one noting an argument between Westover and Mary Ellen at the dinner table, and even a line of testimony insinuating an improper relationship between the brother and sister. The attempt to "blacken" the memory of the famous cowboy star brought about a backlash, and the plaintiffs quickly dropped that line of testimony.

When cross-examination began, defense attorneys said Westover was given $10,000 in Reno as her settlement in the divorce, and that she had told Hart she would "smear him and his sister all over the front pages of the papers in the United States" if she did not receive the money. When asked if she had said this, she said, "I didn't say exactly that. I told it to a lawyer." The defense attorney then challenged Westover that when Hart's attorney told her, "You know, Mrs. Hart, this is blackmail," she replied, "I don't know what you call it as long as it is good at the bank." She denied having said that.

By the time the trial ended, it had lasted over four months, with 119 witnesses, 468 exhibits, and enough testimony to fill 28 book-length novels. It took the jury five days to come up with their verdict—Hart was not of unsound

Winifred Westover around 1920. Although her marriage to William S. Hart lasted barely three months, it produced a son, William S. Hart, Jr., who was born in 1922, shortly after the couple separated. The younger Hart died in 2004.

mind or unduly influenced when he wrote his will. Westover said she planned to file suit to set aside the old property settlement and divorce decree—that she signed away her rights under duress and coercion. Hart, Jr., said he would sue to obtain outright ownership of the ranch. The next month, June 1950, the mother and son requested a retrial, which was denied by Superior Court Judge Harold Jeffrey.

Westover and Hart, Jr. tried unsuccessfully over the next five or six years to gain ownership of the ranch. In the end, the county of Los Angeles made significant improvements to the property, even purchasing additional adjacent land—and on September 20, 1958, the William S. Hart Park at Newhall was officially dedicated. Although there was an assortment of old stars in attendance, Jane was not among them. However, one of the more in-depth articles announcing the upcoming dedication had a large photo of Hart holding a horse with Jane astride.

Say "Good night," Jane.

In the decade prior to all of the Hart-Westover court drama and well into the 1950s, Jane was not totally absent from view. In June 1941, western star Harry Carey was honored on his 33rd anniversary in films at his ranch near Saugus. Actor Frank Morgan presented him with a watch on behalf of Hollywood actors and a scroll with 500 signatures of film notables. Eva and Jane were there to pay tribute to him along with a large contingent of stars. Jane co-starred with Carey in the 1916 serial *Graft* and was once again in the 1936 western *Ghost Town*. Other silent stars on hand to pay tribute were Mary Pickford, William Desmond, and James Kirkwood.

Just six years later, Jane and Eva were among a long list of Hollywood notables who were attending Carey's funeral. He died September 21, 1947, at the age of 69 after battling emphysema and cancer.

Although Jane was essentially inactive during 1941, in 1942 she did have her most active professional year since 1927. She was cast in the low-budget crime-drama *Gallant Lady* (1942) for the poverty row studio Motion Picture Associates and distributed by PRC (Producers Releasing Corporation). Rose Hobart and Sidney Blackmer had the leads. Jane did have a credited part as Lucy Walker, a backwoods wife whose husband has broken his leg. Hobart is a doctor who just escaped from prison, but she comes upon the Walkers' shack in the backwoods and cares for him. The sequence is a good seven minutes long and demonstrates Jane's versatility as a character actress. A far cry from her silent film roles, her dress is raggedy, and her brushed-back hair is unkempt.

Another small role came along that year in the PRC release, *The Yanks Are Coming*, with Henry King and his Orchestra, William Roberts, and Mary Healy. However, this was a fun part for Jane as the giddy, silly stage mother of Vicki (Lynn Starr). Vicki is Rita's (Healy) rival for the affection of crooner Bob (Roberts). She is present through most of the film, and her high-pitched voice and animated gestures are quite effective. Her character is a little wacky and flighty, so it comes as no surprise that she falls for the dimwitted Maxie Rosenbloom.

A personal event that brought joy into Jane's life occurred when she became a proud grandparent in December 1942. Mickey gave birth to a healthy baby girl when her husband was serving as a corporal in the Marines.

Jane was also busy at the end of 1942 filming her next picture, *Man of Courage* with Barton MacLane, Lyle Talbot, and Charlotte Wynters. This, too, was a PRC release and another standard crime-drama. Jane plays a matronly lady who takes care of Wynters's daughter, played adorably by child actress Patsy Nash. Jane appears on and off throughout the film and comes into significance when Nash is supposedly kidnapped while in her care. The film was released January 4, 1943—and would be her last for some time. The dry spell was broken when she was cast in small parts (occasionally with billing) in several major motion pictures produced by Hal B. Wallis and released by Paramount in 1950: *The File on Thelma Jordan* (released in January), starring Barbara Stanwyck and Wendell Corey; *Paid in Full* (in March), featuring Robert Cummings, Lizabeth Scott, and Diana Lynn; and *The Furies* (in August), again with Stanwyck and Corey; *Scared Stiff* (1953), starring the comedy team of Dean Martin and Jerry Lewis; and *About Mrs. Leslie* (1954), with Shirley Booth. Jane's appearance in the latter warranted a paragraph in the newspapers that said she would give a "colorful characterization of a frantic customer" in the boutique scene. However, Jane plays a very low-key customer who leaves just as the business is closing. She takes her packages, thanks Booth, and as she is being let out the door, Booth says, "Good night."

"Good night," Jane replies.

This was Jane's last appearance on film.

SOURCES: See page 287

Chapter 23
The Novak Sisters,
Part II: Eva
୯ର

As Jane was throughout the years associated with William S. Hart, Eva, is most often identified only as Tom Mix's leading lady. She was obviously a favorite of Mix's, co-starring in 10 of his films; however, she made 49 other silent features and a substantial number of shorts. Nevertheless, Eva, as well as Jane, deserves to be remembered for so much more.

Eva was born at home, 2401 South Twelfth Street, in St. Louis, Missouri, on Valentine's Day, February 14, 1898. Her schooling, too, was at Notre Dame High Convent in St. Louis.

She liked to tell a story about the time when she was a young girl, working in a St. Louis department store. Her uncle Joe stopped in one day and told her, "Get out of town as fast as you can and go to California." Eva had no idea why he would say this, except for the fact that he didn't like St. Louis. Eva's older sister Jane was then with Universal in Hollywood; it was time to pay her a visit.

"Jane was showing me around [the studio] when a director fell in love with my tiny little feet. I think I wore a size 1 shoe, she recalled. "Anyhow, he asked me to walk up some stairs for a movie he was shooting. He just wanted to show my tiny little feet and my legs. I was very slim."

Encouraged by this spontaneous appearance in a movie, Eva found work at the L-KO (Lehrman-Knock Out) studio, which was overseen by its founder, Henry Lehrman. A successful director, screenwriter, and producer, Lehrman has the distinction of having directed Charlie Chaplin's first film at Keystone, *Making a Living* (1914). Several years earlier, in 1906, the Austrian immigrant applied for work at the Biograph studio. To get his foot in the door, he mentioned that he had been sent there by the prestigious Pathé-Frères company in France, an obvious fabrication. Nevertheless, he got the job—and the nickname "Pathé." When Mack Sennett left Biograph in 1912 to head Keystone, Lehrman followed as a director. In 1914, he left to form L-KO.

Roped into Slapstick

The first confirmed appearance by Eva in a film is a short entitled *Roped into Scandal*, starring Harry Lorraine and Eva and supported by perennial side-kick Bert Roach; it was released May 30, 1917. A string of low comedies followed: *Hearts and Flour*, *The Sign of the Cucumber*, *Street Cars and Carbuncles*, *A Nurse of an Aching Heart*, *Vamping Reuben's Millions*, *Double Dukes*, and *Hula Hula Hughie.*

L-KO comedies usually rotated two leading men (or sometimes both appeared in the same film): Robert McKenzie, a 37-year-old actor, described as "a small man with a big belly," who has an amazing 352 film credits to his credit; the other was a bookworm type, Eddie Barry, the brother of comedian Neal Burns.

Eva's first year in films was obviously a busy and productive one. She was learning the ropes in one of the most challenging of genres, slapstick—and, thankfully, none of her early films were directed by Lehrman himself, a taskmaster with little regard for his actors' safety.

One of Eva's L-KO comedies from 1918, *Belles of Liberty*, is available on home video. It stars Monty Banks, an Italian comedian who continued with moderate success throughout the silent era. This two-reeler is unadulterated slapstick from beginning to end, with one actor landing in a burning fireplace and running to an indoor pool to douse his smoking rear—then comes a car crashing through the door and into the pool. The end—a chase, of course—has a patrol wagon full of cops—à la the Keystone Cops—chasing the hero and heroine and falling all over themselves. Eva was what pros refer to as a trouper. Whether she is being knocked to the floor by a collapsing stage or transferring from a moving car to a streetcar and back—she is clearly in her element.

Although Jane and Eva were sisters, there was little family resem-

A screen shot from Belles of Liberty *(1918), starring Eva and Monty Banks (pictured). This L-KO short was one of Eva's earliest roles.*

blance. Jane, of course, was a more sophisticated-looking beauty, with her tiny mouth and those lovely, alluring eyes. Eva's appeal was that of an innocent little girl with a roundish face and a big smile. She also didn't mind posing in a bathing suit, as the following newspaper account from July 1917 indicates:

> Moving picture beauties yesterday afternoon paraded in bathing suits over the two miles of Seal Way from Anaheim Landing to Seal Beach. They were watched by more than 30,000 spectators. Three first prizes were awarded to Miss Edith Roberts, Miss Eva Novak and Miss Mildred Lee. Mayor Ord was invited to kiss the prettiest of the trio, but he declined the responsibility.

As 1918 rounded the corner, Eva was still being kept busy at the L-KO studio in support of comedians Hughie Mack, Alice Howell, Rube Miller, Gale Henry, Eddie Barry, Eddie Boland, and former Keystone comedian Harry Gribbon. A sign of her increasing popularity, Eva Novak became a featured name in trade magazine advertisements. The pace was grueling and non-stop at the comedy studios of the teens as evidenced by the 18 two-reelers she made that year, and six more in the first half of 1919. Personal appearances were a requirement, as well. Eva appeared at Quinn's Rialto in Los Angeles October 2, 1918, in connection with her picture *Nuts and Noodles*. The blurb mistakenly identified her as Jane's cousin. At least they spelled her name right!

The Speed Maniac

After slightly more than two years in pictures, Eva finally landed her first feature-length role. As one announcement put it, "Now it's the Novak family which is revealing itself as containing another genius beside the lovely Jane. Miss Jane's sister, Eva Novak, has just been engaged as leading woman for Tom Mix." *The Speed Maniac*, released October 19, 1919, would be the first of 10 films she would make with the rising star.

Although Mix is a cowboy in this film, it is hardly one of his typical westerns. He's a ranch owner who goes to San Francisco with his engine invention. He befriends a little boy whose father is a prizefighter serving time in prison for a crime he did not commit. Mix cares for the boy and his three siblings until the father is released—eventually taking his place in the ring when enemies drug him. The climax involves a big race, using the motor Mix has perfected. Eva makes her entrance when Mix rescues her on a runaway horse in the park.

The car race was, of course, staged, with hundreds of extras hired to fill the stands. However, Mix always insisted that the cars travel at racing speed, a

The Feud (1919) was the second film Eva made with Tom Mix; there would be eight more.

blurring 60 miles per hour. As the cameras were being cranked, Mix took too sharp a turn, and his car rolled over several times. The onlookers gasped in horror, assuming the driver had been killed. However, Mix emerged from the wreckage, unscathed and waving to the crowd.

Mix was a speed maniac in real life, and he raced as a hobby. When this film was in production, he entered the Pacific Coast Amateur Championship held at Ascot Park in Los Angeles. The proceeds were to go to the Actors' Fund. Mix drove a Stutz Special in the 25-mile race—and won.

As popular as Mix had become by this time, *The Speed Maniac* was not well reviewed. It was criticized as lacking plot and characterization and serving only as a vehicle for Mix's athleticism. *Variety* was particularly harsh, saying it was "thin in story value and bordering on the rankest kind of melodrama . . . What saves it from being mere trash are three of the biggest climaxes that were ever combined in five reels." The climaxes referenced allowed Mix to display his skills on a horse, in the ring, and on the track.

Apparently, critics didn't take notice of Eva in this picture, which may be just as well considering its poor reception. Nevertheless, she was back with Mix in his next venture, *The Feud*, released in December. Set in Kentucky, it tells the story of a typical mountain feud. Mix and Eva are the offspring of the opposing families. *Motion Picture News* described it as "a picturesque tale and one that interests from inception to conclusion." Almost as an afterthought, the critic adds: "Eva Novak appears opposite Mix and gives a charming portrayal."

The Roaring Twenties

The beginning of the new decade saw Eva's popularity rising rapidly. Comedy shorts were a thing of the past, replaced by features and stardom.

Eva's motion picture output wasn't as prolific as her sister's, but with six feature film releases in 1920, she was certainly busy. She opened the year with her third Tom Mix film in a row, *The Daredevil*, which hit theater screens in March. It's a simple story of a wealthy young man (Mix) whose father sends him to Arizona for "safe keeping." Once there, he falls in love with a girl (Eva) whose father is about to lose his position as superintendent of the railroad due to a rash of robberies. By the fade-out of the fifth and final reel, Tom has captured the robbers and saved the day.

Newspaper editors loved to print stories of humorous happenings on movie sets, whether real or manufactured. One such incident that supposedly happened on the set of Tom Mix's *The Daredevil* involved a prank that Mix and fellow actor Sid Jordan pulled on Eva. Mix told Eva that Jordan could contact the spirit world, so, completely taken in by the excitement of it all, Eva wanted Jordan to ask the spirits if she'd be "a hit" as Alice Spencer in *The Daredevil*. The scene was set when Jordan closed his eyes and a mysterious clicking sound was heard—leading Eva to believe he really had made contact with an apparition. Finally, he told her, "Eva, the spirits say you will score your biggest hit as Alice Spencer." Later, Mix cooled Eva's excitement when he told her it was all a ruse and that Jordan had broken his big toe once when he and Mix were "punching broncos." Ever since, he was able to make a clicking sound with that toe.

Mix pic No. 4 was next for Eva, released only one month later and entitled *Desert Love*. However, the lovely Francelia Billington took the female lead as Tom's love interest. Eva plays Billington's younger sister in this tale of an outlaw killing a boy's parents. He grows up, becomes sheriff, and his one mission in life is to avenge his parents' death. Of course, he must also save his girl from the outlaw.

Desert Love was a dud. *Harrison's Reports* called it "punk" and recommended it for third-class theaters only. Eva's part apparently was rather small, as there is no mention of her in the reviews.

But now it was Eva's turn to shine. For her next two films, she would receive top billing. The first, *Up in Mary's Attic*, was made for Ascher Productions (this was apparently their only film) and sold to Fine Arts. It was a comedy—a genre with which Eva was only too familiar. Her leading man was Harry Gribbon, who had worked at the Keystone company during the teens. Mary (Eva), a student at a girls' school, and Jack (Gribbon), the physical education instructor, are secretly married lest she lose her inheritance (it is stipulated in the will that she may only wed with her guardian's consent). They have a baby, but she must hide it in the school attic. Their lives are complicated by Waldo (Cliff Bowes), the son of her guardian, who is in love with her and tries to keep Eva and Jack apart at every chance. In the end, Mary comes of age and can now reveal her marriage and baby and claim her inheritance.

Released in July, *Up in Mary's Attic* received good reviews. *Harrison's Reports* said it was reminiscent of the old Keystones (and why not, with Gribbon in it?) but without the vulgarity. They called it "light" entertainment and said it was "artistically handled." It's interesting to note that the reviewer said the producers were banking on the girls appearing in tights as a draw—but that

Wanted at Headquarters (1920) was only the second film in which Eva was the star—and her first foray into drama. It was a hit with both critics and audiences.

the scenes were "not connected with any salacious thoughts." One wonders: how, exactly, could they make that determination?

Referring to her work in the film, another reviewer stated: "Eva is a comedienne of ability" and "is not one whit behind her sister either in looks or ability. Eva is a typical American girl with the sort of face that one sees on the covers of magazines." Eva was one of 28 actresses who tried out for the role. (The film survives in the UCLA Archive.)

Eva was the butt of a practical joke by Gribbon during the filming. Knowing that she was sensitive about her blonde hair being real, he said to her, "Your wonderful hair, Miss Novak. Is it peroxide?" Indignant, Eva responded, "Certainly not!" and bent over, parted her hair, and demanded, "Look, if I used peroxide, it would be dark at the roots. It's blonde, isn't it!" Humbled, the following day Gribbon presented her with a five-pound box of candy in apology.

The summer of 1920 saw the announcement that Universal had signed Eva for a series of "comedy-dramas," and her first production would be "Kate Plus Ten," from the novel of the same name. This turned out to be the working title for her next film, *Wanted at Headquarters*. This was Eva's first foray into drama, but from its description (it's assumed to be a lost film), it sounds as if it was a fun story—so it's worth a brief description. This time, Eva, as Kate Westhanger, is the mastermind of a gang of crooks. She gets a job in a gold syndicate to learn about a shipment she wants to steal. She meets a criminologist, Michael Pretherson (Leonard Shumway), to whom she is attracted, even though she chides him for his amateur sleuthing. He knows of her plans, but she challenges him to stop her. She and her gang succeed in robbing the train, but they are about to double-cross Kate. Kate, along with Michael, plans to turn the tables and double-cross the gang. The gang captures the couple intending to kill them. Fortunately, the police arrive in the nick of time and a big fight ensues. In the end, Kate decides she loves Michael more than crime. She returns the gold, is exonerated, and marries him.

The film was completed in August and opened in theaters in October. Reviewers were not kind. *Variety* called it "a poor type of melodrama." *Harrison's Reports* was slightly more generous, offering the backhanded compliment "[*Wanted at Headquarters* is] an entertaining melodrama for non-critical audiences."

As Eva's star continued to rise, her name regularly turned up in newspapers and magazines. One accompanying an announcement of a double bill at the local theater proclaimed that "Eva Novak is Better Than Alice Brady at Star Theater." In spite of what the critics had to say, the article was claiming

Like her sister, Eva played opposite William S. Hart as well. This is a scene from the first of her two films with him, The Testing Block *(1920). Playing the part of their son is child star Richard Headrick (pictured).*

This is a candid shot taken during the filming of The Testing Block *(1920). It is unclear what Hart (in the tall hat) and Eva are doing; it appears they are on their lunch break.*

Eva's *Up in Mary's Attic* was a better picture than the veteran Alice Brady's *The New York Idea*, which was also playing. Harshly, the article closes by saying, "Eva Novak, though, in *Up in Mary's Attic*, makes one forget Alice."

Stealing Her Sister's Hart

Sliding into Jane's territory, Eva was cast in *The Testing Block*, opposite William S. Hart. Eva plays a traveling violinist who captures the heart of outlaw "Sierra" Bill (Hart, of course). The six-reeler was made for the star's own company and released through Paramount Artcraft December 26, 1920.

After filming *Silk Husbands and Calico Wives* with House Peters for the forgotten Equity Pictures, Universal announced that Eva had been chosen to star in a South Pacific island story entitled "Out of the Sunset." A month later, they announced that Jack Perrin, who had served as an aviator in the war, would play, of all things, an aviator in the film. Velma (Eva) is washed overboard from her husband's yacht and ends up on an island with bootleggers. Lt. Paul Mack (Perrin) lands his hydroplane on the island to refuel, at which time he meets and falls for Velma. So, how do they end up together in the finale? Velma's husband violates doctor's orders and dies from undue liquor consumption.

When released, the film's title was *The Torrent* (not to be confused with the William Fairbanks feature of 1924 or the Garbo film of 1925). It was Eva's first release for 1921.

Next, Eva was once again opposite Hart in *O'Malley of the Mounted* (1921). Hart plays Sergeant O'Malley, a member of the Royal Canadian Mounted Police, who infiltrates a gang of outlaws to capture a murderer. Predictably, he falls in love with Eva—a situation complicated by the fact that she is the suspect's sister.

The only time Hart mentions either Eva or Jane in his autobiography, *My Life East and West*, is in relation to this film: "The heroine was played by a beautiful girl, Eva Novak, the younger sister of dear Jane." He explained that the heroine was to ride by quickly, and Hart would jump on the back of the horse to escape the outlaws. Hank Potts doubled for Eva and took Hart on a wilder ride than he had anticipated. Going under a low branch, Potts was able to duck, but Hart was knocked off and suffered two broken ribs.

Moving Up

Carl Laemmle saw star quality in Eva, which led to her receiving top billing in her next two films for Universal. Considering the minor names in the supporting cast, Laemmle must have been banking solely on Eva's celebrity.

Society Secrets came out about the same time as *O'Malley of the Mount-ed*—in February 1921. Gertrude Claire was a moderately popular star, but she was 69 years old and had been relegated to motherly roles. Nor were the other cast members—George Burrell, William Buckley, and Lee Shumway—box-office draws. The scenario has New York City dwellers, a brother and sister, ashamed to host a visit from their small-town parents. Eva steps in and makes sure their New York debut is a success.

Then came *The Smart Sex* in March. Once again, not much in the way of supporting players—Frank Braidwood, Geoffrey Webb, and Mayre Hall. Rose (Eva), a stranded showgirl, meets a young man who gladly offers her a place to stay at an adjoining farm. Naturally, the man's mother objects to this liv-ing arrangement. Rose is suspected of a jewel robbery but uncovers the thief herself—and the wedding date is set. The original title was "The Girl and the Goose," but savvy Universal execs knew a more enticing title would be *The Smart Sex*.

Throughout its filming in the first months of 1921, *Wolves of the North* was being advertised as "The Evil Half," with the name change coming shortly after its completion at the end of March. Eva and the Universal unit, under the direction of Norman Dawn, had just spent the past two weeks in Northern California, filming snow scenes. Set in Alaska, two men are in love with Eva, with a climactic avalanche determining which man she ends up with.

Back in the Saddle

After three non-westerns in a row, Eva's next five out of six pictures would be in support of Tom Mix.

The Rough Diamond (October 1921 release) took advantage of the "mythi-cal kingdom" fad—and it seemed that virtually all such stories had some sort of revolution as a backdrop. Of course, Mix almost single-handedly defeats the villains for the king and his daughter (Eva).

The Last Trail (November 1921) was another picturization of a Zane Gray story, this one starring Maurice "Lefty" Flynn, who made a few forgettable westerns in the silent era; if he is remembered at all, it is due to his brief mar-riage to Viola Dana. This is another of those stories in which a secret bandit (known as "The Night Hawk," the original title of the film) is wreaking havoc with the building of a dam, but the mysterious stranger who takes him down is, in the end, revealed to be a company agent. Filming was completed in late June or early July.

Back with Mix in *Trailin'* (released December 21), Mix hunts for a man who killed his father in a duel. The neat twist to this one is that he eventually learns

A lovely—and sexy—photo of Eva from The Last Trail *(1921), a western that paired her with Maurice "Lefty" Flynn. A standout athlete at Yale in the teens, Flynn had 40 films to his credit in the silent era, but never achieved true star status.*

Tom Mix rescues Eva in Sky High *(1922), her sixth film with the western star. Eva made a total of 10 films with Mix.*

the murderer is his real father, and the man who was killed had run off with his mother years earlier. Eva, a hotel waitress, is there to warn him of unforeseen dangers.

Opening in January 1922 was *Sky High*, one of Mix's most notable ventures for the scenes filmed on location in the Grand Canyon. Cinematographer Blaine Walker was awarded a gold medal by Fox Film Corporation for obtaining the first motion picture footage of the Grand Canyon from an airplane, a flight that was deemed "perilous." The story concerns Grant Newburg (Mix), an immigration officer seeking to uncover a gang smuggling Chinese migrants across the border. He comes across Estelle (Eva), who is lost in the canyon and places her high up on a ridge for safety; he even steals food for her. The story has the heavy threatening Estelle, Mix jumping from an airplane, leaping into the Colorado River, and swimming to where Estelle is being held captive to save her.

Chasing the Moon (released February 1922) was a departure for Mix that wasn't well received by critics or theater owners. He's a blasé millionaire who thinks he has been exposed to some poison and is going to die in 30 days unless he finds the professor with an antidote. Several of Mix's westerns were labeled as "comedy-westerns" because of the lighter moments he included in his films and characterizations, but it sounds as if this one was more of a comedy than a western.

Eva's ninth film with Mix was *Up and Going* (released April 1922)—another tale about the Royal Canadian Mounted Police, this time involved in tracking down bootleggers. The climactic rescue of the heroine is another highlight. Truckee, California, served as the Canadian Northwest for this film.

As noted earlier, Eva's 10 films with Mix established her legacy, just as Jane was forever referred to as William S. Hart's leading lady. Eva was justly proud of the films she had made with Mix. And, if the frequency with which she appeared with him implies a romantic relationship, there is nothing to back that up. He was married during these years to Victoria Forde, who had been his leading lady in so many of his one- and two-reelers. Additionally, Forde gave birth to their second daughter during the filming of *Sky High*.

Marrying Well

In 1922, the trades carried an announcement of the newly formed Eva Novak Productions. E. L. Butler and William R. Reed were listed as executive heads; they had even leased space at the Fine Arts Studio. Although one report stated that camera work would commence within the week, another said an initial story had not yet been completed, although its working title was "The Blue Sedan." As so often happens with development deals in Hollywood, no such film was ever made. As a matter of fact, no film was issued under the "Eva Novak Productions" banner. What *did* occur from this aborted plan was Eva finding a husband, the aforementioned William R. Reed, whom she married on June 21, 1922, in Los Angeles.

One source stated that Reed was a former cameraman who had moved into production. Another said he was an actor, a claim that could not be confirmed. Reed was the brother-in-law of well-known director Alfred E. Green, whose career lasted from 1916 to the 1950s. Green had married Reed's sister, actress Vivian Reed. Since Green had directed Eva in *Silk Husbands and Calico Wives* in 1920, this could also have been how she met Reed. He would soon direct her again, this time in the Thomas Meighan vehicle, *The Man Who Saw Tomorrow* (1922). That Paramount-released fantasy film offers Eva as a beguiling Russian sorceress. Unfortunately, this is a lost film.

The Man from Hell's River was released in May, starring Irving Cummings and made for his eponymously named production company. It's another James

Eva's beauty radiates in this early 1920s fan magazine portrait. It was taken at the time she first received star billing.

Oliver Curwood outdoor story, filmed on location in Yosemite National Park. Its most significant claim to fame is that it was Rin Tin Tin's first film.

1922 was rounded out for Eva with a George Larkin western, a comedy with William Russell, and with Jack Holt in a soap opera-style drama.

It wasn't until October that Eva and Reed were able to take a honeymoon. Eva told a reporter that they would be motoring north in the state for about a month. The article also teased fans with a tidbit that Eva and Jane were planning, for the first time, to appear together in a picture. The gist of the interview was Eva's warning to aspiring starlets to stay at home. "It's a hard life!" she averred. "Stay at home, girls, and help mother if you would be happy." However, for those who aspire, she added, "[S]tars aren't made in a day, as many people believe. Whatever a star is comes generally after years and years of ceaseless toil. It takes years to make even an acknowledged actress." The interview was done at the Hotel Johnson in Visalia, about 190 miles north of Los Angeles. Since she only had one scene to do there, her stay was short, and she returned to Los Angeles November 9 to complete studio work.

Besting Jane

As 1923 rounded the corner, Eva was suddenly becoming more active in films than Jane. The year saw six features in the theaters with Eva in the cast—not as many as the year before, but still twice as many as Jane who had only had three in 1923. However, Eva, like sister Jane prior to her Chester Bennett association, had not had a studio contract, instead moving from one studio to another, from low-budget outfits to major production companies.

For Eva, 1923 was a mix of these. *Dollar Devils* came out at the end of January, and it was made for the well-known and much-respected director Victor Schertzinger's namesake company. The stars were minor—except for Eva, of course. But there were some recognizable players in supporting roles—Hallam Cooley, Cullen Landis, and Lydia Knott. It's about a small New England town where oil is discovered (there's oil in New England?) and how the hero and his girlfriend's little sister (Eva) expose the swindler.

Temptation was an April release for Columbia Pictures. Bryant Washburn was the star of the film, with Eva and June Elvidge in support. Washburn and Eva are a couple corrupted by their sudden wealth, but when a police raid on a roadhouse finds them with different companions, they are brought to their senses and their wild lifestyle comes to a screeching halt.

Eva was back at a major studio, Paramount, in *The Tiger's Claw*, released in April. Sam Sandell (Jack Holt) is in India, building a dam. He marries a half-caste, Chameli (Aileen Pringle). His former English sweetheart, Harriet (Eva),

This lobby card from The Tiger's Claw *(1923) shows Eva with co-star Jack Holt. Not pictured here is the third star, Aileen Pringle, who plays a half-caste whom Holt marries, but she proves unfaithful and dies in the end from a bullet intended for Holt. In the end, Holt reunites with his former sweetheart, Eva.*

takes the marriage well and even introduces Chameli to society. But Chameli is faithless, and later, is killed by a bullet meant for Sam. The dam is blown up by thugs, and Sam rescues Harriet from the flood. *Whew!*

Boston Blackie, a Fox feature, came out the following month (May) and co-starred Eva with William Russell. In this one, Blackie (Russell) is released from prison but vows to expose the warden for his cruel treatment of prisoners. Mary (Eva), his girlfriend, is his helper and contact outside the prison walls. Although Boston Blackie is best known from sound movies, radio, and early TV as a detective, author Jack Boyle originally depicted him as a safecracker and jewel thief. Boyle was serving time in San Quentin when he began writing these stories, the first being published in 1914. This film was considered quite realistic in its depiction of cruelty in the prison, a fact appreciated by critics if not exhibitors.

Eva's next two assignments would be for Metro Pictures, Inc., soon to merge with Goldwyn and Louis B. Mayer's company to form Metro-Goldwyn-Mayer. The first of her Metro offerings would be *A Noise in Newboro*, a comedy starring Viola Dana and David Butler. It boasted a good cast that included Allan For-rest, Betty Francisco, Malcolm McGregor, and former Keystone comedian Hank Mann. Martha Mason (Dana) is snubbed by her hometown, leaves, and returns seven years later, a celebrity. Ben Colwell (Butler) has political ambitions. He plans to marry Anne (Eva), daughter of the richest man in town. However, when he learns Martha has $30 million, he turns his attentions on her. Martha encour-ages him but finally reveals his true character to the whole town. With Colwell's political ambitions shattered, Martha leaves town, satisfied.

As noted earlier, Jane and Eva appeared in only one film together, *The Man Life Passed By*. Filming started in September bringing Eva back with Victor Schertzinger Productions—and with Jane on loan from Chester Bennett—the sisters supported the film's star, debonair Englishman Percy Marmont. Jane was reunited once again with Hobart Bosworth, and Eva was back with Cul-len Landis and Lydia Knott for the second time this year. Also in the cast were George Siegmann, George Beranger, Lincoln Stedman, and Francis X. Bush-man, Jr. Marmont plays inventor John Turbin, who vows vengeance when "Iron Man" Moore (Bosworth), a wealthy iron industrialist, steals his plans. Pover-ty and disappointment make him a derelict, but he forgives his enemy after Moore's daughters, Hope (Jane) and Joy (Eva), befriend him.

It was big news that both Jane and Eva were to appear together. In one of those fluff pieces released by a PR department, it was reported that Jane was becoming frustrated with her long hair. In one scene as Hobart Bosworth, play-ing her father, crushes her to him, Jane's hair would become disheveled with each take. It took four takes for the scene, each time with Jane returning to the hairdresser for about 35 minutes to repair her hair.

Record-Breaking Eva

Eva must have set some records in 1924 that would have been hard to beat. First, she had 14 features released. Second, seven of those were as Wil-liam Fairbanks's costar. And finally, how many stars had three of their pictures released on the same day?

Robert J. Horner, author and director, ran a full-page ad in the December 29, 1923, issue of *Exhibitors Herald*. It read that he had just finished producing a series of pictures featuring the stars on "this page," which he would offer on a states-rights basis—basically meaning a distributor could obtain the films with exclusive rights to a particular state. This was done in lieu of distributors like Paramount, Metro, First National, etc. The stars pictured were Marjorie Daw, Jack Perrin, Ranger Bill Miller, Patricia Palmer, George Chesebro, and Eva.

Horner was the director and writer of Eva's first release for 1924, *Safe-guarded*, a typical western in which she played opposite cowboy star Neal Hart. The producer was Morris J. Schlank, who specialized in B-westerns. In this one, the heroine (Eva, of course) inherits some oil deeds, and the hero must save her when she is kidnapped by swindlers and rumrunners.

 Safeguarded was representative of Eva's career, as her production companies tended to be the short-lived outfits. Although silent western fans will no doubt recognize Morris J. Schlank's name, Eva worked for others that would more likely fit the "fly-by-night" category: Sacramento Pictures Corporation, Choice Productions, Norman Dawn Alaskan Company, and Hercules Film Productions. The William Fairbanks features were all made for Columbia, specifically when it was operating under its original name, C.B.C. Film Sales. (It was often referred to, snidely, as "Corn Beef and Cabbage.")

No new Eva Novak releases were seen in March and April, but the comedy *Listen Lester* appeared in May. Eva was among the principals, but Louise Fazenda was the star, supported by Harry Myers, George O'Hara, Lee Moran, Alec B. Francis, and Dot Farley. With her background in comedy shorts, Eva said, "It's just like being home again to work with this company. The only thing that bothers me in my semiserious role here is that I constantly work in fear of being decorated with an overstuffed custard pie at any moment."

Fans were desperate for any tidbits about the stars, and newspapers were only too ready to oblige. Consider the following fish story:

> William Reed stole away from the office of the Waldorf Studios and borrowed his wife, Eva Novak, from *Listen Lester* yesterday afternoon. In two hours, Mr. Reed and Miss Novak reduced the crowded population of the lake by taking the limit of five bass and 10 perch apiece. Miss Novak's largest fish, a small mouth bass weighing four pounds, struck at her Dowagiac minnow with such enthusiasm that although he missed the bait, he landed in the boat. "I don't know whether he was more surprised than I was," commented Miss Novak. "I screamed and jumped around so that Bill said I'd upset the boat, but I got the best over Mr. Bass—and here he is."

Five days after *Listen Lester* came *Missing Daughters*, co-starring Eva, Eileen Percy, and Pauline Starke. Veteran heavy Walter Long kidnaps the three girls with the assistance of his gang members, each of whom is being sought by the government for illegal activities. Just before the fade-out, a U.S. Secret Service agent (Rockcliffe Fellowes) rescues them.

Eva supported William Fairbanks in eight of his films, only two fewer than she made with Tom Mix. In The Battling Fool *(1924), Fairbanks shows off his boxing skills.*

Eva was on location at Ventura's Seaside Park racetrack sometime during the summer for the filming of "Goldcup Derby," which was eventually released on August 8, 1924, as *Racing for Life*, with William Fairbanks. An article covering the shoot pointed out that William Reed was assisting B. Reeves Eason in the direction. "Isn't it odd that it is we people [the actors] who always get the publicity, and, after all, it is the others who really do most of the work," Eva was quoted as saying. "Yes, I like having Billy for a director. We really get along fine together."

She went on to say, "Although I've passed through Ventura several times, this is the first time I've ever stopped. I think it is beautiful and so interesting. The mission interests me so much, especially the stories of the olden days."

Racing for Life was the third film in which she supported Fairbanks. Two had been released on the same day just one week before—*A Fight for Honor* and *The Battling Fool*. And that wasn't all. After *Racing for Life*, she would make five more films with Fairbanks, making her association with him just two films fewer than she had made with Tom Mix. The upcoming Fairbanks/Novak films were *The Fatal Mistake*, released September 1, 1924; *The Beautiful Sin-*

The Fearless Lover *(1925) is another of the films Eva made with William Fairbanks. Fairbanks is the policeman, and Eva is to his left.*

ner, released October 1, 1924; *Women First*, released November 1, 1924; *Tainted Money*, released December 15, 1924; and *The Fearless Lover*, released February 1, 1925. With eight Fairbanks films to her credit, one would think she was the actor's favorite leading lady. However, that honor must go to Dorothy Revier, with whom he made nine films. Apparently, numbers matter.

Although not a stunt man like Richard Talmadge or Yakima Canutt, Fairbanks was ruggedly athletic. The seven films Eva made with him in 1924 were all dramas, with the hero foiling a train robbery, winning an automobile race, capturing a gang of crooks, and preventing a jewel theft. Occasionally, they might take a surprising turn, as in *Tainted Money*, which features a Romeo and Juliet theme—Eva and Fairbanks are the offspring of feuding lumber magnates. In another, Fairbanks is a racehorse trainer, but when some competitors drug him and the jockey, Eva is the one donning the silks and winning the race.

The third picture released on August 1 to feature Eva was *The Lure of the Yukon*, described as a gold rush story "with plenty of red-blooded action for those who like the wild and frozen north film." *Photoplay* said it included such

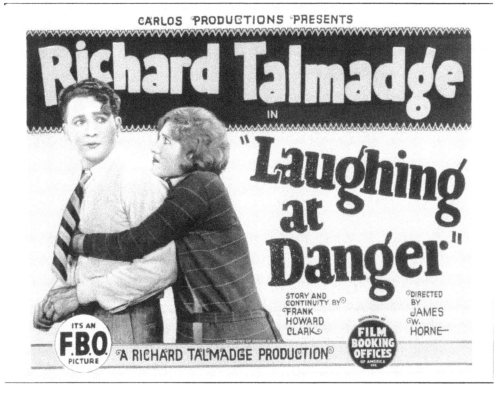

Richard Talmadge was one of several stuntmen who transitioned into starring roles—the attraction of their films being essentially a presentation of dangerous stunts. Eva is Talmadge's co-star in Laughing at Danger *(1924).*

"hair-raising catastrophes as avalanches, fights, logjams, dog chases and death from hardship." You can't ask for more than that for a dime admission.

November saw the release of *Laughing at Danger*, another Richard Talmadge action-comedy stunt picture, which *Moving Picture World* said had "a pippin of a story." Eva's last film released in 1924 was *Battling Mason*, a comedy/drama co-starring the muscular Frank Merrill (who went on to play Tarzan a few years later). In this, he's a fighter who runs for public office on the condition he will not fight his opponent. He keeps the pledge through insults and provocations, but when his girl is attacked by ruffians, he gives them their comeuppance.

To keep up with such a physically fit co-star, Eva told a reporter that she performed a "daily octette" to keep in shape. It was described as "a series of exercises that would make the average girl hesitate." According to Eva: "You've got to keep up day in and day out. But it certainly keeps you feeling fit. Also, I love horseback riding, and that is another great exercise."

A Different Kind of Output

Eva's output of three pictures in 1925 paled in comparison to the year before. There is a good reason for this. Vivian Barbara Reed was born July 15, 1925, in Los Angeles. She came into the world at 1:17 p.m. and weighed six pounds. Newspapers around the country carried a photo of the proud Eva and her new daughter in the hospital.

About the same time, her husband was performing a stunt in a movie that resulted in serious injury. The stunt required him to make a leap from the roof of a building to the crossbar on a telephone pole. He missed with one hand, and when the other slipped, he fell approximately 35 feet, striking a hitching post. First reports said he suffered a fractured skull, a fractured jaw, a broken nose, cuts and bruises on his face and head, and a possible broken back. The report went on to say he probably missed being killed by striking the edge of another roof, which helped to break his fall. He was doubling for Buck Jones in a picture entitled *A Man Four Square*. Filming was taking place near Westwood, beyond Beverly Hills.

The good news was that the day after the accident, newspapers were reporting that Reed was recovering slowly, with non-life-threatening injuries.

Prior to this activity in the summer of 1925, Eva was engaged in a salary dispute. She filed a wage claim in April, asserting that she was still owed $666.67 for a picture she made for Sequoia Productions; it was financed by Dr. Jasper Mayer of 1118 Story Building in Los Angeles. She said she played the lead, and the movie required eight days of filming. No record of such a movie could be found. *The Lure of the Yukon* could likely be the film referenced in the complaint, although the production company is listed as the "Norman Dawn Production Company."

What Goes Up . . .

Eva moved down the celebrity ladder a bit with her next film, *Sally*, a successful starring vehicle for Colleen Moore. Eva was listed fourth among supporting players, with Leon Errol, David Hughes, and Dan Mason preceding her in the credits.

Following her maternity break, Eva was back at work on *The Northern Code* for the low-budget Gotham Productions. Yet another tale laid in the Canadian Northwest, Marie (Eva) shoots her drunken trapper husband when he attacks her. Thinking that he is dead, she flees, is befriended by Louis Le Blanc (Robert Ellis), and they eventually marry. However, the husband returns,

Eva was the star of The Lure of the Yukon *(1924), a story of the Alaskan gold rush days. This lost film was said to include such "hair-raising catastrophes as avalanches, fights, logjams, dog chases and death from hardship."*

and the two men have a brutal fight, one that results in her ex-husband falling from a cliff to his death.

Eva's six features in 1926 were double the number her sister had released. She started off the year once again supporting Colleen Moore, this time in *Irene*, released February 21, 1926. Her part is minuscule, at best. Lloyd Hughes is the typical rich kid, and Moore is the poor Irish girl in whom he's interested. Society girl Eva is Mom's pick for Hughes's future wife. Although Eva is beautiful, Hughes is obviously not interested. So, other than a few flashes of her seated at the climactic fashion show, her total screen time is less than 30 seconds.

In April, Eva took a quick side trip to the Hal Roach studios, where she co-starred with Roach stalwart Glenn Tryon in the two-reeler *Say It with Babies*, which was released the following month. Other Roach regulars in this film include Oliver Hardy (before officially teaming with Stan Laurel), and female foils Vivien Oakland and Martha Sleeper, the latter of whom often supported Charley Chase.

Eva expresses either surprise or shock in this still from The Millionaire Policeman *(1926), starring Herbert Rawlinson in the titular role. The film also starred veteran actress Eugenie Besserer, left, as Eva's mother.*

By the end of April, she had completed her next feature, *The Millionaire Policeman*, directed by Edward Le Saint. Herbert Rawlinson has the lead as the uncourageous son of a rich man. He leaves town, joins the police force, and falls in love with Mary Gray (Eva). Things get complicated when he must arrest Mary's brother for a crime. Although *Film Daily* called the story "trite," it did say Eva was "thoroughly pleasing as [the] daughter."

It was announced in June that Eva and Cullen Landis had been signed for *The Dixie Flyer*, which came out at the end of July. The vice-president of the railroad is trying to oust the president. He has a saboteur among the ranks. Landis is the foreman, and Pat Harmon (remember him as the football coach in Harold Lloyd's *The Freshman*?) is the saboteur. Eva is, of course, the president's daughter and in love with Landis. It's an engrossing story, but when fight scenes are called for, it's difficult to see Landis as a match for Harmon.

At the end of August, Eva could be seen for the tenth, and final, time with Tom Mix, in *No Man's Gold*. In this one, Mix must fulfill his promise to a dying man and keep a mine from getting into nefarious hands. In addition, he must

Eva's tenth, and final, film with Tom Mix was No Man's Gold *(1926). She made more films with him than any of his leading ladies in feature films; from that point on, any mention of her career would include the legendary cowboy star.*

rescue Eva, who had been kidnapped. *Film Daily* said, "Eva Novak plays the lead, and she is just about the most winning lady Tom has ever worked with."

The Land Down Under

In the summer of 1926, Eva and Reed went to Australia, where they stayed for a combination vacation and business trip. After a stopover in Tahiti, the couple arrived in Sydney in early August to a greeting from "thousands of people who congregated on the wharf."

While there, Eva made one film for the Australasian Film Company, *For the Term of His Natural Life*, co-starring American actor George Fisher. This is a brutal film about Australian convicts in the early days. The shoot, which took place in Sydney and Tasmania, ran into trouble when authorities threatened to deny approval for export because of brutal scenes depicting flogging and other graphic horrors for fear it would "blacken Australia's name." It didn't have its world premiere until the following year at the Theatre Royal, Newcastle, NSW, June 20, 1927, and proved to be a success. It was intended to launch the Australian film industry into the world market, but its release in the U.S. was delayed until 1929, causing this silent film to have little impact among the many sound films released that year.

Due to the success of *For the Term of His Natural Life*, Phillips Films Productions, Ltd., was formed with a capital of 100,000 pounds to produce six films with Eva. Their first release, *The Romance of Runnibede*, was to have been directed by American import Scott Dunlap, but his arrival was delayed, forcing Reed to take up the megaphone. The story, based on a popular novel, had Eva's character kidnapped by aboriginals while returning from school; her rescue is coordinated by two men, both of whom are in love with her.

The film was previewed in September 1927 and was praised by the *Sydney Morning Herald* critic. It premiered in Australia January 9, 1928, to a dismal showing at the box office.

Eva returned to the San Francisco port November 29, 1926, on the Oceanic Liner Sierra. As a side note, the newspapers ran a photo of two ladies who came in on the Sierra. Apparently they accidently left their luggage in Sydney, so Eva loaned them some of her clothes.

When Eva returned from Australia in late November, Reed had stayed behind with the company. But, after spending Christmas at home, Eva completed two more pictures before rejoining her husband in Australia — *Red Signals*, a railroad melodrama with Wallace MacDonald and Earle Williams, and *Duty's Reward*, a gangster melodrama with Allan Roscoe and George Fawcett.

Earlier reports had said Eva would return to Australia in February 1927, but, shortly after filming *Red Signals* in early February, Reed cabled her that she would not be needed until April to begin her contract with Phillips Film Production, Ltd. But then it was reported the sailing date was moved to May 1. A cable came in early April that she should return immediately, so she, her mother and daughter Vivian sailed out of San Francisco on the Wilhelmina for Honolulu where they would connect with the Vancouver for Australia. Because Eva was contracted for six films, Reed was also busy looking for a home for his wife and Vivian.

In early summer, sister Jane and daughter Mickey boarded the steamer Malolo for a vacation in Hawaii. While in Hawaii, they met Eva who had just returned from her second trip to Australia. Eva was soon to have a baby, so the Reeds hurried to leave Australia and have daughter Pamela Eve born on American soil — that is, Honolulu. According to reports, the Reeds arrived in Honolulu just one day ahead of the baby's birth, June 28. Jane, Mickey and the Reeds returned to San Francisco, along with 336 other passengers, aboard the liner City of Honolulu July 20.

Eva's return to Australia turned out to be all for nothing. *The Romance of Runnibede* flopped, and Phillips Film Production, Ltd., would soon be in liquidation. When Eva returned to the States in November 1926, she was still owed 3,000 pounds in salary, which was quite a sum in those days.

Speak Up!

With two children—one a newborn—Eva decided to take a break from acting for a while. She wouldn't be seen in a new movie until 1930. This was *The Medicine Man*, vaudeville comedian Jack Benny's feature film debut and Eva's first talkie. The leading lady role went to Betty Bronson, who is best remembered for her charming performance in the title role of *Peter Pan* (1924). Eva is cast as a beautiful Swedish girl, Hulda, who follows traveling medicine man Benny to his next stop. It's up to Benny's cronies to get rid of her, which they do, but only after giving her quite a bit of money for travel, hotel, etc. Later we see her meet up with her father, and we learn it was all a ruse, with Hulda walking away with the swag. Eva is both convincing and engaging as the swindling Swedish girl—and her accent isn't bad, either!

So many female stars from the silent era found themselves as the feminine lead in B-westerns of the 1930s that it became a symbol of their diminishing stardom. Eva felt right at home on a western set, however, having appeared in so many during her career. In *Phantom of the Desert* (1930), she was cast as Jack Perrin's leading lady. It has the typical plot concerning a stolen herd and

Jack Perrin was active in the silent era, mostly in westerns, and easily made the transition to sound films. Phantom of the Desert *(1930) was the second time Eva and Perrin were together in a film; the first time was in* The Torrent *(1921).*

Perrin saving the day for Eva's father. After this oater, the roles would be few, small, and far between.

In July 1935, *The Signal* of Santa Clarita announced the culmination of "Placeritos Days," an annual celebration of Newhall and the Little Santa Clara Valley. Eva Novak Reed was cited as one of the recipients of an honorable mention, although it is not clear what the award was for—possibly the equestrian event. It also named "W. S. Hart and Wm. Reed" among the three-person judging committee.

The next month, it was announced that William Reed was to go to Singapore to produce films for a Chinese company. Eva and Mrs. Buck Jones were to travel with him, and, once Buck Jones' contract with Universal was complete, he would join them. There was no other mention of Reed's involvement with a Chinese film company or the making of any film in Singapore.

Singapore's newspaper, *The Sunday Tribune*, reported on October 6 that Mrs. Buck Jones and 17-year-old daughter Maxine were in Singapore in the course of a round-the-world trip. There was no mention of Eva.

In 1936, Eva had one film, the crime drama *Dangerous Intrigue* starring Ralph Bellamy. Unfortunately, her brief appearance as a nurse in the film was an uncredited part.

Eva was announced to have bit parts in two films in 1937. The first of these was *Angel*, a Paramount picture starring Marlene Dietrich and Herbert Marshall. Eva and fellow silent star Ethel Clayton were to appear, but neither of them is among the film's cast listing, not even as uncredited.

The working title of the second picture was "The Great Diamond Mystery," directed by Malcolm St. Clair and starring Cesar Romero. When released, the film was titled *Dangerously Yours*, and, once again, Eva, if she did appear somewhere in the film, is not listed among the cast.

In December 1938, Louella Parsons reported in her column that Eva Novak and former silent star Barbara Bedford had "checked in" for roles in MGM's upcoming *Honolulu*—released February 3, 1939, and starring Eleanor Powell, Robert Young, and the comedy team of George Burns and Gracie Allen. In October of that year, Eva was among the many former stars who attended the premiere of *Hollywood Cavalcade*, a tribute to the silent movie days, at the 4 Star Theatre in Los Angeles. The film starred Don Ameche and Alice Faye and featured such familiar silent players as Buster Keaton, Hank Mann, Heinie Conklin, Jimmy Finlayson, Ben Turpin, Chester Conklin, Edward Earle, Franklyn Farnum, Harold Goodwin, Snub Pollard, Victor Potel, and Mack Sennett. The admission fee was $10 per person, with all proceeds going to the Motion Picture Relief Fund. With an attendance of 730, $7,300 was raised for the fund.

Working "Extra"

It appears that Eva didn't want to give up films entirely and continued to take work in films where she received no credit—and in which she may not even be recognized in the final product. She was announced for three more such films. Trade magazines in late 1939 and early 1940 reported that several "former great stars" would be appearing in *Mr. Smith Goes to Washington* (whose initial release was actually October 1939), director Frank Capra's classic starring James Stewart. The "former great stars" were Maurice Costello, Vera Stedman, Eva Novak and Fisk O'Hara.

For the next film, Eva was mistakenly identified as a serial queen of the silents and that she would be working as an extra in RKO's *Dance, Girl, Dance* (1940) starring Maureen O'Hara.

While hyping Jeanette MacDonald and Nelson Eddy's latest Technicolor operetta, *Bitter Sweet* (1940), it was mentioned that "10 former luminaries" would appear in the ballroom scene. The names given were King Baggott,

Barbara Bedford, May McAvoy, Lillian Rich, Mahlon Hamilton, Mason Hopper, Rosemary Theby, Rhea Mitchell, Naomi Childers—and Eva Novak.

The war had started in December 1941 for the United States, and anything Hollywood did to support the war effort was news—even a tidbit reported by Louella Parsons in December 1942 that Eva was taking a course in welding in Brooklyn, not only to do her bit for Uncle Sam, but "to keep her family together." It may be that with Reed away serving his country, Eva needed the extra income, although there was never anything throughout the years to indicate she and her husband had financial difficulties.

No Time to Grieve

In October 1943, Louella Parsons announced that Eva was in town and available for movie jobs. She was reported to have been doing defense work "in the East," [Brooklyn, New York] but was returning home with her husband, who had been ill. Three months later, on January 7, 1944, William Reed passed away at the untimely age of 49. Eva would live another 44 years, but she never remarried.

In July of that year, a Hollywood columnist mentioned that Eva was back at work, along with Roscoe Arbuckle's one-time wife Minta Durfee, playing bit parts in David O. Selznick's *Since You Went Away*. Whether these still-working actresses made the final cut is anybody's guess. Film after film followed, and sometimes there might even be a line or two of dialogue. The studios varied from obscure, such as Argosy and Enterprise, to the respectable and small Republic studio, and an occasional major studio, such as Warner Bros. An uncredited part as a nun in director Leo McCarey's 1945 hit, *The Bells of St. Mary's*, was one of Eva's most recognizable roles during this period.

In the early 1950s, Eva was a board member on the Screen Extras Guild and was a candidate for director in 1954. That same year, she was one of four judges for the Sun Valley Fiesta Queen. And in 1955, she became a grandmother for the sixth time.

On April 3, 1956, Mary Pickford hosted a party at Pickfair in honor of author Daniel C. Blum—one of his books being the prodigious *A Pictorial History of the Silent Screen* (G.P. Putnam's Sons, 1953). In attendance were Jane and Eva, ZaSu Pitts, Louise Fazenda, Annette Kellerman, Frances Marion, Mary Philbin, Marguerite Fischer, Louise Dresser, Irene Rich, Francis X. Bushman, Laura La Plante, Viola Dana, Betty Blythe, Shirley Mason, Harold Lloyd, Eleanor Boardman, Marion Davies, Claire Windsor, May McAvoy, Pat O'Malley, Antonio Moreno, Ramon Novarro, Edward Everett Horton, Ralph Graves, Johnny Mack Brown, Reginald Denny, Gilda Gray, Hoot Gibson, Mahlon Hamilton, Charles Rosher

(Pickford's cameraman), Anita Stewart, Clara Kimball Young, Marguerite Snow, Louise Glaum, William Boyd, Eileen Percy, James Kirkwood and others.

That same month, Hedda Hopper's column announced that Jane and Eva were signed by John Payne and brothers Frank and Walter Seltzer (Jane's son-in-law) for *The Boss*. Hedda Hopper mistakenly said this was the first time the sisters had ever appeared in the same picture—they had worked together in *The Man Life Passed By* in 1923. Unfortunately, neither Jane nor Eva can be found among cast credits, credited or uncredited.

Between 1950 and 1957, Eva appeared in 14 films. She has an uncredited part as a "courtier" in Gloria Swanson's famous *Sunset Boulevard* in 1950, one of many silent stars whose faces show up at one time or another in the film. She was in *The Eddie Cantor Story* in 1953; the comedy *How to Be Very, Very Popular*, with Betty Grable and Bob Cummings in 1955; and even a Ma and Pa Kettle movie in 1957. Of those 14 films, her only credited part was for Republic Pictures' *The Blonde Bandit* (1950), in which she played a prison matron.

In late 1957, Eva appeared in a movie . . . at least her photograph did. Producer/director Dick Powell's *Enemy Below* is a World War II drama about an American destroyer escort's encounter with a German U-boat. Curt Jurgens, as the U-boat commander, keeps a photo of his wife (Eva) in his quarters. Eva's compensation for the sitting was a check in the amount of $21.51.

There were also extra roles in four westerns, one starring Randolph Scott. It's clear that Eva enjoyed performing in westerns—her days with Tom Mix would attest to that. So, it is not surprising that the final eight years of acting included several TV westerns—of which there were plenty in the late 1950s and early 1960s. She can be seen in *Tales of Wells Fargo*, *Laramie*, *Wagon Train*, and *Laredo*. In 1962, she played an uncredited townswoman in the acclaimed John Ford film *The Man Who Shot Liberty Valance*, starring John Wayne and James Stewart.

In 1965, she had a credited part in *Wild Seed*, starring Michael Parks and Celia Kaye. She was Kaye's mother, but the viewer can only see a flash of her as she and her husband discover their runaway daughter at a hotel, and she rushes in to hug her. There is a lengthy scene with Parks and Kaye in a dark bar with Eva and her husband in the background, but it is so dark you can't even make out their faces. That's about it. Interestingly, one newspaper article about her appearance in the film said it was a return to the screen after an absence of 46 years!

SOURCES: See page 287

Chapter 24
The Novak Sisters
Part III: Fade-Out

෭ඁ

The Novak sisters disappeared from public view for several years. Then, in 1974, Jane was suddenly being recognized for her new cookbook, filled with chicken recipes, all her own. It will be remembered that all the way back in the silent days, Jane was described as a "homebody" who loved to keep house and cook. Jane said that long years of sharing the kitchen with Mickey and her husband led to the collaboration on the cookbook. Jane selected and tested the recipes, and Mickey did the typing and editing. *A Treasury of Chicken Cookery* was published by Harper & Row and proved to be a good seller.

In 1974, Jane's name was once again in the newspapers with the release of her cookbook, Treasury of Chicken Cookery, *featuring over 300 of her favorite recipes.*

With this renewed recognition, interviewers frequently prevailed upon the sisters to discuss their days in the silent movies. In one article in *The Los Angeles Times*, Jane recounted her decision to move from St. Louis to Los Angeles. Noting that the press of the day was enjoying the publication of anything scandalous involving film players, she said, "My mother had better sense. She knew there were just as many opportunities to become a fallen woman in St. Louis, if I wanted to." She once again gave her aunt, the Vitagraph actress Anne Schaefer, credit for introducing her to films. During the short period she worked for Hal Roach, she noted, "We never had a script. We'd just come up with an idea, and then others would embellish it, and the next thing we were shooting it."

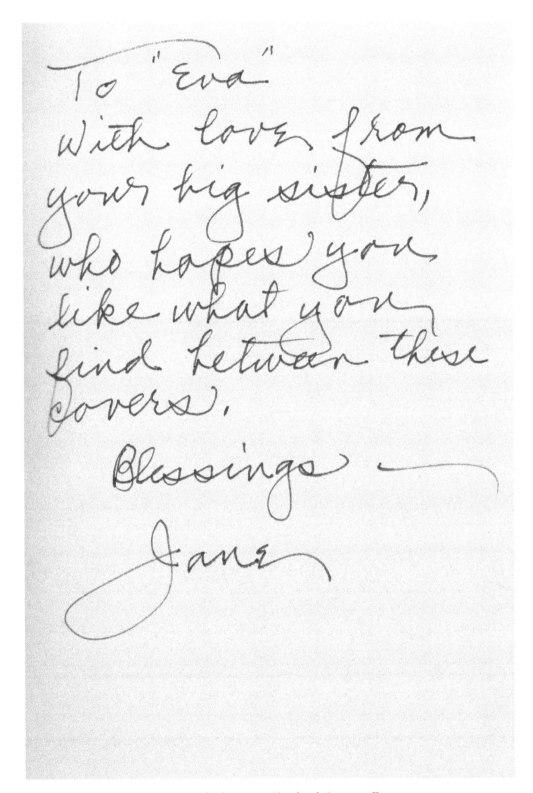

To "Eva"
With love from
your big sister,
who hopes you
like what you
find between these
covers.
Blessings —
Jane

Jane inscribed a copy of her book for sister Eva.

It was during this interview that Jane finally admitted that she and William S. Hart had once been engaged. "She worked with Hart and his horse, Fritz, and was engaged to the Western star for nearly five years," the article reads. "In that time, they twice came close to tying the marital knot, but both times she backed off for reasons she said she cannot recall exactly." Jane did appear once earlier in the year in a photo at the re-dedication of the refurbished William S. Hart mansion in Newhall at the Hart Park. She was pictured with two of the park's officials and a gentleman named Joe McNinch, Hart's friend, who also willed his ranch to the county.

On April 17, 1988, the following announcement ran in newspapers around the country:

> Silent movie actress Eva Novak, who starred as Tom Mix's love interest in 10 of his Westerns and did her own stunts, as well, has died after a bout with pneumonia. She was 90. Miss Novak died Sunday evening at the Motion Picture Country Hospital.

Two years later, on Thursday, February 3, 1990, Jane suffered a stroke and died at the age of 94. Like Eva, she had been a patient at the Motion Picture and Television Hospital. Following a private memorial service, Jane was laid to rest near her sister at the San Fernando Mission Cemetery.

Jane's final on-camera appearance was for Kevin Brownlow and David Gill's 1989 documentary, *Harold Lloyd: The Third Genius*. In a brief clip, the nonagenarian recalls the time she first met Hal Roach, in 1915.

The last-known interview with both sisters had occurred seven years earlier, in 1982. Jane (86 at the time) and Eva (84) had remained close over the years, living only five minutes apart in the San Fernando Valley. They were interviewed in the home of Walter and Mickey Seltzer, where Jane had resided for many years. According to the article, Seltzer referred to the sisters "with affectionate good humor" as "two dippy old broads from St. Louis."

In the interview, Eva said Tom Mix thought she reminded him of a baby sister. He liked working with her because she did all the stunts with him, she said. Then Jane interjected, "We all did our own stunts in those days." Eva said she met Tom Mix and his wife, Victoria, in a restaurant, and he offered her a three-picture contract right there. She recounted that in one movie she had to lie down by the side of a horse while the cattle were stampeding. "They will go around the horse and not harm us," Mix told her. "I wasn't even scared. You're never scared when you're young."

More than once, then-and-now photos of the sisters were shared with the media. These were taken from 1921 and 1950, respectively.

Jane claimed that at one time she was making $2,000 a week. Eva said she never made that much money. Jane also said she was still receiving about 10 fan letters a week, one having arrived recently from Germany.

The article pointed out that Jane had one daughter and one grandchild. Eva, it noted, had two daughters, six grandchildren, and eight great-grandchildren.

Finally, the interviewer asked if there was ever any rivalry between them in their acting days.

"Oh, no, never," Eva said.

"Not at all," Jane added.

SOURCES

NEWSPAPERS

Akron (OH) Beacon Journal, 1921

Albuquerque (NM) Morning Journal, 1917

The American Film Institute Catalog of American Feature Films (afi.com)

The Boston (MA) *Globe*, 1928

The Chicago (IL) *Tribune*, 1917

The Chronicle-Telegram (Elyria, OH), 1915

Colton (CA) *Daily Courier*, 1924

Corsicana (TX) *Daily Sun*, 1923

The Daily Record (Long Branch, NJ), 1926

Engineering News Record, 1923

Exhibitors Herald, 1922–1923

Film Daily, 1915–1927

The Fresno (CA) *Morning Republican*, 1918–1927

The Los Angeles (CA) *Times*, 1919–1982

The Marshall County News (Maryville, KS), 1921

Modesto (CA) *Herald*, 1921

New York (NY) *Herald*, 1921

The New York (NY) *Times*, 1920

Oakland (CA) *Tribune*, 1919–1933

Oroville (CA) *Daily Register*, 1919–1926

Press and Sun-Bulletin (Binghamton, NY), 1921

The Sacramento (CA) *Bee*, 1920–1921

Santa Ana (CA) *Register*, 1922

The Signal (Santa Clarita, CA), 1935–1950

The Sunday Tribune (Singapore, China), 1935

Sydney (Australia) *Morning Herald*, 1927

The Ventura County (CA) *Star*, 1924

The Ventura (CA) *Daily Post*, 1924

Visalia (CA) *Morning Delta*, 1922

OTHER PERIODICALS

Harrison's Reports, 1920–1921

Motion Picture Classic, 1924

Motion Picture Magazine, 1922

Motion Picture News, 1919–1922

Motion Picture World, 1924–1925

Photoplay, 1915–1924

Picture Play, 1920–1921

The Silent Picture, Issue No. 14, Spring 1972

Variety, 1915–1929

INTERNET

Internet Archive (archive.org)

The Internet Movie Database (IMDb.com)

The Library of Congress (loc.gov)

SCVhistory.com

Wordpress.com

BOOKS

Brownlow, Kevin. *Behind the Mask of Innocence: Sex, Violence, Prejudice, Crime: Films of Social Conscience in the Silent Era*. Berkeley and Los Angeles: University of California Press, 1990.

Davis, Lon. *Silent Lives: 100 Biographies of the Silent Film Era*. Albany, GA: BearManor Media, 2008.

Hart, William S. *My Life East and West*. Chicago: R.R. Donnelly & Company, 1994.

Jensen, Richard D. *The Amazing Tom Mix: The Most Famous Cowboy of the Movies*. New York: iUniverse, 2005.

Johnston, William Allen, ed. *Motion Picture Studio Directory and Trade Annual 1921—Primary Source Edition*. Eagle, ID: Silver Creek Press, 2013.

Koszarski, Diane Kaiser. *The Complete Films of William S. Hart: A Pictorial Record*. New York: Dover Publications, 1980.

Lahue, Kalton C. *Ladies in Distress*. New York: A.S. Barnes and Company, 1972.

Liebman, Roy. *Silent Film Performers: An Annotated Bibliography of Published, Unpublished and Archival Sources for Over 350 Actors and Actresses*. Jefferson, NC: McFarland, 1996.

Lloyd, Annette D'Agostino. *The Harold Lloyd Encyclopedia*. Jefferson, NC: McFarland, 2004.

Slide, Anthony. *The New Historical Dictionary of the American Film Industry*. Lanham, MD, and London: The Scarecrow Press, 2001.

———. *Silent Players: A Biographical and Autobiographical Study of 100 Silent Film Actors and Actresses*. Lexington, KY: The University Press of Kentucky, 2002.

About the Author

Tim Lussier has served as webmaster for the respected silent movie web-site SilentsAreGolden.com for 23 years. In 2018, his book *Bare Knees Flap-per: The Life and Films of Virginia Lee Corbin* was published by McFarland & Company, Inc. A former newspaper reporter, journalism teacher and school public relations director, Lussier has had a 46-year love affair with silent mov-ies. He has amassed a collection of over 1,200 silent features and hundreds of shorts, as well as hundreds of silent movie-related books and vintage movie magazines. Lussier is retired and lives in North Carolina with his wife, Debbie, where they spend time traveling and enjoying their six grandchildren.

Index

Numbers in **bold** indicate photographs

100% American 109
101-Bison Ranch 64, 65
143rd Field Artillery Battalion 105, 107, 110
Abbott and Costello 129
About Mrs. Leslie 251
Abysmal Brute, The 126
Academy Award® 5, 6, 46
Across the Border 133
Affairs of Anatol, The 172
African Film Company 51
Agnew, Robert 243
Aherne, Brian 96
Air Hawk, The 140, 184
Air Patrol, The 141, 148
Alias the Bad Man 195, 196, 197
All Quiet on the Western Front 82
Allen, Gracie 281
Allison, May 65, 66, **67**, **69**, 70, 239
Ameche, Don 281
American Aircraft Company 139
American Film Criticism 82
American Film Manufacturing Company (American Flying "A") 57, 65, 66
American Lifeograph Company 218, 239
American Releasing Company 181
American Vitagraph Company (see Vitagraph Company of America)
Anderson, "Broncho Billy" 153, 212
Anderson, Robert **229**
Andy Hardy series 213
Angel 281
Anna Karenina (1935) 129
Anne of Little Smokey 221
Anne of the Trails 202
Arab, The 167
Arbuckle, Roscoe "Fatty" 130, 132, 154, 282
Argosy Pictures Corporation 282
Arlington Cemetery 151
Army Air Corps. 143, 147
Arnold, Stanford F. 190

Around the World in 80 Days 130
Arrow Film Corporation 236, 239
Artists Booking Exchange 229
Ascher Productions 258
Ashtrays Unlimited 7
Ask Father 10, **11**
Assault on a Queen 130
Associated Cinema Artists 245
Asther, Nils 91, **92**, 93, **94**, 95, 96, 97
Asther, Evelyn 95
Astor, Mary 126
At the Sign of the Lost Angel 202
Australasian Film Company 278
Ayres, Agnes 194, 245
Ayres, Lew 82, 96
Back Pay 46, 48
Bad Boy 123
Baggott, King 281
Bainbridge, John 86, 87, 90
Ballak, Mrs. J.T. 244
Balloonatic, The 20, **23**, 29, 117, 118
Balshofer, Fred J. 66, 67
Bancroft, George 1, 238
Bankhead, Tallulah 86
Banks, Monty **254**
Banner Productions 230, 231, 239
Bara, Theda 243
Barbarian, The (1921) ix
Barbarian, The (1933) 129
Barker, The 5, 6
Baroud 167, 168
Barrie, J.M. (James) 170, 184
Barron Field (TX) 143
Barry, Eddie 254, 255
Barrymore, John 125
Barrymore, Lionel 188
Barthelmess, Richard **6**, 125, 170, 176, 177
Batman 130
Battle Cry of Peace, The 104
Battle of Santiago Bay 151
Battle of Shiloh, The 74
Battling Butler 86

Battling Fool, The **271**
Battling Mason 273
Bayer, William 197, 199
Bayne, Beverly 65
Beautiful Sinner, The 271, 272
Bedford, Barbara 281, 282
Beery, Noah 181, 183, 225
Beery, Wallace 13, 79, 181, 215, 216, 224-225, 238
Behind the Door 215, 216
Bellamy, Madge 59, **60**, 235-236
Bellamy, Ralph 281
Belle of Alaska 224
Belle of Broadway, The **4**
Belles of Liberty **254**
Bells of St. Mary's, The 282
Ben Hur 136
Ben Wilson Productions 187
Bennett, Chester **224**, 225, 226, 230, 235, 236, 239, 240, 267, 269
Bennett, Whitman 230
Benny, Jack 279
Beranger, George 269
Bernhardt, Sarah 88
Bernstein, William 197
Besserer, Eugenie **276**
Betty Takes a Hand 102
Betz, John 74
Betzwood Studio 74
Big City, The 5, 7
Billington, Francelia vii, 55, **56**, 57, **58**, 59, **60**, **61**, 62, 257
Biltmore Productions 195
Biograph Company 73, 137, 153, 175, 215, 253
Birth of a Nation, The 207
Bitter Sweet 281
Bitter Tea of General Yen, The 95
Black Beauty 158
Black Oxen, The 47
Blackmer, Sidney 251
Blacksmith, The 25
Blackton, J. Stuart 77-78, 150, 151, **152**, 153, 155, 158, 178
Blackwell, Carlyle 56
Blackguard, The (aka *Die Prinzessin und der Geiger*) **233**, 234, 247
Blazing Arrows 60, **61**

Blind Husbands 55, 57, **58**
Blonde Bandit, The 283
Blue Blazes 59
Blue Danube, The 92
Blue Light, The 38
"Blue Sedan, The" 265
Bluebeard 96
Blum, Daniel C. 282
Blythe, Betty 282
Boardman, Eleanor 38, 86, 182, 282
Boat, The 18, 21, 29
Body Punch, The 192
Boer War 105, 151, 152
Boland, Eddie 255
Bold Bank Robbery, The 72
Bonner, Priscilla 192, 197
Booth, Shirley 251, 252
Borzage, Frank 74, 235
Boss, The 283
Boston Blackie 268
Boston Braves 47
Bosworth, Hobart 204, **205**, 206, 215, 216, 269
Bow, Clara 86, 170, 172, 228, 238, 239
Bowes, Cliff 119, 258
Bowers, Charlie 111
Bowers, John 59, 230
Boyd, William 283
Boyle, Jack 268
Bradbury Mansion 12, 202
Brack, Tony 148
Bracken, Eddie 96
Brady, Alice 259, 261
Braidwood, Frank 262
Brando, Marlon 247
Breaking Through 157
Breese, Edmund 242
Brenon, Herbert 92
Brent, Evelyn 182
Brewster, Eugene V. 178
Brian, Mary 86, 197, 238
Bringing Up Betty 125
Briscoe, Lottie 74
Broadway Arizona 102
Broken Blossoms 176
Bronson, Betty 170, 238, 279
Brooks, Louise 88, 89, 90
Brooks, Sammy **11**, **14**

Brown, Clarence 88, 90

Brown, John Mack 93, 94, 282

Brown of Harvard 86

Brown, Dr. Spencer 183

Brownell, Vincent 190

Browning, Elizabeth Barrett 224

Browning, Tod 79

Brownlow, Kevin vi, 1, 7, 38, 40, 53, 54, 90, 127, 130, 131, 149, 286

Bruce, Kate 174

Bruce, Nigel 129

Brunton, Robert 180

Buckley, William 262

Buhler, Richard 73

Bulldog Drummond 129

Bunny, John **153**, 154, 157

Bumping Into Broadway 15

Burglar On the Roof, The 151

Burn 'Em Up Barnes 176

Burning the Wind 194

Burns, George 281

Burns, Neal 254

Burns, Vinnie 73

Burrell, George 262

Bushman, Francis X. vii, 65, 245, 282

Bushman, Francis X., Jr. 269

But the Flesh is Weak 95

Butler, David 269

Butler, E.L. 265

Byron, Marion 111, **112**, 113

Cabanne, Christy 57

Cabinet of Dr. Caligari, The 18

Calgary Stampede, The 185, 186, 197

California Straight Ahead **126**, 127

Campbell, Webster 45

Cameraman, The 19, 28

Camille (1936) 88

Camp Kearney (CA) 105, 106, 107

Canutt, Yakima 136, 272

Capital Films 59

Capra, Frank 194, 281

Captain Blood 158

Captain Kidd's Kids **14**, 15

Card, James 97, 170, 177

Cardboard Lover, The 92

Carewe, Edwin 74

Carey, Gary 86, 90

Carey, Harry 183, 189, 206, 221, **244**, 245, 250

Carr, Dixie 206

Carradine, John 96

Carter, Owen 133

Cat Ballou 130

C.B.C. Film Sales (see Columbia Pictures Corporation)

Century Comedies 113

Chadwick Pictures Corporation 4

Chaney, Lon viii, 2, 5, 6, 92, 119, 170, 172, 177

Changing Husbands 79

Chaplin, Charlie 8, 9, 32, **33**, 34, 35, 36, **37**, 38, **39**, 40, 67, 74, 78, 80, 82, 109, 111, 130, 153, 154, 253

Chase, Charley 111, 121, 122, 123, 130, 245, 275

Chasing the Moon 264

Cheat, The 211

Cheerful Fraud, The 127

Cherrill, Virginia 36, **37**, 38, 39

Chesebro, George 269

Chester Bennett Film Laboratories 240

Chesterfield Pictures 193

Chicago 119

Chicago Daily Tribune 207

Childers, Naomi 282

Chip of the Flying U 185, **186**, 197

Choice Productions 270

Christian, The 155

Christie, Al 2

Christie Brothers 2, 113, 118

Christy, Howard Chandler 98, 178

Cinema Director, The (see *Luke's Movie Muddle*)

Cineograph 72

Circus, The 35, 36

City Lights 36, **37**, 39, 74

City Slicker, The 15

Civilization 104

Claire, Gertrude 262

Clark, Maguerite 63

Clarke, Frank 139

Clary, Charles 240

Claws of the Hun, The 210, **211**

Clayton, Ethel 73, 74, 125, 281

Closed Gates 242

Cloud Dodger, The 141

Cloud Rider, The **140**

Clune Studio 207

Colbert, Claudette 172

Colleen of the Pines **225**, 226

College 19, 23, 29

Collier, William 194

Collins, John 49, 50, 51, 52

Colorado Motion Picture Company 133

Columbia Pictures Corporation 4, 195, 235, 247, 267, 270

Committee for Honoring Motion Picture Stars, The 47

Compson, Betty ix, **x**, 1, 2, 3, **4**, 5, **6**, 7, 80, 245

Compson, Eleanor Lucime (Betty Compson) 2

Conklin, Chester 281

Conklin, Heinie 281

Conklin, William 221

Conley, Lige 119

Continental Producing Company 207

Convict 13 20

Coogan, Jackie 32

Cooley, Hallam 267

Cooper, Miriam 208

Coquette 6

Corbett-Fitzsimmons Fight 72

Corbin, Virginia Lee vi, **81**, **140**, 290

Corelli, Marie 227

Corey, Wendell 251

Cortez, Ricardo 3, **85**

Cosmopolitan Pictures 92

Cossacks, The 92

Costello, Maurice 153, 245, 281

Count Your Change 15

Courtot, Marguerite 242

Covered Wagon, The 3, 170

Crawford, Joan 86, 92, 93

Crawford-Saunders Field 139

Creeth, Bud 146

Cricket on the Hearth, The 181, 197, 198

Crisp, Donald 207, 242

Criterion Theatre (New York) 155

Crowd, The 38

Cruze, James 2, 3, 4, 5, 7

Cummings, Irving 265

Cummings, Robert "Bob" 251, 283

Cuneo, Francelia 60

Cuneo, Jack 60

Cuneo, Lester 59, 60, **61**

Curious Dream, A 152

Curley, Pauline 67

Curwood, James Oliver 218, 223, 266-267

Cutts, Graham 233, 234

Dale, Dora 212

Dalton, Dorothy 43

Dana, Viola v, 49, **50**, 51, 52, 53, 54, 79, 262, 269, 282

Dance, Girl, Dance 281

Danger Patrol 193, 194

Danger Signal, The 235

Dangerous Intrigue 281

Dangerous Virtue (see *The Prude's Fall*)

Dangerously Yours 281

Daniels, Virginia "Bebe" ix, 2, 8, 9, 10, **11**, 12, **13**, **14**, 15, 16, 17, 80, 117, 157, 239

D'Arcy, Roy 245

Dardis, Tom 11, 12, 15, 17

Daredevil, The 257

Das Geheimnis der Herzogin 92

Dash Through the Clouds, A 137

David Harum 65

Davies, Marion 38, 92, 238, 282

Davis, Lt. Benjamin 100

Davis, Bette 129, 238

Davis, Gilbert 245

Davis, Mildred 11, 15

Davis, Ulysses 206

Daw, Marjorie 269

Dawn, Norman 262, 270, 274

Dawn of Tomorrow, The 79, 83

Day, Laraine 247

Day, Marceline 19, 28

Day of Faith, The 78, 83

Day She Paid, The 58

Daydreams 21, 25

de Grasse, Joseph 183

de Mille, William 106

de Remer, Rubye 67

De Voortrekkers (see *Winning of a Continent*)

Dean, Priscilla 79

Deely, Ben 223

Del Rio, Dolores 86

DeMille, Cecil B. 13, 14, 17, 79, 96, 106, 107, 109, 139, 172, 173, 174, 176, 178, 211, 238

DeMille Pictures 92

Denny, Reginald vii, 124, **125**, **126**, 127, **128**, 129, 130, 131, 282

Dent, Vernon 119

Desert Love 59, 257

Desmond, William 180, 183, 250

Devil's Chaplain, The 194

Devil's Masterpiece, The 190

Devoe, Norman 146

Devore, Dorothy 182

Die Prinzessin und der Geiger (aka *The Black-guard*) **233**

Dietrich, Marlene 86, 129, 281

Director of the Cinema (see *Luke's Movie Muddle*)

Divine Lady, The 45, **46**, 47

Divorce 230

Dix, Richard 241

Dixie Flyer, The 276

Dizzy Heights and Daring Hearts 137

Docks of New York, The ix, 1, 5

Doctor Cupid 154

Dollar Devils 267

Donnell, Dorothy 223

Donovan Affair, The 194, 197

Don't Change Your Husband 172

Double Dukes 254

Double Speed 172

Doubling for Romeo 180, 197

Dougherty, Jack 190, 191, 192, 194, 198

Doyle, Arthur Conan 184

Doyle, Billy 62

Dr. Kildare's Wedding Day 96

Dream of Love 92

Dresser, Louise 188, 282

Dressler, Marie 109

Drew, Sidney 157

Duffy, Oliva (see Olive Thomas)

Dugmore, Reginald Lee (see Reginald Denny)

Dumas, Alexander 181

Duncan Sisters 92, 95

Duncan, Vivian 92, 95, 96

Duncan, William **159**

Dunlap, Scott 278

Durfee, Minta 282

Durham, Dick 190

Durning, Bernard 52

Duse, Eleonora 88

Duty's Reward 278

Dwan, Allan 238

Dwyer, Ruth 126

Eagle's Talons, The 139

Earle, Edward 281

Eason, B. Reeves 271

Eddie Cantor Story, The 283

Eddy, Helen Jerome 221

Eddy, Nelson 281

Edeson, Robert 242

Edison Motion Picture Company 49, 50, 51, 52, 63, 72, 73, 137, 153, 161

Edison, Thomas 150, 153, 161

Educational Pictures, Inc. 113

Electric House, The 27

Ell-bee Pictures 187

Elliott, Milton "Skeets" 145

Ellis, Robert 274

Elvidge, June 267

Embarrassing Moments 129

End of the Road, The **69**

Enemy Below 283

Enemy Sex, The 3

Engineering News-Record 243, 288

Enterprise Productions, Inc. 282

Equity Pictures 261

Errol, Leon 274

Erwin, Stu 113

Espionage Act of 1917 105, 207

Essanay Film Manufacturing Company 32, 65, 73, 75, 153, 156

Eva Novak Productions 265

Evans Studio 2

Even Break, An 102

Everson, William K. 38, 40, 50, 54

Everybody's Sweetheart 102, 103

Evil Half, The (see *Wolves of the North*)

Exclusive Rights 121

Excuse My Dust 172

Exhibitors Herald 225, 269, 288

Eyes of the Forest 146

Eyes of the World, The 207, 232

Eyman, Scott 101, 102, 108, 110

Eyton, Bessie 67

Fair, Elinor 2, 180

Fairbanks, Douglas viii, 38, 47, 63, 67, 70, 80, 101, 102, 105, 109, 134, 135, 187, 234

Fairbanks, Douglas, Jr. 5, 238

Fairbanks, William 188, 261, 269, 270, **271, 272**

Faire, Virginia Brown vii, viii, 178, **179**, 180, 181, 182, 183, **184**, 185, **186, 187**, 188, **189**, 190, 191, 192, **193**, 194, 195, **196**, 197, 198, 199

Famous Players-Lasky 3, 14, 65, 79, 82, 106

Farley, Dot 270

Farnum, Franklyn 148, 281

Farnum, William 245

Fast Worker, The 126

Fatal Mistake, The 271

Fates of Flora Fourflush or The Massive Ten Billion Dollar Vitagraph Mystery Sequel, The 157

Fawcett, George vii, 170, 174, **175**, 176, 177, 278

Faye, Alice 281

Fazenda, Louise 270, 282

Fearless Lover, The **272**

Fellowes, Rockcliffe 270

Ferguson, Elsie 125

Feud, The **256**

Fielding, Romaine 75

Fight for Honor, A 271

Fightin' Mad 180, 182

File on Thelma Jordan, The 251

Film Booking Offices (F.B.O.) 181, 239

Film Daily 43, 204, 236, 237, 240, 276, 278, 288

Films in Review 48, 97, 169, 197, 198

Finch, Flora 154, 245

Fine Arts Corporation 258

Fine Arts Studio (New York) 230, 265

Finlayson, James "Jimmy" 281

Fire Flingers, The 212

First Division Pictures 240

First National Pictures 5, 32, 42, 43, 45, 46, 47, 183, 185, 193, 217, 239, 269

Fischer, Marguerite 282

Fisher, George 278

Fisher, Harrison 98

Fitzmaurice, George 43

Flagg, James Montgomery 178

Flapper, The 102

Flesh and the Devil 5, 87, 88, 177

Flugrath, Edna 49, 50, **51**, 53, 54, 145

Flugrath, Leonie (see Shirley Mason)

Flugrath, Virginia (see Viola Dana)

Fluttering Hearts 123

Flyin' Thru 140

Flying Fool, The 146

Flying Mail, The 140

Flynn, Maurice "Lefty" 262, 263

Fonda, Jane 130

Fontaine, Joan 129

For Heaven's Sake 86

For the Term of His Natural Life 278

Ford, Harrison 118

Ford, John 283

Forde, Victoria 265, 286

Foreign Correspondent 247

Forest Ranger (see *Eyes of the Forest*)

Forman, Tom 237

Forrest, Allan 269

Four Horsemen of the Apocalypse, The 58, 164

Fox Comedies 117

Fox, Earle 224

Fox Film Corporation 4, 52, 53, 78, 113, 145, 146, 161, 181, 183, 188, 208, 215, 235, 239, 264, 268

Fox, Virginia 25, 29, 116, 118

Francis, Alec B. 270

Francis, Kay 96

Francisco, Betty 182, 269

Frazer, Robert 80

Free Lips 240, 242

Freshman, The 276

Frohman and Shubert 63

From Italy's Shores 203

From Soup to Nuts 113, **114**

Frozen North, The 20

Furies, The 251

Furst, Mildred 243

Furthman, Jules 117

Gaemon, Charles 138

Gainsborough Films (England) 233, 234

Gall, Filvius Jack 7

Gallant Lady 251

Gamble, The 66

Garbo, Greta vii, 5, 84, **85**, 86, 87, **88**, 89, 90, 91, 92, 93, **94**, 95, 96, 97, 129, 177, 187, 188, 261

Garbutt, Frank 14

Garden of Allah, The 166, 167, 168
Garden of Eden, The **42**, 47
Garon, Pauline 182
Garvin, Anita vii, 111, 112, 113, **114**, 115, 123
Gassaway, Gordon 223
General, The 18, 26, 29, 81, 82
General Film 154, 156, 158
George Eastman House 47, 170
George, Maude **42**
Gest, Morris 124
Ghost City, The 140
Ghost Town **244**, 250
Gibson, Hoot 62, 126, 185, **186**, 189, 194, 282
Gilbert, John 2, 5, 87, 92, 170, 172, 177, 181, 183
Gill, David 38, 40, 53, 55, 286
Gilmore, Lillian 184
Girl and the Goose, The (see *The Smart Sex*)
Girl of Today, The 41
Girl Who Stayed at Home, The 176
Gish, Lillian 177
Glass, Gaston 146, 195, 235
Glaum, Louise 283
Gleason, Jackie 47
Glyn, Elinor 239
Goddard, Paulette 38, **39**, 40
Goddess, The 157
Gold Rush, The 33, 34, 38
Goldcup Derby (see *Racing for Life*)
Golden Trail, The 218
Goldstein, Robert 207
Goldwyn Pictures 42, 78, 79, 218, 239, 268
Gonzalez, Myrtle 202
Good Morning, Judge 127
Goodwill Pictures 190
Goodwin, Harold 281
Gordon, Huntley 239
Gordon, Julia Swayne 153, 155
Gordon, Robert 235
Gordon, Robert "Bobby" 192
Gosfilmofond 47
Gotham Film Company 193, 274
Grable, Betty 283
Grace, Dick 132, 136, 137, 145, **146**, 147
Graft 206, 244, 250
Grand Central Palace (New York) 77
Grant, Cary 129
Graves, Ralph 282

Gray, Gilda 282
Gray, Zane 262
Great Accident, The 218
Great Air Robbery, The 58, 143, **144**, 145
Great Circus Mystery, The 148
Great Diamond Mystery, The (see *Dangerously Yours*)
Great Divide, The 74
Great Train Robbery, The 63, 72, 137
Greatest Question, The 176
Greely, Evelyn 125
Green, Alfred E. 265
Greenwood, Charlotte 129
Grey, Lita 32, 34, 35
Gribbon, Harry 255, 258, 259
Griffith, Corinne 41, **42**, 43, **44**, 45, **46**, 47, 48, **159**, 243
Griffith, D.W. 104, 174, 175, 177, 207, 215
Griffith, Raymond ix, 1, 77, **78**, 79, 80, **81**, 82, 83, 130
Grim Game, The 143
Guaranty Liquidating Corporation 247
Gudrun 96
Gun Gospel **189**, 190
Haas, Hugo 47
Hagney, Frank 240
Haisman, Irene "Renee" 124, 128
Hal B. Wallis Productions 247, 251
Hale, Alan 170
Hale, Creighton 193, 245
Hale, Georgia **34**, 35, 38
Hall, Mayre 262
Halliday, John 245
Hamilton, Lloyd 111, 119, 120, 121
Hamilton, Mahlon 59, 240, 243, 282
Handcuffed 194
Handworth, Octavio 73
Hanson, Lars 91, 177
Hands Up! **81**, 82
Harbaugh, William 133
Hard Luck 20, 25, 26, **27**, 29
Hardy, Oliver 74, **112**, 275
Harlan, Kenneth 230, **231**
Harmon, Pat 276
Harold Lloyd: The Third Genius 286
Harris Theatre (New York) 155
Harrison, Arthur 8

Harrison's Reports 186, 187,188, 198, 222, 249, 250, 257, 258, 259, 288, 289

Harron, Robert "Bobby" 174, 176

Hart, Mamie (see Mary Ellen Hart) 220

Hart, Mary Ellen 249

Hart, Neal 270

Hart, William S. ix, 63, 67, 68, 200, 205, 208, 210, 212, **214**, 218, **219**, 220, 221, **222**, 223, 239, 242, 245, **248**, 253, **260**, 261, 265, 280, 286

Hart, William S., Jr. 248, 249, 250

Hatton, Raymond 238

Hauschild, Lewis J. 183

Haver, Phyllis 20, **23**, 24, **117**, 118

Hawley, Ormi 74

Haworth Pictures Corporation 211, 212, 215

Hawthorne of the U.S.A. 172

Hayakawa, Sessue 211, **212**, 213

Hazardous Valley 190

Headrick, Richard **260**

Healy, Mary 251

Hearn, Edward **225**

Hearst-Vitagraph Weekly News 154

Hearst, William Randolph 238

Hearts Adrift 65

Hearts and Flour 254

Hearts Are Trumps 59, 164

Hearts of the World 174

Hecht-Lancaster Productions 247

Hell's Angels 142

Henley, Hobart 206

Henry, Gale 255

Henry King and his Orchestra 251

Henstell, Bruce 82

Hepburn, Katherine 86, 129

Her Gethsemane 202

Herbert, Holmes 239

Hercules Film Productions 270

Herndon, Booten 101, 102

Hersholt, Jean 218, 242

Hertel, Aage 91

Heston, Charlton 247

Hiatt, Ruth 119, **120**, 121

High Gear Jeffrey 59

Hill, Thomas J. 138

Hines, Johnny 176

His Debt **212**, 213

His First Flame 121

His People 186, 197, 198

Hitchcock, Alfred 2, 129, 234, 247

Hitchcock, Reginald Ingram Montgomery (see Rex Ingram) 161

Hobart, Rose 251

Hollywood (film) 3

Hollywood: A Celebration of American Silent Film 53, 54

Hollywood Boulevard 245, 246

Hollywood Cavalcade 281

Hollywood, The Pioneers 53, 54

Hollywood Producers Association 14

Hollywood, The Years of Innocence 2, 7

Holmes, Helen 245

Holmquist, Sigrid 231

Holt, Jack 107, 194, 238, 267, **268**

Honolulu 281

Hoodooed On His Wedding Day 202

Hope, Bob 129

Hopper, Hedda 283

Hopper, Mason 282

Horner, Robert J. 269, 270

Horton, Edward Everett 282

Houdini, Harry 143

House of a Thousand Scandals, The 66

House of Shame viii, 193, 197, 198

How to Be Very, Very Popular 283

Howard, Leslie 129

Howe, Herbert 54, 83, 166

Howe, James Wong 184

Howell, Alice 255

Howes, Reed 187, 188

Huff, Theodore 32, 34, 35, 37, 38, 40

Hughes, David 274

Hughes, Howard 82, 142, 238

Hughes, Lloyd 275

Hula Hula Hughie 254

Hulette, Gladys 153

Humdrum Brown 162

Hunchback of Notre Dame, The 172

Hunt, Marsha 245

Hurst, Fanny 58

Hutchison, Charles **135**

I Cover the Waterfront 172

Ibáñez, Vicente Blasco 187

In the Clutches of Milk 224

Ince, Ralph 157
Ince, Thomas 8, 60, 64, 104, 161, 215
Incredible Eve, The 245
Ingram, Rex ix, 58, 59, 161, 162, **163**, 164, 165, 166, 167, 168, 169
Innocent Delilah, An 202
Innocent Sinner, The 208
Internal Revenue Service 237
International Film Company 98
International Novelty Company 150
Intolerance 38, 104
Irene 275
Iron Hand, The 206
Irving, Mary Jane 211-212
Isobel; or the Trail's End 218
Jack White Comedies 119
Jaeger, Daniel 192
James Ormont Productions 240
Jamison, Bud 8, **11**
Jazz Age 176, 239
Jealous Husbands 230
Jean, The Vitagraph Dog 157
Jennings, Al 249
J.L. Frothingham Productions 221
Johanna Enlists 109
John Petticoats 221
Johnson, Arthur 74
Johnston, Julanne 234, 235
Jones, Buck 188, 221, 235, 274, 280
Jones, Maxine 280
Jones, Phil 142
Jordon, Sid 257
Joy, Leatrice 79, 176
Joyce, Alice 56, 157, **159**, 228
Julian, Rupert 212
Jurgens, Kurt 283
Just Nuts 202
Kalem Company, The 55, 56, 78, 153, 157, 200, 201, 205
Karloff, Boris 129
Katchmer, George A. 62, 124, 131
Kate Plus Ten (see *Wanted at Headquarters*)
Kauffman, Stanley 82
Kaye, Celia 283
Kaye, Danny 129
Kazan 223, 224

Keaton, Buster vii, viii, ix, 18, **19**, 20, 21, 22, **23**, **24**, 25, 26, **27**, 28, 29, **30**, 31, 78, 81, 111, **115**, 116, 117, 118, 123, 129, 130, 170, 171, 172, 177, 281
Keaton, Eleanor 31, 117, 118, 123
Keefe, Cornelius 194
Kellerman, Annette 153, 282
Kennedy, Edgar 113, 122
Kennedy, Merna 35, **36**, 129
Kent, Barbara 127
Kerr, Walter 9, 81, 82, 83
Kerrigan, J. Warren 170
Kerwood, Dick 148
Key, Kathleen 182
Keystone Cops 254
Keystone Film Company 32, 132, 137, 253, 255, 258, 269
Kid, The 32, 33
Kid Boots 86
Kiki 129
Kinetoscope 150
King, Burton 2331
King, Carlotta 192
King, Henry (director) 74, 170
King of Kings, The 172
Kingsley, Grace 208, 223, 224, 234, 242
Kipling, Rudyard 180
Kirkwood, James 250, 283
Kiss, The 96
Kline, Jim 115, 123
Knott, Lydia 267, 269
Kobal, John 2, 7, 54, 149
Kodak 238
Koster and Bial's Music Hall 151
Koszarski, Richard 127, 131
La Buna, Virginia 178, **179**
Ladies Must Live 2
Lady of the Pavements 176
Laemmle, Carl 57, 125, 127, 128, 143, 203, 261
Lahue, Kalton C. 61, 62, 289
Lamarr, Hedy 96
Lancaster, Burt 247
Lancaster, John 229
Landis, Cullen 187, 267, 269, 276
Landis, Margaret 181
Lane, Lupino 111, 130
Lane, Nora 129
Langdon, Harry 111, 119, 120, 121, 130

La Plante, Laura 86, 126, 127, **128**, 182, 282

Laramie 283

Laredo 283

Larkin, George 267

Lascelle, Ward 61

Lasky Home Guard 106

Lasky, Jesse 3

Last Trail, The 262, **263**

Laugh, Clown, Laugh 92

Laughing at Danger ix, **273**

Laurel & Hardy viii, 111, **112, 114**, 115, 123, 130

Laurel, Stan **112**, 113, 115, 275

Lawford, Peter 96

Lawrence, Florence 74, 153

Lazybones 235, 236

Le Saint, Edward 276

Leahy, Margaret 182

Lease, Rex 192, 193, 195

Leather Pushers, The 125, 126, 127

Lee, Lila 6, 239

Lee, Mildred 255

Lee, Raymond 245

Lehrman, Henry 253

Lehrman Knock-Out (L-KO) Comedies 78, 79, 253, 254, 255

Lessey, George 206

Lester Cuneo Productions 59, 61

Let's Go 135, 137

Lewis, Jerry 251

Lewis, Randolph 180

Liberty Loan Drive 64, 67, 109, 110, 212

Liebman, Roy 182, 199, 289

Life (magazine) 84

Life of an American Fireman, The 63

Life of Moses, The 155

Lightning Hutch 135

Lilac Time 147

Lilies of the Field 46, 48

Lily Christine 47

Limousine Love 121, 122, 123

Lincoln, E.K. 73

Lindberg, Per 92

Lindbergh, Charles 141

Linder, Max 130

Listen Lester 270

Little American, The 107, 108, 109

Little, Ann 67

Little Brother of the Rich, A 205

Little Lord Fauntleroy 77

Little Minister, The 129

Livingstone, Jack 207, 218

Lloyd, Annette D'Agostino 9, 12, 15, 17, 203, 289

Lloyd, Harold ix, 8, 9, **10, 11**, 12, 13, 14, 15, 16, 17, 78, 111, 117, 127, 130, 136, 202, 203, 276, 282, 286, 289

Locklear, Ormer 53, 58, 143, **144**, 145

Lockwood, Alma 63, 66, 68

Lockwood, Harold 63, **64**, 65, 66, 67, 68, **69**, 70

Lockwood, William (Harold Lockwood, Jr.) 63, 70

Loff, Jeannette 192

Logan, Jacqueline 79

London, Jack 126

Lonesome Luke 8, 9

Lonesome Luke (film) 8

Long, Walter 270

Lorensbergsteatern (Gothenburg) 92

Lorraine, Harry 254

Los Altos Apartments 238, 239

Los Angeles Times, The 208, 215, 223, 234, 238, 242, 243, 284

Lost Patrol, The 129

Lost World, The **184**, 185, 197

Love 87, 177

Love Nest, The 20, 22, 29

Loves of an Actress 92

Love's Prisoner 102

Lowe, Edmund 239

Loy, Myrna 129

Lubin Manufacturing Company 71, **73**, 75, 153, 156

Lubin, Siegmund "Pop" **71**, 72, 73, 74, 75, 153

Lubinville 73, 74

Lubitsch, Ernst 234

Lugosi, Bela 96

Luke's Model Movie (see *Luke's Movie Muddle*)

Luke's Movie Muddle 8, 9, 10

Lullaby, The **229**, 230

Lumiere, Samuel 178

Lure of the Yukon 272, 274, **275**

Lusitania 104, 107

Lynch, Helen 182
Lynn, Diana 251
Lyon, Ben 16
Ma and Pa Kettle 283
Mack, Hughie 255
Mack, Marion 18, 26
MacArthur, Archie 63
MacDonald, Jeanette 281
MacDonald, Wallace 157, 278
Mackaill, Dorothy 5
MacLane, Barton 251
MacLean, Douglas 243
MacPherson, Jeannie 13
Mad Whirl, The 176
Maddux Air Lines 142
Magician, The 167, 168
Making a Living 253
Male and Female 14, 172, 174
Maltin, Leonard 9
Man From Hell's River, The 265
Man Four Square, A 274
Man Life Passed By, The 230, 269, 283
Man of Courage 251
Man Who Lost Himself, The 96
Man Who Saw Tomorrow, The 265
Man Who Shot Liberty Valance, The 283
Man Without a Heart, The 231
Mantrap 170, 172
Mann, Bertha 82
Mann, Hank 132, 269, 281
Manners, Dorothy 192
Man's Desire 213
Mansfield, Martha 67
Manslaughter 176
Mare Nostrum ix, 166, **167**, 168
Margaret Ettinger Agency 247
Margarita and the Mission Funds 65
Marion, Edna 123
Marion, Frances 88, 98, 104, 282
Markey, Enid 161
Marlowe, June 240
Marmont, Percy 230, 269
Marsh, Gene 8
Marsh, Mae 38
Marshall, George 47
Marshall, Herbert 247, 281
Marshall, Tully 170

Martin, Dean 251
Marvin, Lee 130
Mason, Buddy 132, 134
Mason, Dan 274
Mason, Shirley 49, 50, **52**, 53, 54, 282
Mature, Victor 96
Maurice Tourneur Productions 239
Mayer, Dr. Jasper 274
Mayer, Louis B. 50, 51, 268
Maynard, Ken 189, 190, 195, 196
Mayo-Wright Properties 238
McAvoy, May 176, 282
McCarey, Leo 282
McCrea, Joel 247, 249
McGregor, Malcolm 269
McGuire, Kathryn 18, **19**, 21, 22, 25
McHugh, Grace 133
McKee, Raymond 119, 242
McKenzie, Robert 254
McKim, Robert 187, 215
McKinley, President William 152
McLaglen, Victor 129
McNinch, Joe 286
McVey, Lucille 157
Medicine Man, The 279
Meet Dr. Jekyll and Mr. Hyde 129
Meighan, Thomas 2, 174, 243, 265
Melford, George 56
Meliés Manufacturing Company 153
Menjou, Adolphe 79
Mercury Aviation Company 139
Merrill, Frank 273
Merry Widow, The 177
Metro Pictures 50, 51, 53, 162, 230, 268, 269
MGM (Metro-Goldwyn-Mayer) 5, 51, 89, 92, 93, 94, 95, 96, 136, 168, 177, 191, 213, 247, 268, 281
Milestone Films 102
Miller, Marilyn 102
Miller, Ranger Bill 269
Miller, Rube 255
Million Bid, A 155
Millionaire Policeman, The **276**
Millionaire Vagabonds, The 65
Millner, Cork 158, 160
Milton, Joyce 34
Miracle Man, The 2, 5

Miss Bluebeard 80

Missing Daughters 270

Mitchell, Rhea 282

Mix, Ruth 61

Mix, Tom ix, 47, 59, 132, 133, 145, 146, 212, 230, 253, 255, **256**, 257, 262, **264**, 265, 271, 276, **277**, 283, 286, 289

Modern Times 38, **39**

Mohan, Earl 8

Money Corral, The 212

Monogram Pictures 96

Monte Cristo 181, 197, 198

Montez, Maria 129

Montgomery, Peggy 119

Montgomery, Robert 95

Montmartre (Paris) 100, 101, 223

Moore, Colleen 45, 48, 106, 147, 228, 239, 274, 275

Moore, Owen 183, 185

Moore, Tom 73, 218

Moran, Lee 119, 270

Moreno, Antonio 87, 157, **159**, **167**, **187**, 188, 282

Morey, Harry 41, **159**

Morgan, Frank 250

Morning Telegraph 67, 68

Morosco, Walter 45

Morris, Gouverneur 215

Morris R. Schlank Productions 192, 240

Morrison, Chick 133

Morrison, Pete 59, 140

Motion Picture Associates 251

Motion Picture Classic 7, 48, 54, 62, 83, 169, 178, 179, 198, 223, 288

Motion Picture Home 107

Motion Picture Magazine 16, 48, 54, 63, 66, 67, 68, 70, 75, 124, 130, 169, 172, 177, 198, 223, 288

Motion Picture News 2, 7, 66, 75, 158, 160, 216, 218, 222, 225, 257, 288

Motion Pictures Patents Company (MPPC) 72, 73, 75, 153, 154, 156

Motion Picture Relief Fund 281

Mounted Stranger, The 62

Movie Weekly 79, 83

Moving Picture World 8, 17, 63, 164, 169, 235, 273

Mower, Jack 202

Mr. Blandings Builds His Dream House 129

Mulhall, Jack 176, 245

Murray, Charles 245

Murray, Mae 43

Mutual Film Corporation 32, 138

Mr. Smith Goes to Washington 281

My Favorite Brunette 129

My Life East and West 261, 289

My Life With the Redskins 47

My Wonderful World of Slapstick 30, 31

Myers, Carmel 67, 157

Myers, Harry 74, 270

Mysterious Escort, The 204

Nan of Music Mountain 172

Nash, Patsy 251

Naval Air Service 145

Navigator, The 18, **19**, 21, 22, 29

Nazimova, Alla 104

Neft Apartments 243

Neft, Max 243

Negri, Pola 43, 92, 243

Neilan, Marshall "Mickey" 78, 101, 217, 218, 239

Nervous Wreck, The 118

Nestor Studio 63, 64

New York Evening World 150

New York Idea, The 261

New York Times, The 46, 48, 80, 97, 174, 180, 195, 215-216, 218

Newburg, Frank 201, 205, 216, 217

Newburg, Virginia Rita "Mickey" (also see Mickey Seltzer) 208, 216, 217, 226, 227, 230, 236, 237, 240, 247, 279

Newmeyer, Fred 127

Niblo, Fred 87, 187, 188

Nichols, George 215

Night Hawk, The (see *The Last Trail*)

Night Monster 96

Niven, David 130

Nixon, Marian 81, 127, 192

No Man's Gold 276, **277**

Noise in Newboro, A 268

Nolan, Mary 127

Non-Stop Kid, The 10

Norman Dawn Alaskan (Production) Company 270, 274

Normand, Mabel 35, 67, 68, 137, 157

Northern Code, The 274

Novak, Barbara 200, 244

Novak, Eva xii, ix, 200, **209**, 219, 220, 223, 226, 230, 235, 236, 238, 240, 243, 244, 250, 253, **254**, 255, **256**, 257, **258**, 259, **260**, 261, 262, **263**, **264**, 265, **266**, 267, **268**, 269, 270, **271**, **272**, **273**, 274, **275**, **276**, **277**, 278 279, **280**, 281, 282, 283, 284, 285, 286, **287**, 288, 299

Novak, Jane vii, ix, 4, 157, 200, **201**, 202, 203, 204, 205, 206, 207, 208, **209**, 210, **211**, **212**, 213, **214**, 215, 216, 217, 218, **219**, 220, 221, **222**, 223, 224, **225**, **226**, 227, **228**, **229**, 230, **231**, 232, **233**, 234, 235, 236, 237, **238**, 239, 240, **241**, 242, 243, **244**, 245, **246**, 247, 248, 249, 250, 251, 252, 253, 254, 255, 261, 265, 267, 269, 279, 282, 283, 284, 285, 286, **287**, 288, 289

Novak, Joseph 200

Novak, Joseph, Jr. 244

Novarro, Ramon 129, 166, 282

Noy, Wilfred 236

Nurse of An Aching Heart, A 254

Nuts and Noodles 255

Oakdale Affair, The 125

Oakland, Vivien 275

Oakman, Wheeler 193, 194, 237

O'Brien, Eugene 221

O'Donnell, Spec 113

Of Human Bondage 129

Ogden, Helen 220

Oh, Doctor! 126

O'Hara, Fisk 281

O'Hara, George 270

O'Hara, Maureen 281

O'Leary, Liam 162, 167, 169

Olcott, Sidney 242

Olivier, Lawrence 129

Olmsted, Getrude 126, 127

O'Malley of the Mounted 261, 262

O'Malley, Pat 188, 242, 282

Omar the Tentmaker 181, 198

One Hysterical Night 129

One Increasing Purpose 239

One Week 18, **115**, 116

O'Neil, Sally 86

Open All Night 79

Opportunity 50

Osbourne, "Speed" 134, 148

Other Man's Wife, The 202

Other Woman, The 221, 222

Our Dancing Daughters 93

Our Hospitality 19, 20, 25, 29, **30**, 116

Out All Night 127

Out of the Air 138

Out of the Sunset (see *The Torrent* [1921])

Out Yonder 102

Owen, Seena 138

Paid in Full 251

Paige, Jean 158, **159**

Pair of Tights, A 111, 113

Palmer, Patricia 202, 269

Palmer Photoplay 60

Palo Alto Film Corporation 57

Pantages 2

Panzer, Paul 153

Papa's Delicate Condition 47

Paradise Alley 47

Paralta Plays 162

Paramount-British 47

Paramount-Artcraft 215, 261

Paramount Pictures 2, 3, 4, 92, 96, 125, 238, 239, 241, 245, 246, 251, 265, 267, 269, 281

Paris, Barry 89

Parker, Jean 96

Parks, Michael 283

Parlor, Bedroom and Bath 129

Parry, Harvey 132, 136

Parsons, Louella 104, 110, 281, 282

Pathé 2, 8, 16, 153, 253

Paths to Paradise ix, 1, 3, 80

Paton, Raymond 234

Patrick, Jerome 221

Payne, John 283

Pennebaker Productions 247

Percy 133

Percy, Eileen 270, 283

Perdue, Derelys 182

Perkins, Gene 132

Perrin, Jack 189, 196, 261, 269, 279, **280**

Peter Pan 170, 183, 184, 197, 198, 279

Peters, House 74, 218, 261

Phantom Flyer, The 141, 184

Phantom of the Desert 279, **280**

Philadelphia Evening Bulletin 247

Philbin, Mary 282

Phillips, Dorothy 191
Phillips Films Productions, Ltd. 278, 279
Photoplay 11, 43, 48, 54, 62, 68, 70, 77, 83, 93,
     97, 104, 105, 110, 148, 166, 169, 172, 177, 184,
     193, 198, 205, 221, 223, 229, 272, 288
Photo-Play Journal 11, 16, 17, 104, 110
Pickfair 282
Pickford, Charlotte 100
Pickford, Jack 98, 100, **101**, 102
Pickford, Lottie 192
Pickford, Mary vii, viii, 6, 43, 63, 65, 67, 70, 98,
     100, 101, 102, 104, 105, 106, **107**, **108**, 109,
     110, 129, 178, 239, 250, 282, 283
Pictorial History of the Silent Screen, A 282
Picture Play 5, 7, 48, 54, 148, 162, 169, 217, 220,
     223, 288
Pictures (magazine) 82, 83
Pidgin Island 66
Pitts, ZaSu 282
Playhouse, The 25, 29
Pollard, Harry (director) 125, 127
Pollard, Harry "Snub" (actor) 8, 11, 281
Pony Express, The 3, 4
Porter, Edwin S. 63, 65, 72, 137
Potel, Victor 245, 281
Potts, Hank 261
Poverty Row 4, 193
Powell, Dick 283
Powell, Eleanor 281
Powell, William 238
Powers, Pat 203
Pratt, Jack 73
PRC (Producers Releasing Corporation) 96,
     251
Prevost, Marie 78, 86, 117
Price, Kate 221
Priesser, June 96
Prince of Pep, The 135
Princess and the Violinist, The (see *Die Prinz-
     essin und der Geiger*)
Pringle, Aileen 267, 268
Prior, Herbert 226
Prisoner of Zenda, The 165
Private Lives 129
Producers Distributing Corporation 183
Prude's Fall, The (aka *Dangerous Virtue*) 4,
     234, 235, 247

Purviance, Edna 32, **33**, 34
Quaker Girl, The 124
Queen of the Chorus 192**, 193**, 197, 198
Race for Life, A 192
Racing for Life 271
Radio City Music Hall 96
Raiders from the Double L Ranch, The 201
Rainbow Riders 196
Ralston, Ether 238, 245
Ralston, Jobyna 15, 86, 182
Rathbone, Basil 129
Rawlinson, Herbert 245, **276**
Ray, Charles 133, 210, **211**, 221, 245
Rayart Productions, Inc. 187, 193
Raymond, Gene 245
Reader, Ronald A. 150
Reardon, Mildred 174
Rebecca 129
Reckless Age, The 126
Red Lights 78
Red Signals 278, 279
Redskin **241**, 242
Reed, Mrs. W.R. (Eva Novak) 247
Reed, Pamela Eve 240, 279
Reed, Vivian (Mrs. Alfred E. Green) 265
Reed, Vivian Barbara 274, 279
Reed, William R. 240, 247, 265, 267, 270, 271,
     274, 278, 279, 280, 282
Reeves, Billie 73
Reid, Dorothy 13
Reid, Wallace 13, 63, 106, 157, 172, 173, 177
Reliance-Majestic Pictures 56
Republic Pictures 96, 282, 283
Restless Souls 59
Return of Jack Bellew, The 202
Revier, Dorothy 194, 272
Rex Film Company 63, 204
Rex, the King of the Wild Horses 133
Rice, Frank **140**
Rich, Irene 282
Rich, Lillian 282
Richard III 125
Richard, Viola vii, **121**, 122, 123
Ricketts, Thomas 65
Ridgeway, Fritzi 181
Riefenstahl, Leni 38
Rilla, Walter **233**, 234

Rin Tin Tin 188, 190, 192, 267
Rink, The 39
River of Romance, The 66
River's End, The 217-218, 220
Roach, Bert 254
Roach, Hal 8, 9, 12, 13, 14, 16, 111, 112, , 113, 114, 121, 123, 133, 202, 203, 275, 284, 286
Roaring Road, The 172, 177
Robards, Jason, Sr. 188
Roberts, Edith 255
Roberts, Joe 22, 27, 118
Roberts, William 251
Roberts, Theodore 170, 172, **173**, 174, 177, 238
Robertson-Cole Company 215
Robinson, David 37
Rock, Joe 113
Rock, William "Pop" **152**, 158
Rockett-Lincoln Film Company 60
Rogell, Al 192, 242
Rogers, Will 47, 180
Roland, Ruth 200, 201
Rolin Films 8, 12, 16, 202, 226, 227
Romance of Happy Valley, A 174, 176
Romance of Runnibede, The 278, 279
Romance Ranch 183
Romeo and Juliet 129
Romero, Cesar 281
Roosevelt, Theodore 151, 151
Roped Into Scandal 254
Rosary, The 224, 229
Roscoe, Allan 278
Rosenbloom, Maxie 251
Rosher, Charles 282
Rough Diamond, The 262
Rough Shod Fighter, A 61
Royal Danish Theatre 91
Royal Dramatic Theatre (Stockholm) 92
Royal Flying Corps. 124, 162
Royal Oak 2
Ruggles of Red Gap, The 172
Russell, William 57, 59, 61, 193, 221, 267, 268
Ryan, Joe **159**
Sacramento Pictures Corporation 270
Safeguarded 270
Safety Last 136
Sally 274
Salter, Thelma 210

Salvation Hunters, The 34
Samson and Delilah 96
Santschi, Tom 188, 190
Saturday Afternoon 119, 120, 121
Saturday's Children 46
Saturday Evening Post 47, 218
Saunders, John Monk 146
Say It With Babies 275
Scared Stiff 251
Scarlet Days 176
Scarlet Seas **6**
Scarlet Sin, The 204, 205
Schaefer, Anne 157, 200, 202, 284
Schenck, Joseph 92
Schertzinger, Victor 241, 267, 269
Schickel, Richard 14, 15, 17, 177
Schildkraut, Rudolph 186
Schiller Aviation School 138, 139
Schlank, Morris J. 192, 240, 270
Scholl, Dan 47
Schulberg, B.P. 121
Scott, J.B. 134, 148
Scott, Lizabeth 251
Scott, Randolph 283
Screen Extras Guild 282
Screenland 60, 62, 80
Sea Bat, The 95
Sea Horses 238
Sebastian, Dorothy 93, 169
Secret Life of Walter Mitty 129
Secretary of Frivolous Affairs, The 65
Seely, Sybil 18, 111, **115**, 116, 118
Seiter, William A. 127
Selfish Yates 210
Selig Polyscope Company 59, 64, 65, 73, 75, 153, 156, 157, 204, 229
Selig-Rork 224
Selig, William 239
Sellers, Peter 88
Seltzer, Frank 283
Seltzer, Mickey (see Virginia Rita Newburg) 247, 248, 284, 286
Seltzer, Walter 247, 283, 286
Selznick, David O. 129, 282
Selznick Pictures 42, 181
Semon, Larry 130, 157, **159**
Sennett Bathing Beauties 113, 115, 117

Sennett, Mack 78, 79, 113, 115, 117, 119, 120, 132, 137, 149, 253, 281

Sequoia Productions 274

Seven Chances 24

Seven Sinners 129

Shannon, Ethel 182

Share and Share Alike 240

Shaw, George Bernard 224

Shaw, Harold 51, 53

Shearer, Norma 129

Sheik, The 56, 93

Sherlock Holmes and the Voice of Terror 129

Sherlock, Jr. **24**, 25

Sherman Antitrust Act 156

Sherman, Lowell **42**

Sherwood, Robert 84, 87

Shipman, Nell 57

Shore Acres 162

Should Married Men Go Home? 123

Shumway, Leonard "Lee" 259, 262

Siegmann, George 269

Sign of the Cucumber, The 254

Sign of the Wolf, The 195, 197

Signal, The 280

Silk Husbands and Calico Wives 261, 265

Sills, Milton 5

Sinatra, Frank 130

Since You Went Away 282

Single Standard, The 91, 94

Sisson, Vera 67

Skinner's Dress Suit 86, 125, 127, **128**

Sky High 145, **264**, 265

Sky High Saunders 141, 149

Sky Pirate, The 137

Sky Skidder, The 141

Skywayman, The 53, 58, 144, 145

Sleeper, Martha 123, 275

Slide, Anthony 17, 46, 154, 177, 197

Sloane, Paul 92

Smart Sex, The 262

Smith, Albert E. 77, 150, 151, **152**, 153, 154, 155, 157, 158, 160

Smith Family, The (series) 119

Snow, Marguerite 283

Snowshoe Trail, The **226**, 227

Soanes, Wood 243

Social Code, The 53

Society Secrets 262

Son of Lassie 96

Sorrell and Son 92

Source, The 172

Spanish-American War 151

Spanish Influenza 52, 64, 68

Sparkhul, Theodor 234

Speed Maniac, The 255, 256

Sperling, Cass Warner 158, 160

Spirit of '76, The 207

Sporting Youth 126

St. Clair, Malcolm 281

St. John, Al 132, 242

St. Johns, Adele Rogers 42, 44, 48

Standard Cinema Corporation 113

Standing, Jack 208

Stanley, George 202

Stanton, Richard 206

Stanwyck, Barbara 95, 251

Starke, Pauline 270

Starr, Lynn 251

Starveling, The 225, 226

Steamboat Bill, Jr. 19, 22, 29, 111, 113, 171, 172

Stedman, Lincoln 269

Stedman, Vera 281

Steiffel, Isobel 128

Sterling, Edith 249

Sterling Pictures 193

Stewart, Anita 155, 157, 283

Stewart, James 281, 283

Stewart, Roy 203, 226-227

Stiller, Mauritz 91, 94, 188

Stoffer, Charles 147

Stone, Lewis 93, **94**, , 165, 213, 218, 220

Storey, Edith 155

Stormswept 182

Street Cars and Carbuncles 254

Strong Are Lonely, The 96

Studio Babelsberg (Germany) 233

Sturgeon, Rolin 41

Substitute Wife, The 236

Such a Little Queen 65

Suddenly a Woman (see Gudrun)

Sugar Daddies 123

Sullivan, Billy 192

Sunday Tribune, The 280, 288

Sunrise 46

Sunset Boulevard 283
Sunset Productions 146
Swain, Mack 81
Swanson, Gloria 2, 13, 117, 174, 283
Sweater Girl 96
Sweet, Blanche 176
Sydney Morning Herald 278
Taaffe, Alice Frances (see Alice Terry) 161
Tainted Money (1924) 272
Talbot, Lyle 251
Tale of Two Cities, A 155
Tales of Wells Fargo 283
Talmadge, Constance 74
Talmadge, Natalie 30, 116
Talmadge, Norma 43, 157, 239
Talmadge, Richard **134**, 135, 137, 272, **273**
Tangier 129
Target, The 206
Tarzan of the Apes (1918) 161
Tearle, Conway 221
Tell It To the Marines 86
Temple of the Dusk, The 211
Temptation 267
Temptress, The 84, 86, 87, **187**, 197
Ten Commandments, The 174, 177
Ten Nights in a Barroom 77
Tenderfoot's Luck, The 201
Tennyson, Gladys 224
Terror of the Range, The 2
Terry, Alice ix, 59, 161, 162, **163**, 164, 165, 166, **167**, 168, 169, 238
Tess of the D'Urbevilles 176
Tess of the Storm Country 65
Testing Block, The **260**, 261
Tex 61
That Man From Tangier 96
That's My Daddy 127
Theby, Rosemary 74, 282
Thelma 227
Thief of Bagdad, The 234
Thomas, Olive 98, **99**, 100, 101, 102, 103
Thomson, Fred 133, 140, 157
Thornby, Robert 202
Three Miles Up 141, 149
Three Word Brand 218, **222**
Thrill Chaser, The 126
Thunder 119

Thunder, the Dog 188
Thundergate 183, 185
Tie of the Blood, The 65
Tiffany Productions 239
Tiger Man, The 208, 210
Tiger's Claw, The 267, **268**
Tilford Cinema Corporation 3
Timms, Wally 139
Tinee, Mae 207
Todd, Arthur 127
Todd, Michael 129
Tol'able David 170, 171
Toll of Fear, The 75
Tomick, Frank 146
Tony Pastor's New Fourteenth Street Theatre 150
Too Much Speed 172
Torrence, Ernest 22, 170, **171**, 172, 177, 238
Torrent (1925*)* 84, **85**, 86
Torrent, The (1921) 261, 280
Torres, Raquel 95
Tourneur, Maurice 178, 230, 239
Tracked by the Police 188, 197, 198
Tracy Rides 196, 197
Trailin' 262
Tramp, Tramp, Tramp 86
Treasury of Chicken Cookery **284**
Treat 'Em Rough 212
Triangle Film Corporation 78, 98, 203
Trilby 181
Truant Husband, The 59
True Heart Susie 176
Tryon, Glenn 275
Tucker, George Loane 2
Tully, Frank 148
Tully, Richard Walton 181
Turconi, Davide 79, 83
Turner, Florence 153, 245
Turner, Fred A. 138
Turpin, Ben 130, 281
Twain, Mark 152
Twelve Miles Out 172
Twin Pictures Corporation 231
Two Men and a Woman 65
Two Reels and a Crank 151, 160
Two Shall Be Born **231**
Tyler, Tom 189, **196**

UCLA Archive 259

Unholy Three, The 6

United Artists 42, 92

Universal Pictures 4, 57, 60, 62, 96, 125, 126, 127, 129, 139, 141, 161, 178, 179, 180, 184, 185, 192, 202, 203, 204, 205, 206, 207, 215, 253, 259, 261, 262, 280

Unknown Chaplin 38, 40

Untamed Justice 195

Unwritten Code, The 52

Up and Going 265

Up in Mabel's Room 86

Up in Mary's Attic 258, 261

Vale, Vola 208

Valentino, Rudolph viii, 2, 43, 47, 80, 90, 93, 95, 129, 170

Vamping Reuben's Millions 254

Van Loan, H.H. 182, 183, 198

Vance, Jeffrey 31, 118, 123

Vanderveer, Elinor 113

Vanity Fair 155

Variety (magazine) 5, 7, 45, 46, 48, 95, 97, 141, 148, 149, 180, 181, 190, 193, 194, 195, 198, 204, 213, 218, 222, 256, 259, 288

Vengeance of the Deep 181

Venice Flying Field 138

Victor Schertzinger Productions 267, 269

Victorine Studios 166

Vidor, Florence 183, 238

Vingarna 92

Vitagraph Company of America 8, 41, 42, 43, 45, 60, 73, 75, 77, 78, 104, 150, 151, 152, 153, 154, 155, **156**, 157, 158, 159, 160, 161, 200, 201, 202, 214, 215, 231, 284

Vitagraph Monthly News of Current Events 154

Vitagraph Theatre 155

Vitaphone 6

VLSE 75, 76, 156

von Sternberg, Josef ix, 1, 5, 34

von Stroheim, Erich 55, 57, **58**, 93, 177

Wageknecht, Edward 176, 177

Wagon Tracks **214**

Wagon Train 283

Waite, Malcolm 35

Walker, Blaine 264

Walker, Johnnie 243

Wallis, Hal B. 247, 251

Walsh, Raoul 208

Walthall, Henry B. 162

WAMPAS (Western Association of Motion Picture Advertisers) 182, 199

Wanted at Headquarters **258**, 259

War Brides 104

Ward, Alice 119

Ward, Burt 130

Ward, Fannie 211

Ward, Warwick 234

Warner Brothers 158, 160, 182, 188, 247, 282

Warner, Harry 158

Washburn, Bryant 245, 267

Washington Redskins 47

Wayne, John 136, 189, 196, 283

Weary River 6

Webb, Geoffrey 262

Wedding March, The 177

Weinberg, Irving 7

Welch, Niles 236

Wellman, William 141, 146

Wells, H.G. 224

West, Adam 130

West of the Divide 196, 197

Westover, Winifred 221, 248, 249, **250**

Wet Paint 82, 83

What a Wife Learned 59

What Price Glory 86

What Price Love? 240, 242

When the Earth Trembled 74

Whispering Canyon 237

White, Pearl 132

White Scar, The 205

White Shadows 2

White Sin 59, **60**

White Tiger, The 79

Whitfield, Eileen 101, 103, 105, 110

Whiting, Dwight 12, 14

Whitlock, Lloyd 192, **193**, 194, 196

Why Pick On Me? 10

Wide Open 146

Wild Orchids 91, 93, **94**, 96, 97

Wild Seed 283

Willat, Irving V. 216

William S. Hart Park (Newhall, CA) 250, 286

Williams, Earle 41, 59, 155, 157, **159**, 214, 230, 278

Willie Runs the Park 202

Willie Work 8, 202, 203

Wilson, Al 132, **138**, 139, 140, 141, 142, 145, 146, 183, 184

Wilson, Lois 170, 245

Wilson, Woodrow 104, 207

Windsor, Claire 228, 282

Wings 141, 146

Winning of a Continent 51

Wisteria Productions 221

Witching Hour, The 77

Without Benefit of Clergy 180, 181, 197, 198

Wolf, The 214, 215

Wolheim, Louis 82

Wolves of the North 262

Woman of Affairs, A 88

Woman of Paris, A 33

Woman to Woman 2

Women First 272

Won in the Clouds 141

World Film Corporation 125

World War I 52, 59, 75, 102, 104, 107, 146, 166, 174, 207, 210, 211, 224

World War II 147, 168, 197, 247, 283

Worne, Duke 193, 194, 195

Worthier Man, The 202

Worthington, William 211

Wrath of the Seas, The 95

Wright Brothers 137, 152

Wright, Harold Bell 207, 232

Wynne, H. Hugh 137, 138, 143, 149

Wynters, Charlotte 251

Yanks Are Coming, The 251

Yellow Dove, The 68

Yorke-Metro 66

Young, Clara Kimball 157, 283

Young, James 181

Young, Loretta 92

Young, Robert 281

Ziegfeld, Florenz 98

Ziegfeld Follies 98, 99, 102, 113

Zukor, Adolph 65

Lightning Source UK Ltd.
Milton Keynes UK
UKHW030257080223
416652UK00004B/977